THE POLITICAL ROLE OF LAW COURTS IN MODERN DEMOCRACIES

The Political Role of Law Courts in Modern Democracies

Edited by

Jerold L. Waltman

Professor of Political Science
University of Southern Mississippi

and

Kenneth M. Holland

Associate Professor of Political Science
University of Vermont

M
MACMILLAN

First published 1988
Reprinted 1989

Published by
THE MACMILLAN PRESS LTD
Houndmills, Basingstoke, Hampshire RG21 2XS
and London
Companies and representatives
throughout the world

Printed in Great Britain by
The Ipswich Book Company Ltd
Ipswich, Suffolk

British Library Cataloguing in Publication Data
The political role of law courts in modern
democracies.
1. Courts   2. Jurisdiction
I. Waltman, Jerold L.   II. Holland,
Kenneth M.
342.7'12   K2100 .
ISBN 0–333–39405–4

Contents

Preface

This book grew out of a conversation the editors once had lamenting the lack of materials for their courses in comparative judicial politics. Even basic information about the court systems of the major democracies has been very difficult to find in English. What we have sought to provide, therefore, is an accessible guide for students and teachers of comparative judiciaries.

We have done more than compile a catalogue, however. Each chapter not only provides information but also addresses the important question of the courts' political roles and how these may be changing. The authors pose other specific queries, such as: How do courts allocate values? What are their links with other political institutions? Who are the judges and what difference does their social background make?

The governments of modern democracies are under stress from several directions, and the courts' political roles may be expected to undergo a metamorphosis as the political system both reacts to and generates change. These stresses have, in fact, made the question of whether democracy will continue, at least in the form we know it, within the bounds of respectable political discourse. Economic uncertainty, increasing crime and wanton terrorism combine to interrupt the routines of peaceful and stable democratic government. If democracy's fate is not certain, the question of the evolving judicial role is urgent indeed.

Courts, logically and historically, have been undemocratic institutions. An increased role for the courts, then, could render a political order less democratic. At the same time, courts have often maintained individual rights in the face of majoritarian pressure, thereby helping to keep intact the substratum upon which democracy rests. Citizens of the modern state, especially given its size, may need judicial protection for their liberty as much as they need to secure participation in the governmental process. Thus, there is a tension inherent in any expanded or altered role for the courts. The result could serve either to enhance or undermine democracy.

To be sure, the context of judicial change varies markedly from country to country. A fascist heritage, especially where the courts cooperated with the fascist regime, engenders a different political climate from that of the more long-standing democracies. The legacy of anti-unionism in Britain and the sovereignty of Parliament, as further examples, contrast sharply with conditions in Sweden. Yet, in spite of these and other examples, there are common threads of change and several of them are developed in the concluding chapter.

We would like to thank Mr T. M. Farmiloe of The Macmillan Press for both his initial enthusiasm concerning the project and the patience he showed during its development. Our thanks are also due the contributors. They laboured under our deadlines and acceded gracefully to our requests for alterations, some of which must have seemed unreasonable.

Lastly, we would like to thank our institutions, especially for the degree to which they allowed us to enrich the telephone company. The Vice-President for Research and Extended Services of the University of Southern Mississippi provided funds for typing a portion of the final draft. Also, a summer grant from the University of Southern Mississippi greatly facilitated Waltman's work on the concluding chapter.

JEROLD L. WALTMAN
University of Southern Mississippi

KENNETH M. HOLLAND
University of Vermont

Notes on the Editors and Contributors

Jerold L. Waltman is Professor of Political Science at the University of Southern Mississippi. He holds a PhD from Indiana University, edited a volume entitled *Dilemmas of Change in British Politics* (with Donley Studlar), and is the author of *The Political Origins of the US Income Tax* and *Copying Other Nations' Policies*.

Kenneth M. Holland is an Associate Professor of Political Science at the University of Vermont, and received his doctorate from the University of Chicago. His previous publications have appeared in the *Journal of Political Science*, the *American Bar Foundation Research Journal*, the *Justice System Journal*, and *Law and Policy Quarterly* among others.

Carl Baar is now on the faculty of Brock University of Ontario. He gained a PhD at the University of Chicago. In addition, he has been affiliated with the Canadian Judicial Council. His published works include *Subservient but Equal: Court Budgeting in the American States* and several articles on Canadian judicial administration.

Joseph B. Board is Robert Porter Patterson Professor of Government at Union College. He was educated in law and political science at Oxford and Indiana Universities. He is the author of *The Government and Politics of Sweden* as well as numerous articles in legal and political science journals and the recipient of several fellowships and awards both in the United States and Sweden.

Giuseppe Di Federico is Director of the Research Center for Judicial Studies at the University of Bologna and Professor of Political Science. His advanced degrees in law and political science were earned at the University of Florence and Michigan State University. He has published numerous works on the Italian court system such as *La Corte di cassazione* and *Gil incarichi extragiudiziari dei magistrati* and served repeatedly as a consultant to the Italian Superior Council of the Judiciary.

Carlo Guarnieri is an Associate Professor of Political Science and a member of the Research Center for Judicial Studies at the University of Bologna. Educated at the University of Florence, he has written *L'indipendenza della magistratura* and *Pubblico ministero e sistema politico*.

Hiroshi Itoh is now Professor of Political Science at the State University of New York at Plattsburgh. He gained a PhD from the University of Washington. Among his publications are *Constitutional Law of Japan* and *Japanese Politics: An Inside View*.

Dallis Radamaker holds law degrees from Louisiana State University and the College of Europe. He has lived in France for a number of years and is now practising law in Amsterdam.

Roman Tomasic is Principal Lecturer in Law at the School of Administrative Studies, Carberra College of Advanced Education. He gained a law degree at the University of Sydney, an advanced law degree at the University of Wisconsin, and a PhD in Sociology at the University of New South Wales. He has written and edited a number of books, including *Lawyers and the Community*, *Legislation and Society in Australia*, and *Business Regulation in Australia*.

*To James B. Christoph and
the memory of Herbert J. Storing*

1 Introduction
Jerold L. Waltman

No less than their pre-industrial counterparts, modern democracies find courts indispensable political institutions. At a minimum, those accused of crime must be adjudged guilty or innocent and a legal forum has to be provided for settling the multitude of disputes that emanate from an advanced industrial society. Often, of course, courts are also connected to channels that lead more directly to the seats of political influence.

Courts remain, however, both suspect and little understood. The suspicion flows in the first place from the difficulty in reconciling democracy with the operations of judicial institutions. Law cannot be both democratic and untainted by partisan politics. Every attempt to democratise the courts therefore opens them to the seamier side of politics and soon brings law into disrepute. On the other hand, to the extent that courts are insulated from democratic accountability, the state is less than fully democratic by definition. And the greater the role of courts in the political system, the thornier this dilemma becomes.

The suspicion is exacerbated by the courts' links, where applicable, with pre-democratic monarchical and aristocratic political orders. They are the only survivors of the autocratic polity still to exercise real power. In Germany, Italy, and Japan the politicisation of the courts under fascism has left another bitter legacy. How to protect judges from another such episode while not giving them too much power, sometimes in fact to rely on the very laws and traditions of that era, is a vexing question. Furthermore, in some countries the courts are still tinged with anti-progressive stances judges took in the late nineteenth century and during much of the twentieth century.

The lack of understanding derives in part from the fact that courts tend to play such different roles in each political system. In part, too, modern research has been stifled by the fall of public law from its once central place in political science and the concomitant emphasis on parties, elections, and the like, and more recently on economic policy. Moreover, the immense role played by courts in the United States has inhibited political scientists there from seeing the important functions judicial institutions perform in other polities, diminished though they may be by United States standards.

1

The vitality of the democratic state is a concern of democratic theorists everywhere. Buffetted by international economic upheavals and changing socioeconomic structures, *immobilism* seems an apt description of political systems some distance from the Fourth Republic in time and space. Whether created by these events or whether flowing from other sources, there has been a seeming erosion of the legitimacy of the state. While it is not yet deep enough to label a 'crisis' of political authority, the sense of unease is widespread.

The legitimacy of the state cannot be disconnected from law, for law is what connects people to government both substantively and symbolically. It provides a frame of reference for the conduct of ordinary citizens as well as linking the state with a moral order. Consequently, the courts will be one of the first institutions to suffer from a decline of legitimacy. At the same time, the courts' activities will also help arrest or push forward an incipient decline in legitimacy.

Our authors were asked to add the theme of the courts changing role in each country's democracy to their descriptive material. We believe the ensuing chapters will demonstrate that important changes are occurring in most of the countries analysed here. Even though it is difficult to discern exactly what commonalities exist, an attempt is made in the final chapter to extract a few common threads. What does seem evident is that debates are taking place in several nations about the structural interrelationships among the major political institutions, including the role accorded the courts.

As Western societies move toward the twenty-first century, such a political evolution is not unexpected. The institutional configuration of the post-war era could not be expected to remain static. New issues were bound to generate demands for new decision making structures. To take two examples, an amorphous set of concerns labelled 'quality of life' and a resurgence of questions about individual rights have forced their way on to the political agenda in several nations. Nowhere has the response of executive and legislative institutions been entirely satisfactory, and courts have been pulled into these areas. Indeed, these two issues illustrate two of the forces shaping the agenda of contemporary politics. One is the shift to a post-industrial economy, bringing with it an altered social and economic structure, the other a resurgence of the fundamental issue of how the individual relates to the polity.

Whatever the political future holds for the courts, though, they are performing important functions in contemporary politics and worthy of sustained analysis. We asked the authors to work from a common general outline, although each was free to organise his material as he believed appropriate. It consists of six dimensions: legal culture, the structure of the courts, judicial personnel, the scope of authority, decision making, and links with other political institutions.

Legal culture can be defined as one scholar defined 'legal tradition', as 'a set of deeply rooted, historically conditioned attitudes about the nature of law, about the role of law in the society and the polity, about the proper organization and operation of the legal system, and about the way law is or should be made, applied, studied, perfected, and taught'.[1]

A distinction should probably be drawn between mass and elite legal cultures. At the mass level, the legal culture interacts with the general political culture, usually in a supportive way. Of major importance are mass perceptions of the nature of law and the general expectations citizens have of the law and legal actors.

Moving to the general political elite, it is important to know what role is ascribed to law. It could be that law is revered in some abstract sense, but not seen as important in the political process. Or, it could be that law is factored into certain policy areas, say family issues, but left out entirely in others, for example economic questions. Furthermore, it is relevant to ascertain how decisions of parliament and executive agencies are viewed. Are they 'law'? If so, how much respect is accorded them by virtue of that fact?

For the legal elite, the legal tradition is of paramount importance. Legal elites are socialised into certain habits and approaches, making the philosophy of law they share the starting point for any analysis of the legal system. It is also an interesting question how much this legal philosophy is linked to elite political ideologies. Does one segment of the political elite share the legal philosophy and another not? Do the legal elites keep the legal philosophy on narrow grounds to avoid running counter to the political elite? Of course, much depends on whether the legal elite is part of or isolated from the mainstream political elite.

No institution can be studied apart from its *structure*. We need to know how many courts there are and whether or not there are specialised courts. If there are specialised courts, what are they and who uses them? Most especially, are there special courts for constitutional interpretation? Analysing structure also means describing how the courts are linked together. Are there separate hierarchies? If so, do they converge at some point?

Turning to *personnel*, legal institutions are almost always composed of people appointed by others, at least formally. Are there, though, different recruitment patterns for different levels and types of courts? What kinds of career patterns are observable? Is a judgeship a capstone for a successful legal career or is it a lifetime occupation entered soon after completing one's legal education? Is the judiciary attractive to the best of the legal profession, or is it a burial ground?

Is any special training required for judges? Are there special requirements for certain courts, either formal or informal? Are there any lay judges, say at the lowest levels, and how are they selected? In lateral entry systems, do certain occupations, for instance legal academia, provide expedited access to the bench? And, of course, what about retirement and removal?

What socioeconomic backgrounds do judges come from? Quite naturally, one would expect them to be overwhelmingly from elite backgrounds, by virtue of their educational attainments if nothing else. But how much of an elite? And are there differences according to the level of court? What is the standing of judges compared to other political elites?

Scope of authority is akin to the legal idea of 'jurisdiction', but with a political accent. On the one hand, it can be asked what is the range of judicial authority? Are courts confined to narrow areas, or do they roam over wide turf. On the other hand, what is the depth of their authority in areas they touch? Do they have a large degree of control over the areas they deal with, or do they share authority with other institutions?

Courts, more than any other public body, are for the purpose of *making decisions*.[2] How they go about it, though, naturally varies from country to country and from one type of court to another. At the trial court level, is there a single judge or a panel? Is the judge full time? Is there lay participation, either as jurors or quasi-judges? What is the role of counsel or advocates? In criminal cases, what is the role of the prosecuting authorities? At the appellate level, are there panels or does the whole court sit on each case? Is there a screening device for appeals? If panels are present, who selects the panels? Is there a chief judge, and if so what is his influence? What of the influence of those outside the court: legal academics, prominent counsel, the nation's chief legal officer?

What role does precedent play, formally and informally? What deference is accorded trial or intermediate appellate courts? What can be said of dissents? Are they kept private or made public? Do the judges' political perceptions, or the politically possible, colour their decisions?

Without question, the most important and continuing *link* a court can have *with other political institutions* is judicial review, the power to invalidate acts of legislators and executives.[3] When courts possess this power, they will inevitably be involved in delicate political manoeuvring of the first order.

Even when there is no judicial review, courts are often structurally linked with the bureaucracy, providing a channel for communication and numerous occasions for co-operation and conflict. Even without formal links, courts often hear cases involving government officials and, of course, interpret statutes, and everywhere judicial decisions require implementation by other officials.

Courts are, in sum, part of every political system, and the politics of none can be understood without an appreciation of their role. Yet modern political science has tended to downplay or even ignore judicial institutions, and to the extent that it has done this, its analyses of politics remain incomplete. As we more fully comprehend the roles of courts in each modern democracy, we will be in a better position to construct genuine comparative theories both about courts themselves and modern political development.

NOTES

1. John H. Merryman, *The Civil Law Tradition* (Stanford: Stanford University Press, 1969), p. 2; quoted in Henry Ehrmann, *Comparative Legal Cultures* (Englewood Cliffs, N.J.: Prentice-Hall, 1976), p. 8.
2. For a thorough analysis, see Lawrence B. Mohr, 'Organizations, Decisions, and Courts', *Law and Society Review* (Summer, 1976) pp. 621–42.
3. See the review essay by Donald Kommers, 'Comparative Judicial Review and Constitutional Politics', *World Politics*, XXVII (January, 1975), pp. 282–97.

2 The Courts in the United States

Kenneth M. Holland

INTRODUCTION

In most political communities, courts play a secondary role in governing. John Locke, who helped articulate the separation of powers concept for the modern world, designated the three powers of government as legislative, executive, and federative ('the power of war and peace, leagues and alliances').[1] He spoke of the judicial function as a part of the legislative one and did not insist upon their separation. For the most part, courts have resolved disputes in accordance with rules made by other institutions. Regarding judges during the colonial period as agents of the tyranny of the British crown, the eighteenth-century authors of the state and federal constitutions envisioned a limited role for courts in the United States. Even the embodiment of the judicial dignity of the new nation, the United States Supreme Court, failed to distinguish itself during its first fifteen years. The first Chief Justice of the United States, John Jay, relinquished his unexalted post to serve as governor of New York in 1795. His successor, Oliver Ellsworth, resigned as chief justice in 1800 to become ambassador to France.[2]

The Supreme Court took on new life and greater dignity with the appointment of John Marshall as the third chief justice in 1801, a position he held until his death in 1835. Marshall exerted great influence upon the political and economic development of the fledgling nation through a series of landmark judicial decisions supporting the growth of federal power and authority. The most important decision of the Marshall Court occurred in *Marbury* v. *Madison*,[3] where the court claimed the power of judicial review, the authority to declare null and void laws repugnant to the Constitution. In 1832, Alexis de Tocqueville saw that this power had given courts in the United States a unique role:

6

An American judge can pronounce a decision only when litigation has arisen, he is conversant only with special cases, and he cannot act until the cause has been duly brought before the court. His position is therefore exactly the same as that of the magistrates of other nations; and yet he is invested with immense political power. How does this come about? If the sphere of his authority and his means of action are the same as those of other judges, where does he derive a power which they do not possess? The cause of this difference lies in the simple fact that the Americans have acknowledged the right of judges to found their decision on the *Constitution* rather than on the *laws*. In other words, they have permitted them not to apply such laws as may appear to them to be unconstitutional.[4]

A sign of just how bold the Supreme Court became in the exercise of judicial review was *Dred Scott* v. *Sandford*,[5] in which the Court attempted a final solution of the slavery issue by enjoining Congress from prohibiting the spread of slavery into the western territories. This judicial audacity, however, failed in its object and helped precipitate a great civil war.

The legacy of *Marbury* (1803) is a state and federal judiciary that is the most potent and active in the world. Courts at all levels routinely participate in the making of public policy and the allocation of resources. Some, for example Theodore Lowi,[6] regard this fragmentation of power as a barrier to the enactment of policies serving the public interest; others, such as Michael J. Perry[7] and Arthur Selwyn Miller,[8] view this powerful judiciary as the principal bulwark of liberty, equality, and justice.

LEGAL CULTURE

The United States is the most litigious country in the world. In 1982 18,363 state and federal courts processed more than 25 million criminal and civil cases.[9] There are nearly 13,000 state and federal judges and more than 550,000 lawyers in the United States, approximately one for every 400 Americans.[10] Lawyers are part of the occupational elite. Like physicians, they enjoy high social status and high income. The vast majority of lawyers are native-born white males from higher social backgrounds. Although comprising 11 per cent of the population, blacks make up only one per cent of the legal profession. An increasing number of women, however, are now entering law school.[11] Members of the legal fraternity enjoy more prestige than civil servants or politicians, and judges enjoy even more prestige than attorneys.

As opposed to oriental countries, where the inhabitants highly value social harmony and are thus very reluctant to initiate law suits, Americans prize their rights and are relatively quick to go to court in order to redress violations of those rights. Many grievances, which in the East are not recognised as legal injuries, in the United States are classified as 'causes of action' and can give rise to litigation. In the United States suits by patients against their physicians, clients against their attorneys, parishioners against their pastors, and family members against each other are common. Courts have even entertained suits by children against their mothers and fathers, alleging 'malpractice of parenting'.[12] Legalism permeates United States society. Public and private institutions, including government agencies, universities, industrial corporations, and professional sports teams, are increasingly relying on formal mechanisms to resolve disputes. The American Revolution, essentially an assertion of what the colonists took to be their rights as Englishmen and as human beings, gave 'to American political thought and culture a preoccupation with the assertion and maintenance of *rights*'.[13]

In addition to rights consciousness, scholars have pointed to other explanations for the relatively high litigation rate in the United States: the decay of the ethnic group, the church, the neighbourhood, and the family, each of which provided informal means for settling conflicts; the impersonality of American society, which is the most mobile on the globe (people are much more likely to sue a stranger than someone with whom they share an ongoing relationship); and the paucity of any inexpensive alternative forum, such as neighbourhood justice centres or conciliation services, to which the aggrieved could bring their complaints.

The struggle for equality has taken the form of a contest for legal entitlements. Engaging in this 'politics of rights' have been women, blacks, native Americans, and Hispanics.[14] For instance, frustrated by its lack of success before governors, presidents, and legislative chambers, in the 1920s the National Association for the Advancement of Colored People (NAACP) turned to the courts, a tactical man-oeuvre that paid off handsomely with the constitutional invalidation of racial segregation by the Supreme Court in *Brown* v. *Board of Education*.[15] Homosexuals and victims of AIDS (Acquired Immune Deficiency Syndrome) are only the most recent groups to employ the litigation strategy to improve their economic opportunities.

Issues that in many nations are determined by legislative and executive organs frequently come before the courts. No matter where a change originates, the policy making process is not complete until the new policy has received judicial approbation. As de Tocqueville noted: 'Scarcely any political question arises in the United States that is not resolved, sooner or later, into a judicial question.'[16] Because of the participation of the judiciary, the process of formulating public policy in the United States is comparatively intricate and slow.

The popular belief in a law higher than man-made rules reinforces the power of judicial review.[17] The Declaration of Independence speaks of 'the Laws of Nature and of Nature's God' and traces man's 'unalienable Rights' to the beneficence of his 'Creator'. In *Marbury* (1803), Chief Justice Marshall counselled against calling future constitutional conventions because by a happy coincidence the Constitution penned in 1787 conforms to the dictates of natural reason. Adherents to the natural law doctrine were the most vocal and effective critics of slavery and the legal code that made it possible. More recently, many opponents of the Vietnam conflict grounded their opposition on the conviction that it was an unjust war and called, albeit unsuccessfully, upon the courts to declare it unconstitutional.[18] Common during the era of the struggle for black equality, the practice of civil disobedience of unjust laws is also inspired by the rejection of man-made, or positive, law as the ultimate source of rights and obligations.

Justice is the standard not only for evaluating the validity of the laws but also for estimating the legitimacy of civil and criminal trials. Like other English-speaking countries, the United States believes that 'adversarial' proceedings are more fair than the 'inquisitorial' system employed on the European continent. The three major principles of an adversarial proceeding are party initiation, party prosecution, and party presentation. It is believed that truth is more likely to emerge from partisan presentations of the evidence most favourable to each side than from a disinterested investigation by a third party. This is so because the litigants have a selfish interest in seeing that no relevant fact or legal argument is overlooked, and self-interest is believed to be a more reliable motive than professional duty. The judge is a passive umpire, who cannot call or question witnesses, and who can only enforce the rules of evidence and due process when one of the parties objects to a violation committed by his opponent.

The chief virtue of a judge is impartiality. United States legal culture highly values judicial independence of other branches of government and of public opinion as a means of insuring neutrality.[19] The survival of the judiciary as a co-equal partner in government depends upon popular support. Most of the research in this area has focused on the Supreme Court. Surveys of public opinion reveal strong *diffuse support* directed toward the Court as the legitimate arbiter of the Constitution but a decline in *specific support* for many of its constitutional decisions since the 1960s. Between 10 and 30 per cent of the adult population neither know nor care anything about the Supreme Court's behaviour. In one survey 59 per cent of the respondents indicated they had paid no attention to what the Court had done in reent years. The Court's *attentive* public, those who know about the Court, have strong opinions about its work and read or hear about the Court, comprise about 40 per cent of the adult population. In general, surveys reveal greater public confidence in the Supreme Court than in the Congress or the Presidency.[20]

The trier of fact, either a lay jury or, in the absence of a jury, the judge, must decide entirely on the basis of what he or she saw and heard in the courtroom. In criminal prosecutions, the accused is presumed innocent, may refuse to testify and answer questions from the prosecutor and must be proven guilty 'beyond a reasonable doubt'. In the words of Felix Frankfurter, a former Associate Justice of the Supreme Court, 'ours is an accusatorial and not an inquisitorial system – a system in which the State must establish guilt by evidence independently and freely secured and may not by coercion prove its charge against an accused out of his own mouth'.[21] There is a tendency in the United States to equate justice with adherence to correct procedure. If an innocent man is found guilty or if a criminal is acquitted, the result is considered just as long as the defendant received a fair trial. By contrast, in Europe the disposition is to define justice as the correct outcome – absolution of the innocent, punishment of the guilty.

In nations that draw upon the tradition of the English common law, judges have the authority to make law when the legislature has failed to regulate a particular field. Legislative activity has increased markedly over the past two hundred years, narrowing further and further the scope of judge-made law. The rule of precedent, or *stare decisis*, however, remains in force. According to this principle of adjudication, judges must decide present cases on the basis of previous cases when similar facts were decided. Departures from precedent are most common when courts are called to rule on constitutional, as opposed to statutory, questions.

STRUCTURE OF THE COURTS

The United States is a federation of states rather than a unitary political community like Britain and France. Unlike local governments in unitary systems, the United States states derive neither their existence nor their powers from the general government. Each state possesses the entire apparatus of a sovereign nation – a governor, a legislature, courts, tax collectors, a police force, municipal governments, even an army and air force. The Tenth Amendment to the United States Constitution makes clear the fact that the people of the states have delegated some powers to the federation and reserved the remainder for the states. Within this residual sphere, the states are sovereign.

Because each state has erected a structure of trial and appellate courts, federal courts of the first instance, strictly speaking, are unnecessary. Article III of the Constitution accordingly enjoins Congress to establish only one federal court – a Supreme Court – with the task of insuring the uniformity and supremacy of federal law. The Constitution thus permits the *integrated* court system in which, as in Germany, all the trial courts are state or provincial tribunals. The First Congress, however, in 1789 chose the *dual* system and established federal trial and intermediate appellate courts as well as a Supreme Court. The Congress, dominated by members of the nationalist, or Federalist, party, feared that state judges, especially in suits between citizens of different states, would be biased in favour of their state's interests. The advocates of the interests of the states nevertheless obtained several significant concessions. Federal district court jurisdiction coincides with state boundaries. No district includes more than one state. Circuit court jurisdiction groups districts and thus also respects state boundaries. Each district judge is a resident of the district in which he or she is appointed.[22]

There are 18,252 state and local courts and 111 federal courts. State and local courts dispose of more than 99 per cent of all civil and criminal cases filed in the United States. Article III of the Constitution limits the jurisdiction of the federal courts to cases involving the Constitution, laws, or treaties of the United States, to cases of admiralty and maritime jurisdiction, and to cases where an ambassador, the federal government, two states, or citizens of different states are parties. As a result of this limited federal jurisdiction, most crimes and violations of private rights can only be adjudicated in the state courts. The federal courts also enjoy an *exclusive jurisdiction*.

Bankruptcy, patent, and copyright cases and prosecutions of federal crimes can only occur in federal court. The state and federal courts share *concurrent jurisdiction* over suits between citizens of different states and cases arising under the federal Constitution or laws. In the former category, the federal judge must apply the relevant state law to the dispute and in the latter group the state judge must apply federal law. Article VI of the Constitution requires each state judge to take an oath to 'support this Constitution' and declares that

> this Constitution, and the Laws of the United States which shall be made in Pursuance thereof; and all Treaties made, or which shall be made, under the Authority of the United States, shall be the supreme Law of the Land; and the Judges in every State shall be bound thereby, any Thing in the Constitution or Laws of any State to the Contrary notwithstanding.

The largest proportion (71 per cent) of cases filed in state and local courts involve traffic violations. The remaining major categories are civil cases (15 per cent), criminal cases (12 per cent), and juvenile cases (2 per cent). In 1977, 143,300 appeals, or 0.5 per cent of the total state case load, were filed in state appellate courts. In several states case filings are increasing at between 10 and 25 per cent each year.[23]

Each state and each municipality has its own peculiar court structure. It is therefore difficult to describe the 'typical' state court system. In general, state judiciaries consist of four tiers, as shown in Figure 2.1. At the bottom are courts of limited or special jurisdiction. Approximately 77 per cent of all state courts are of this type.[24] These courts may hear only minor civil or criminal cases involving divorce and child custody. Juvenile, traffic, and small claims courts are examples of courts of limited jurisdiction. More than 90 per cent of criminal cases are processed at this level.[25] State legislatures established these courts in a non-systematic and piecemeal fashion with the result that many courts share overlapping jurisdiction and that the citizenry is confused about where to initiate proceedings. There is a trend in the states to simplify and unify the state and municipal courts and to reduce the number of courts of limited jurisdiction.

At the next level are courts of general jurisdiction. These constitute the states' major trial courts. Generally, the state is organised into judicial districts or circuits that include one or more counties. These courts can hear any civil or criminal case, unless it is one of those over which the federal courts have exclusive jurisdiction. These serve as courts of first instance for most serious criminal cases (felonies) and

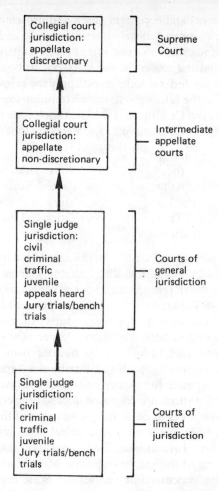

Figure 2.1 Prototype state court system

most civil suits where large sums of money are in controversy. In some states, courts of general jurisdiction may hear appeals from courts of limited jurisdiction. Generally, losers in the latter courts may demand a new trial, a trial *de novo*, in a court of general jurisdiction.

Half the states have intermediate courts of appeals as well as a supreme court. A principle of United States law is that each losing litigant (except the prosecution in a criminal case) is entitled to one appeal, so in those states lacking an intermediate appellate court the state supreme court must accept all petitions for review. Appellate courts must accept the lower court's findings of fact and may only decide legal questions.

The Federal judiciary is organised into three tiers. The district courts are the federal system's major trial courts. There are also specialised tribunals – the Court of International Trade, the Claims Court, and the Tax Court. In 1985 there were 94 district courts staffed by 576 district judges. In 1983, 241,842 civil cases and 35,872 criminal cases were filed in the United States District Courts. Because 94 per cent of the civil cases were settled out of court and 82 per cent of the criminal cases were disposed of by guilty pleas or dismissed by the prosecutor, there were only 14,601 civil trials and 6656 criminal trials.[26] Each of the fifty states, the District of Columbia, Guam, the Virgin Islands, the Northern Mariana Islands, and Puerto Rico has at least one district. The most populous states have four. Each district court is staffed by between one and twenty-seven judges.

The district courts have only original jurisdiction. A single judge tries a case, except when it involves voting rights, civil rights, or legislative reapportionment, when a special three-judge district court is convened. Approximately twenty-five such proceedings occur each year.[27]

The twelve United States Courts of Appeals hear appeals from decisions of the district courts located in their particular circuit. There are 168 appeals court judges. They also hear appeals from the decisions of many federal regulatory and administrative agencies, such as the Immigration and Naturalization Service, which possess quasi-judicial as well as quasi-legislative and quasi-executive powers. In 1983, 25,039 appeals from the district courts and 3069 petitions to review administrative orders were filed in the courts of appeals, about six times the number filed in 1963.[28]

Between six and twenty-eight judges sit on each court of appeals. Judges normally sit in temporary panels of three. The chief judge of each circuit puts together the panels for each case. If a case is especially controversial, all the circuit judges hear the case *en banc*. Approximately 0.5 per cent of the hearings are *en banc*.[29]

At the summit of the federal judicial hierarchy is the Supreme Court, perhaps the most visible court in the world. The Court possesses original as well as appellate jurisdiction. It can try cases between two states, between the federal government and a state, cases involving foreign ambassadors, and suits by a state against the citizens of other states or nations. The Court, however, delegates most of these cases to the district courts. Throughout its history the Court has

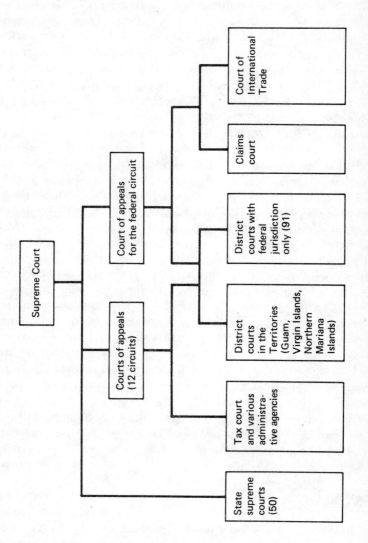

Figure 2.2 Federal court system

ajudicated only 164 cases under its original jurisdiction.[30] The Supreme Court, therefore, is essentially an appellate court.

The Court hears appeals from the decisions of the United States Courts of Appeals and the state supreme courts. Congress has granted the Court complete discretion when the losing party files a petition for writ of *certiorari*. If four of the nine justices vote to grant the petition the full court will consider the case. Only 11 per cent of paid petitions and 3 per cent of unpaid petitions filed by state or federal prisoners are granted each year. In certain cases, such as those in which a lower court has held a federal law unconstitutional, the losing party is entitled to have his case reviewed by the Supreme Court. The Court, however, has carved out discretion with regard to such petitions as well and dismisses about 55 per cent of these appeals for 'lack of substantial federal question'. Many of the remaining 45 per cent are disposed of by summary judgment, without oral argument or a written opinion. Of the 300 cases decided on the merits annually, the Court hears oral argument and writes a detailed opinion in about 150. The remainder are decided by a *per curiam* opinion, which is short and unsigned. The Court operates as a single body and does not decide cases in panels. It receives approximately 2000 petitions for review each year. The degree of discretion enjoyed by the justices makes the Supreme Court unique among United States courts. Unlike most other appellate judges, the justices are free to select those cases they regard as most important. Most of the Court's docket, then, consists of highly controversial issues with significant political implications.

Unlike Germany and Italy, there is no specialised constitutional court in the United States. The Supreme Court resolves many disputes involving federal statutes and administrative regulations that do not involve the Constitution in any way. The Court, moreover, cannot settle conflicts over constitutionality unless they are presented in the context of real legal controversies where the plaintiff alleges a concrete injury to a personal interest.

PERSONNEL

The highest positions of prestige within the legal profession belong to judges. Evidence of this exalted rank is the fact that men and women are commonly called 'judge' even long after they have vacated the office. Judges are lawyers and thus receive the same professional education as attorneys. No special experience or training is required of judges. They are expected to perform their judicial duties without any formal instruction or apprenticeship. Those lawyers who become judges typically do so in middle age and regard a judgeship as the capstone of a successful legal career, a reward for years engaged in the practice of law. The federal judiciary and the appellate state courts are in general attractive to the best of the legal profession.

When analysing who becomes a judge, one must distinguish between *recruitment* and *selection*.[31] Recruitment refers to the mechanisms that induce lawyers to seek judgeships. Selection refers to the process by which judges are selected from the pool of recruited members of the legal profession. Judges, in general, are recruited from the elite of the bar, who themselves are already an elite of the population. Judges tend to have moderate to conservative attitudes.[32]

A disproportionate number of justices of the federal Supreme Court have attended an Ivy League college or law school. Surprisingly, there is no constitutional or statutory requirement that Supreme Court justices be lawyers, although nearly all the states require judges to be 'learned in the law'. In fact, all members of the Supreme Court have had legal training. Because the president appoints the justices, many of them are either political supporters or personal friends of the president or are recommended by someone who is. Although many justices have had no prior judicial experience, they have nearly all held some kind of state or federal political office. More than 90 per cent of the justices come from the middle or upper class. They also generally come from socially prestigious families, from urban areas, are Anglo-Saxon Protestants and are white males. The first and only black was appointed to the Court in 1967, and the first and only woman was appointed in 1981. There is no compulsory retirement age, so five of the presently sitting justices are in their seventies and three are in their sixties. Article III of the Constitution requires the presidential nominees to the Supreme Court be confirmed by a majority vote in the Senate. The Senate has refused to confirm 26 of the 136 Supreme Court nominees submitted to it by the president.[33] They are appointed 'during good behaviour', which in practice amounts to life tenure. Lower federal judges are selected in the same way. The president does not actually select district and circuit judges but defers to the wishes of the Senators of his party who represent the states involved. The tradition of 'senatorial courtesy' insures that the full Senate will conform their colleagues' choices.

The states use five methods for selecting judges: partisan elections (candidates run under the label of a political party – 12 states); nonpartisan elections (the candidate's political party is not identified on the ballot – 12 states); election by the state legislature (4 states); gubernatorial appointment (similar to the federal method – 8 states); and the merit plan (14 states).[34] Under the latter, a judicial nominating board composed of judges, lawyers and laymen screens applications for a vacancy and sends a list of the three to five most qualified candidates to the governor who must choose one person from the list. Since the 1940s all the states that have changed their mode of selecting judges have adopted the merit plan, called the Missouri plan after the first state to adopt it. Most state judges serve limited terms and are eligible for re-election or reappointment. As the difference in selection methods indicates, state judges are expected to be more accountable to the public than federal judges. It is therefore common for state criminal trials to be broadcast on television, while television cameras are absolutely barred from federal courtrooms.

The Sixth and Seventh Amendments to the Constitution guarantee the right to trial by jury in criminal prosecutions and civil suits in federal courts. The Fourteenth Amendment extends this right to defendants in state criminal proceedings as well. The trial, or petit, jury typically consists of twelve laymen, who are randomly drawn from a list of registered voters in the jurisdiction. In a public proceeding, the attorneys examine the potential jurors for bias, and the judge will excuse any who cannot render an impartial verdict. The trend is to use smaller juries (six is becoming common) and even to permit non-unanimous verdicts. Frequently, litigants waive their right to a jury trial and are tried by the judge sitting alone, i.e. in a 'bench trial'. The Fifth Amendment guarantees the right in federal criminal cases of indictment by grand jury. The grand jury decides whether the government possesses sufficient evidence to warrant a prosecution. It consists of twenty-three laymen chosen in the same manner as petit juries. Several states have eliminated the grand jury and permit public prosecutors, who typically are popularly elected for limited terms, to accuse individuals 'by information'. Only one jurisdiction, the State of Vermont, utilises lay judges as distinguished from jurors. Two assistant judges, elected by the voters of the county for four-year terms, sit beside a professional judge, selected by the merit plan, in civil and criminal cases heard in Vermont Superior Court, which is a trial court of general jurisdiction. The lay judges have equal voting rights with the professional judge. Critics believe that the role of laymen should be confined to fact-finding as jurors and should not include deciding other issues, such as sentence, which should be the sole province of the professional judicial magistrate. Vermont has a long tradition of distrust of lawyers and judges and shows no signs of abolishing the assistant judgeships.

The United States Constitution permits the removal of federal judges guilty of treason, bribery, or other high crimes amd misdemeanors. The constitutional authority to impeach, or accuse, is vested in the House of Representatives, and the power to try impeachments rests with the Senate. Only nine federal judges have been impeached by the House of Representatives and only four convicted and removed by the Senate. Samuel Chase was the only Supreme Court justice impeached, but in 1805 the Senate refused to convict, leading President Thomas Jefferson to complain that impeachment was merely a 'scarecrow'. Although federal judges may only be removed by impeachment and conviction, there are up to five removal devices, including impeachment, present in the states.[35] Voters can refuse to re-elect an unethical judge. By means of a recall ballot in some states voters may remove a judge before his term expires. In a few states the legislature by 'address' may vote to remove an official from the bench. A number of states recently have established independent judicial conduct boards. These commissions hear complaints about judicial misconduct and have the authority to discipline errant judges directly or to recommend such action to the state supreme court. Sanctions include private reprimand, public censure, retirement and removal. The United States Supreme Court has held that in the United States 'judges are exempt from liability in a civil action for acts performed in the exercise of their judicial functions'.[36]

SCOPE OF AUTHORITY

State and federal courts in the United States perform a number of functions, some of which find general acceptance and others of which generate significant public controversy.[37] Among the non-controversial functions are the resolution of disputes, the enforcement of social norms, the processing of uncontested cases, the promotion of economic development and the enhancement of governmental legitimacy. When negotiation or mediation has failed to achieve a mutually satisfactory outcome, disputants may bring their conflict to a court if the alleged injury is one recognised by the law. The adjudicator will resolve the dispute in accordance with the relevant law. The decision affects primarily the parties to the case. Besides helping disputants settle their conflicts, judges enforce society's rules of behaviour. Because the interest of a third party, the state, determines the result, both parties often are dissatisfied with the court's decision. In several categories of cases, the defendant does not deny the allegations made in the plaintiff's complaint and therefore there is no dispute. The defendant has simply refused to meet admitted obligations. Many landlord-tenant, creditor-debtor and divorce proceedings are non-contentious. Because the defendant usually declines to appear in court, judges award the plaintiffs in these suits 'judgment by default'. These three actions constitute about 43 per cent of all civil cases disposed of in United States courts.[38]

Growth in the free market economy of the United States requires that capital be freely available. Courts provide incentives for financial investment and lending by reducing the risks associated with these activities. They reduce risk primarily by enforcing contracts, thus establishing an atmosphere of predictability and stability conducive to economic development. One must not underestimate the contribution courts have made over the past two centuries to the emergence of the United States as the world's wealthiest nation. The moral authority of the state and federal governments rests upon their willingness to keep the promises made in the state and federal constitutions. By sanctioning violations of public and private rights, courts force government to abide by these promises. Ironically, by enhancing the legitimacy of government, the judiciary facilitates the ability of government to control society, since no government could survive unless the bulk of the population were in the habit of obeying public authority.

Four judicial functions are quite controversial and have sparked efforts, mostly unsuccessful, to limit the third branch's scope of authority. These functions are defining authority, policy making, changing society and administering institutions. Supreme Court Justice Robert H. Jackson once described the high court as 'the nation's balance wheel, continually tilting the flow of power away from one sufficiently powerful branch of the national government to another and to and from the individual and the states'.[39] The significance of this function is illustrated by *US* v *Nixon*,[40] in which the Supreme Court resolved a dispute between the courts and the president over the extent of the latter's privilege not to comply with subpoenae for information. When the Court interpreted the Constitution in favour of the judiciary, President Richard Nixon resigned. Thomas Jefferson believed that conflicts between the branches over the extent of their respective powers should be resolved by the authors of the constitutional division of power, the sovereign people, not by the popularly unaccountable Supreme Court.

Throughout its history the high court has not only interpreted the law but has made law. A series of highly controversial policy decisions in the 1960s and 1970s in the areas of school prayer, busing to achieve racial balance in the schools, legislative reapportionment, racial preference, the rights of the criminally accused and abortion has led to a continuous wave of criticism directed at the Court for usurping the legislature's prerogative in the formulation of public policy. In these cases, the Court is not primarily concerned with the parties to the litigation challenging existing policy but with the interests of large numbers of people not parties to the suit.

In a number of cases beginning with the Court's decision invalidating racial segregation in *Brown* v. *Board of Education* (1954), the Supreme Court has attempted to effect massive social change by either modifying public attitudes and values or by redistributing wealth and political power. The Court, for example, has attempted to reduce racism and to raise the level of tolerance for religious minorities as well as to help blacks and women acquire a larger share of power and money.[41] Critics question the wisdom and right of federal judges, unaccountable and insulated from public opinion, to engineer changes on such a scale. *Brown* was also significant in that its enforcement required that federal district courts monitor local schools for compliance. When school boards refuse to comply with federal court orders, as happened in Boston in the 1970s, district judges often assume responsibility for the day-to-day management of the schools, including the assignment of teachers and students. Responding to allegations of systematic violation of the constitutional rights of individuals, federal courts, in order to remedy these violations, have administered not only state schools but also state prisons and mental hospitals as well as local police and fire departments found liable for racially discriminatory hiring. States have been forced to raise and spend millions of dollars to improve conditions in psychiatric and penal institutions. Critics complain that the allocation of public revenue and the raising of revenues through taxation are legislative, not judicial, tasks. The judges respond that the democratic process has failed to enforce the terms of the Constitution.

DECISION MAKING

Students of the judicial process have put forward two mutually contradictory models to explain why judges decide cases the way they do. According to the traditional model, a judicial decision is the product of the facts of a case and the law relevant to those facts. Adjudication is, therefore, a logical process, which leaves no room for the judge's personal attitudes, preferences or feelings. Judges are believed to be fungible. The model has been expressed in the formula R (rules) $\times F$ (facts) $= D$ (decision).[42] The mechanical model is most frequently invoked by law school professors.

Admitting that the traditional model expresses the expectations in United States legal culture as to how judges *should* make decisions, social scientists have challenged its power to explain how they *do* in fact decide cases. The sociological model assumes that the attitudes of a judge, whether he is politically liberal, moderate or conservative, explain decisions better than any other independent variable. These attitudes, in turn, are the product of social background characteristics and environmental influences. Research shows that Protestant judges and older judges impose harsher sentences on criminals than Catholic and Jewish and younger judges.[43] The background characteristic with the greatest explanatory power is party affiliation. Democrats are more lenient sentencers than Republicans.[44] There is evidence that judges respond to changes in public opinion. For example, during the early years of the Vietnam War federal district judges most frequently sentenced defendants convicted of avoiding conscription to the maximum penalty prescribed by law – five years imprisonment. Gradually, the American people became disenchanted with the war and in the final years the same judges were handing out the lightest possible sentence – probation – for the same offence.[45]

Personal attitudes only explain decisions when the case involves an issue which divides those on the left and right ends of the political spectrum. Such issues include the punishment of criminals, civil rights and liberties, government regulation of business and labour-management disputes. Unless the case presents one of these, knowing whether a judge is a liberal or a conservative will not aid in predicting his decision. For some judges knowing their political orientation does not aid prediction because they place more importance upon their duty as a judge than upon their policy preferences. Judges either have an activist perception of the role that justifies judicial law making or they perceive the judge's function as limited to interpreting and applying

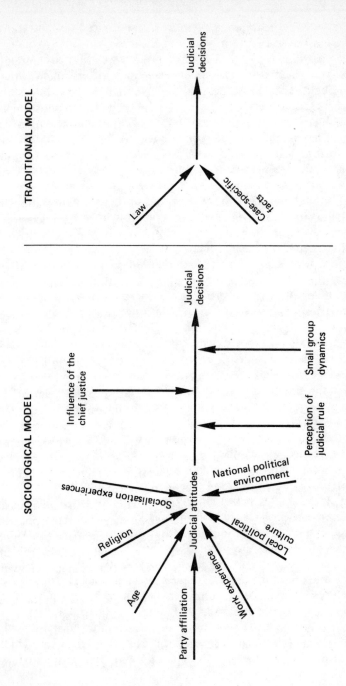

Figure 2.3 Models of judicial decision-making

the law made by legislatures or administrators. Justice Frankfurter, for instance, confessed that as a Jew from Eastern Europe he was most sympathetic with the plight of Jehovah's Witnesses who were subject to what they regarded as widespread persecution in the United States. Yet he upheld such acts of 'persecution' as forcing school children to salute the United States flag, even though it is forbidden by their religious doctrine, on the grounds that such requirements, unjust and foolish as they might be, were consistent with the Constitution.[46]

The sociological model states that judges will reach different decisions if they are members of a collegial body than if they are sitting alone. Because all appellate courts are collegial institutions, small group dynamics help explain the decisions of these tribunals.[42] Social psychologists have discovered that in small groups there is pressure to conform to the views of the majority. Although dissents are permitted, the vast majority of state and federal appellate decisions, in fact, are unanimous. Judges tend to defer to the wisdom of their colleagues who have developed a reputation for expertise in a given subject. Although some state appellate courts do, none of the federal courts follow the practice of designating prior to the hearing one member of the court as the reporter with responsibility for writing the court's opinion.

Judges may also attempt to persuade their colleagues to change their mind, a manoeuvre which is of course impossible on single-judge tribunals. Such appeals to reason are common in the decision making process of the United States Supreme Court. After the Court accepts a case for review, the parties submit written briefs and appear for oral argument, which occurs in nearly every case that results in a full written opinion. Following oral argument, the nine justices meet in a secret conference, discuss the merits of the case and vote. If the Chief Justice is in the majority, he assigns the task of writing the opinion of the court either to himself or one of the associate justices in the majority. If the chief is in the minority, the privilege of assignment falls to the senior associate justice in the majority. Given the fact that some cases are perceived as more important than others, the chief's power to assign the opinion can be used to win and reward 'friends' and to punish 'enemies'. In certain cases Chief Justice Warren Burger allegedly waits until his brethren have voted and then casts his ballot with the majority in order to control the assignment, regardless of his views on the merits of the case.[48]

A justice is free to change his vote at any time prior to public announcement of the Court's decision. In cases where the vote is close, in 5–4 or 6–3 splits, the dissenting justices will attempt to persuade one or two members of the provisional majority to join them. Both factions circulate drafts of the dissenting and majority opinions, and an initial opinion of the Court may become a dissent if the minority is sufficiently persuasive. Judges who agree with the result but disagree with the opinion writer's rationale may file a separate concurring opinion. There is in fact significant fluidity in Supreme Court voting.[49]

The most controversial technique employed by justices attempting to maximise their influence is bargaining. The justice writing an opinion will often make changes in the draft in order to keep or win the vote of critical colleagues. One justice may agree to vote with a fellow justice in a case important to him in exchange for the latter's promise to vote with the former in a subsequent case in which he has a special interest.[50] Allegedly, in a 1972 case Justice William Brennan voted to sustain the conviction of a man charged with murder whom Brennan believed deserving of a new trial, in exchange for Justice Harry Blackmun's promise to vote to invalidate the state's prohibition on abortions.[51]

LINKAGES WITH OTHER POLITICAL INSTITUTIONS

Judges are frequently asked to grace *ad hoc* commissions. Governors and presidents find their reputation for learning and impartiality useful in raising the prestige of such bodies. President Truman asked Associate Justice Robert Jackson to serve as the chief prosecutor in the Nuremburg trials of Nazi war criminals, an assignment that took him away from the Supreme Court for a year. At the behest of President Lyndon Johnson, Chief Justice Earl Warren headed a commission to investigate the assassination of President John F. Kennedy. The controversial character of the Warren Commission's findings have, however, made subsequent Supreme Court justices reluctant to accept such extra-judicial posts.

Courts are subject to a number of outside influences. Articles that appear in law reviews and other legal periodicals influence judicial decisions, especially the reviews published by the most prestigious law schools – Harvard, Yale, Columbia and the University of Michigan.[52] Social scientists also exert influence through the publication of social science data bearing on the policy issues that increasingly come before the courts.[53] Some of the Supreme Court's law clerks, recent law school graduates in their mid-twenties who serve a particular justice for one or two years, have participated in shaping the work of the Court.[54] The

Supreme Court permits individuals and organisations who are not parties to a case but who have an interest in the outcome to file *amicus curiae* briefs. These briefs, like the one filed by the United States in *Brown* v. *Board of Education* (1954), can be quite influential.[55]

In order to maximise their influence in the policy making process, interest groups commonly employ litigation as one in a number of lobbying tactics. When the Federal Communications Commission ruled that stations which carry cigarette commercials must also run anti-cigarette announcements, the tobacco lobby attacked the ruling in court.[56] Civil rights groups have long relied upon the courts to fight discrimination and inequality. The National Association for the Advancement of Colored People (NAACP) is the single most successful interest group in using litigation as a tactic to gain desired policies. Since 1944, this association has accumulated a string of victories in the struggle for racial equality. A close second is the Jehovah's Witnesses in their drive to obtain a maximum of religious liberty.[57] Private organisations like the Environmental Defense Fund and the Center for Law and Social Policy have come into existence to represent groups chronically unrepresented or under-represented in the legislative and bureaucratic processes. Their clients include 'broad classes of people, such as environmentalists and consumers, who have an important collective interest but as individuals have too marginal an interest to warrant hiring an attorney on their own'.[58]

Compliance with Supreme Court decisions is not uniform. There was virtually no compliance with *Brown* for twenty years. In 1964 Congress in the Civil Rights Act prohibited the use of federal funds by an institution or programme practising racial discrimination. The law had no immediate impact because education was almost entirely funded by the states. In the Elementary and Secondary Education Act of 1965 the Congress for the first time made large sums of money available to the states for education on condition they comply with the 1964 proviso. Proving that the carrot is more effective than the stick, large-scale compliance with the order of *Brown* to end racial segregation was underway by 1966. On the other hand, although chiefs of police complained that the Supreme Court was 'handcuffing' the police, there was immediate and general compliance with decisions regulating police searches and interrogations.[59] Although outright defiance of judicial orders is rare, research indicates that compliance is most complete when certain conditions prevail. The conditions relate to the internal characteristics of the court, certain external governmental conditions and a variety of environmental influences.[60]

Congress and the president have taken a number of steps to limit the impact of Supreme Court decisions they find distasteful. Congress may propose constitutional amendments to reverse particular court decisions or to curtail the Court's power. The Eleventh, Thirteenth, Fourteenth, Fifteenth, Sixteenth and Twenty-sixth Amendments reversed Supreme Court decisions. One of the most disputed congressional checks is removal of the appellate jurisdiction of the Supreme Court over a particular category of cases. The Court upheld such a practice in *ex parte McCardle*,[61] and conservative congressmen are presently engaged in efforts to strip the federal courts of jurisdiction over all cases involving school prayer, busing and abortion, thus leaving such cases to the state courts, even though they raise constitutional questions.

The president's principal source of influence over the Supreme Court is the power of appointment. Frustrated by judicial opposition to his New Deal economic recovery programme, President Franklin Roosevelt attempted to pack the Court by persuading Congress to increase the size of the Court from nine to fifteen. Congress declined, but because of deaths and retirements during his four terms in office President Roosevelt appointed nine justices to the Supreme Court, thereby saving the New Deal.

CONCLUSION

In the United States, the power of judicial review is a firmly entrenched component of popular legal culture. As a result, courts participate as an integral partner in a policy making process. The fragmentation of decision making is one of the distinctive traits of the United States political system and provides numerous points of access for interest groups. However, because courts sustain most challenged governmental actions, they are also one of the principal sources of governmental legitimacy and political stability.

NOTES

1. John Locke, *Second Treatise of Government* (Indianapolis: Hackett Publishing, 1980 [1690]), section 146.
2. Michael D. Wormser (ed.), *The Supreme Court: Justice and the Law*, 3rd

edn (Washington, DC: Congressional Quarterly, 1983), p. 21.

3. 1 Cranch 137 (1803).
4. Alexis de Tocqueville, *Democracy in America* (New York: Alfred A. Knopf, 1945 [1835]), vol. I, ch. 6, p. 104.
5. 19 Howard 393 (1857).
6. Theodore Lowi, *The End of Liberalism: The Second Republic of the United States*, 2nd edn (New York: W. W. Norton, 1979).
7. Michael J. Perry, *The Constitution, The Courts, and Human Rights: An Inquiry into the Legitimacy of Constitutional Policymaking by the Judiciary* (New Haven: Yale University Press, 1982).
8. Arthur Selwyn Miller, *Toward Increased Judicial Activism: The Political Role of the Supreme Court* (Westport, Conn.: Greenwood Press, 1982).
9. Sheldon Goldman and Thomas P. Jahnige, *The Federal Courts as a Political System*, 3rd edn (New York: Harper and Row, 1985), p. 15.
10. Mitchell S. G. Klein, *Law, Courts, and Policy* (Englewood Cliffs, NJ: Prentice-Hall, 1984), pp. 100, 63.
11. Klein, *Law, Courts, and Policy*, pp. 63–4.
12. Howard Ball, *Courts and Politics: The Federal Judicial System* (Englewood Cliffs, NJ: Prentice-Hall, 1980), p. 2.
13. James Q. Wilson, *American Government: Institutions and Policies*, 2nd edn (Lexington, Mass.: D. C. Heath, 1983), pp. 78–9.
14. Stuart A. Scheingold, *The Politics of Rights: Lawyers, Public Policy, and Political Change* (New Haven: Yale University Press, 1974).
15. 347 US 483 (1954).
16. de Tocqueville, *Democracy in America*, vol. I, p. 280.
17. Edward S. Corwin, *The Higher Law Background of American Consitutional Law* (Ithaca, NY: Cornell University Press, 1929).
18. See *Massachusetts* v. *Laird*, 400 US 886 (1970).
19. Alexander Hamilton, James Madison, and John Jay, *The Federalist Papers* (New York: The New American Library, 1961 [1788]), no. 78.
20. Goldman and Jahnige, *The Federal Courts*, pp. 109–10.
21. *Rogers* v. *Richmond*, 365 US 534, 540–1 (1961).
22. Richard J. Richardson and Kenneth N. Vines, *The Politics of Federal Courts* (Boston: Little, Brown, 1970), p. 21.
23. Amy K. Rausch, 'The State of the Judiciary: An Agenda for Change', *State Court Journal*, V (1981), pp. 23–5.
24. Law Enforcement Assistance Administration, *National Survey of Court Organization* (Washington, DC: Government Printing Office, 1973), p. 4.
25. Gerald M. Caplan, 'Foreword', in Karen Markle Knab (ed.), *Courts of Limited Jurisdiction: A National Survey* (Washington, DC: Government Printing Office, 1977).
26. *Annual Report of the Director, Administrative Office of the United States Courts* (Washington, DC: Government Printing Office, 1982), pp. 4, 7, 290.
27. *Annual Report*, p. 186.
28. *Annual Report*, Tables B–1, B–3.
29. *Annual Report*, p. 49.
30. Henry J. Abraham, *The Judicial Process*, 4th edn (New York: Oxford University Press, 1980), p. 181.

31. Jerome R. Corsi, *Judicial Politics* (Englewood Cliffs, NJ: Prentice-Hall, 1984), pp. 103–4.
32. Klein, *Law, Courts, and Policy*, p. 97.
33. Abraham, *The Judicial Process*, p. 80.
34. Sheldon Goldman and Austin Sarat, 'Judges: Selection and Background', in Sheldon Goldman and Austin Sarat (eds), *American Court Systems: Readings in Judicial Process and Behavior* (San Francisco: W. H. Freeman, 1978), p. 255.
35. Herbert Jacob, *Justice in America* (Boston, Mass.: Little, Brown, 1978), pp. 116–18.
36. *Randall* v. *Brigham*, 74 US 523 (1868).
37. Willard Hurst, *The Growth of American Law: The Law Makers* (Boston, Mass.: Little, Brown, 1950); Willard Hurst, 'The Functions of Courts in the United States, 1950–1980', *Law and Society Review*, XV (1981), pp. 401–71.
38. Craig Wanner, 'The Public Ordering of Private Relations; Part One: Initiating Civil Cases in Urban Trial Courts', *Law and Society Review*, VIII (1974), p. 422.
39. Wormser, *The Supreme Court*, 2.
40. 417 US 683 (1974).
41. Stuart A. Scheingold, *The Politics of Rights: Lawyers, Public Policy, and Political Change* (New Haven: Yale University Press, 1974).
42. Jerome Frank, *Courts on Trial: Myth and Reality in American Justice* (Princeton, NJ: Princeton University Press, 1949).
43. Stuart S. Nagel, 'Ethnic Affiliations and Judicial Propensities', *Journal of Politics*, XXIV (1962), p. 110; Sheldon Goldman, 'Voting Behavior on the United States Courts of Appeals Revisited', *American Political Science Review*, LXIX (1975), p. 505.
44. Stuart S. Nagel, 'Political Party Affiliation and Judges' Decisions,' *American Political Science Review*, LV (1961), p. 843.
45. Beverley B. Cook, 'Public Opinion and Federal Judicial Policy', *American Journal of Political Science*, XXI (1977), p. 598.
46. *West Virginia State Board of Education* v. *Barnette*, 319 US 624 (1943).
47. Walter F. Murphy, *Elements of Judicial Strategy* (Chicago: The University of Chicago Press, 1964).
48. Bob Woodward and Scott Armstrong, *The Brethren: Inside the Supreme Court* (New York: Simon and Schuster, 1979), pp. 64–9.
49. J. Woodford Howard, 'On the Fluidity of Judicial Choice,' *American Political Science Review*, LXII (1968), p. 43.
50. Murphy, *Elements of Judicial Strategy*.
51. Woodward and Armstrong, *The Brethren*, pp. 224–5.
52. Chester A. Newland, 'Legal Periodicals and the United States Supreme Court', *Midwest Journal of Political Science*, III (1959), p. 72.
53. Abraham, *The Judicial Process*, p. 248.
54. William H. Rehnquist, 'Who Writes Decisions of the Supreme Court?', *US News and World Report* (13 December, 1975), p. 275.
55. Samuel Krislov, *The Role of the Attorney General as Amicus Curiae* (Washington, DC: American Enterprise Institute for Public Policy Research, 1968), p. 91.

56. Jeffrey M. Berry, *The Interest Group Society* (Boston, Mass.: Little, Brown, 1984), p. 195.
57. Abraham, *The Judicial Process*, p. 250.
58. Berry, *Interest Group*, p. 197.
59. *Mapp* v. *Ohio,* 367 US 643 (1961); *Miranda* v. *Arizona*, 384, US 436 (1966).
60. Stephen L. Wasby, *The Impact of the United States Supreme Court: Some Perspectives* (Homewood, IL: Dorsey Press, 1970).
61. 7 Wall. 506 (1869).

3 The Courts in Australia
Roman Tomasic

Compared with the United States, very little research has been undertaken in Australia on its judicial process and its relationship to the wider political order of Australian society. However, even internationally, the study of judicial politics is in an under-developed state.[1] In view of this dearth of available Australian empirical research, this chapter will be traversing largely unchartered ground. Having said this, it should be pointed out that the politicisation and the political role of Australian judges and courts has been a subject of considerable public interest in recent years in Australia. One reason for this has been the frequent use of judges to head Royal Commissions of Inquiry to investigate what are often politically quite sensitive issues. Another has been the recent series of inquiries regarding the appointment or the removal of various state court magistrates in New South Wales as well as the inquiry into the possible misbehaviour of a federal High Court judge and a state intermediate court judge in New South Wales. With all the attendant publicity which has been generated by these scandals it is regrettable that there is so little systematically researched Australian empirical material to draw upon in respect to what we might call the politics of the judiciary. Nevertheless, a few broad outlines and patterns may be discerned.

LEGAL CULTURE

It is appropriate to begin by sketching the broad framework within which the Australian judicature is located. The British heritage of the Australian legal system is particularly evident, despite the resort to United States constitutional precedents at the time of the federation of the six Australian colonies. Since then, local conditions have also had an important influence upon the development of the legal system as well as upon its relationship with the political order at both federal and state levels. Nevertheless, the British imprint still looms large in the legal and political life. This is in part due to the fact that Australia remains a constitutional monarchy, with the British monarch also being the Queen of Australia and its head of state. On a day-to-day basis, the effect of this is that state governors and the Commonwealth or federal Governor General act as representatives of the monarch. While for most practical purposes these are largely figurehead positions, with the government in effect being in the hands of the political party with a majority in the lower house, it is not unknown for governors or Governors General to exercise what has been described as their reserve power and to dismiss the government of the day, despite its continued majority in the lower house. The most recent manifestation of this was, of course, the constitutional crisis of November 1975 which saw the then Governor General dismiss the Whitlam federal Labour government and install the Leader of the Opposition Liberal party.

This event, had major implications for the legal system and for the High Court of Australia, in particular, in view of the fact that Chief Justice of the High Court, Sir Garfield Barwick, who had himself been a federal Liberal Party Attorney General, proffered advice to the Governor General concerning the nature and extent of the latter's reserve powers as representative of the Crown. The tension and trauma generated by this event was to embroil the High Court in controversy for the remainder of the term of the Chief Justice, so that it has been relatively easy for the High Court to be once more involved in political controversy in the light of current accusations against another High Court member, Mr Justice Lionel Murphy. He has been accused of seeking to influence the trial of a Sydney lawyer with high political connections in the state of New South Wales. This incident has become the subject of extensive Senate committee hearings in the federal parliament. It might be mentioned in passing that Murphy was himself a former Labour Party Attorney General in the ousted Whitlam government. Thus, although Australia is clearly a modern constitutional democracy, its elected political figures can nevertheless be dismissed by officials reliant upon more traditional monarchical authority, often in alliance with leading judicial figures. The roots of this situation can be traced back to the fact that the superior Australian common law courts, such as the State Supreme Courts, were directly modelled upon the old English monarchical courts such as Kings Bench, Common Pleas, Exchequer and Chancery, over which the monarch originally had great control by virtue of the fact that these courts emerged out of the court of the king. Even after the English judiciary was more clearly separated from the monarchical administration from about the seventeenth century, Australian colonies still retained the Privy Council of the British House of Lords as the ultimate court of appeal for Australian cases. This has only recently effectively come to an end, with the abolition of most Privy Council appeals, although many members of the Australian judiciary still seem to retain an especially strong commitment to Anglo-monarchical values, if the public statements of some leading judges are to be taken on their face value.

THE STRUCTURE OF AUSTRALIAN COURTS

As we saw above, Australia has a federal system of government, with the High Court of Australia as the pre-eminent appeal court in both state and federal matters. The High Court is also the constitutional court for matters arising under the federal Constitution. Until the mid-1970s there were very few other federal courts apart from the High Court, with most litigation involving matters of federal law being handled by state courts which had for various reasons been invested with federal jurisdiction. However, since the mid-1970s at the federal level, we have seen the establishment of the Federal Court of Australia and the Family Court of Australia. The jurisdiction and workload of these courts is expanding quite rapidly, so much so that there have now been a number of proposals for restructuring the system of Australian courts, partly due to the rapid growth in the size and status of federal courts, such as the Federal Court of Australia. This has been accentuated by the somewhat extensive legalisation of disputes with and within federal administrative agencies as reflected in the growth of what has generally been described as 'the new administrative law'.[2] This has seen the creation of complaints handling devices such as the federal Administrative Appeals Tribunal and the office[a] of the Ombudsman. To a large degree, this phenomenon of the judicialis-ation of administrative dispute handling through rapid growth of the new administrative law may be seen as having reflected an expansion of the executive arm of government into the judicial arm and so has further blurred the executive–judicial divide by increasingly requiring judicial officers to participate in the public policy making process and to deal with administrative disputes which previously were either ignored or dealt with by non-legal mechanisms.[3] At the same time, it also reflects the continuing appeal to the executive of the legitimating qualities of judicialised dispute processing – especially where it is possible to retain a greater degree of control of these proceedings than would be possible for governments having to deal with the more professionalised and tradition-bound higher common law courts.

While this has been especially pronounced in the federal sphere in Australia, it is arguable that, in other respects, it reflects a pattern which has long been evident in state courts, especially within courts of summary jurisdiction or magistrates courts, as we will see further below. Since the creation of the Federal Court in 1976, this court has taken over much of the trial and minor appellate work which previously was dealt with by the High Court. While the High Court still retains an important original jurisdiction in constitutional cases and also deals with appeals from state and federal courts where the amount involved in the claim exceeds $20,000, it has increasingly become evident that the Federal Court of Australia will act as an intermediate court of appeal in many, but not all, federal matters. Given that the case load of the High Court has declined slightly in recent years, the increasing legalisation of problem solving in Australian society has meant that the repeated calls of the Chief Justice for further limits upon the flow of cases are unlikely to see any massive decline in workload, as the figures in Table 3.1 suggest. In fact, in its 1983–84 Annual Report, the High Court specifically stresses that the decline in judgments in 1983 'was not due to a decline in the workload but rather to other factors such as the particularly lengthy hearings in an unusual number of important cases'.[4] This is a reference to the fact that the court seems to be dealing with increasingly complex and politically difficult constitutional questions arising out of rivalry between state and federal governments. As well, the court has seen a steady increase in the number of appeals involving issues of legal principle or public

Table 3.1   Case load of High Court of Australia, 1977–83

		1977	1978	1979	1980	1981	1982	1983
Matters heard								
Appeals from state								
Supreme Court		58	36	48	29	40	43	68
Appeals from a federal								
court		6	12	10	16	20	14	20
Other matters heard		81	103	100	139	133	141	89
	Total	145	151	158	184	193	198	177
Judgements								
Reserved		73	77	78	88	84	78	70
Delivered		103	74	87	72	90	113	59
	Total	176	151	165	160	174	186	139

policy from state and federal courts. We will return to this issue of public policy making by Australian courts in a later section of this paper. Despite the growth in the federal court infrastructure over the past decade, it is still the case that the vast bulk of matters arising under federal law are dealt with in state courts exercising federal jurisdiction. An exception is family law matters which since 1976 have been dealt with primarily by the new federal Family Court of Australia, the largest single federal court, with forty-five judges compared with the thirty who sit on the Federal Court of Australia, and a body with a massive and increasing case load, as Table 3.2 illustrates.

Table 3.2   Applications dealt with by the Family Court of Australia, 1977–83

		1977	1978	1979	1980	1981	1982	1983
Custody		8623	7913	8504	8748	8560	8778	7914
Access		3778	3393	3710	4139	4214	4754	4784
Property		7372	8625	9115	9512	10468	12173	12288
Maintenance		8568	8092	9342	9386	9616	9988	9451
Injunction		2727	2991	4038	4688	4848	5019	4790
	Total	31068	31014	34699	36473	37706	40712	39227

These various statistics on the Family Court case load seem to suggest the increasing penetration of the Court into family relationships in Australia, once again illustrating the progressive legalisation of social relations in Australia. This has not been without its own problems for in recent years there has been a spate of attempted and successful killings of family law judges and the bombing of their homes and court registries. One sociologist has argued that this violence can be understood by reference to the contradictions which presently exist between the legalistic values and style of the Court and its involvement in quite sensitive social problems.[5]

It is useful to compare the above figures and trends with the situation in State Supreme Courts. In New South Wales, for example, the total number of criminal appearances in 1982 in the higher criminal courts was 5693, of these 4842 were proceeded with after committal. These matters related to 3975 distinct persons who were found guilty, a 1.7 per cent increase over the previous year.[6] Some trends in the handling of criminal cases are shown in Table 3.3. As is evident from Table 3.3, robbery, fraud, theft and other property offences account for over 60 per cent of cases handled in higher criminal courts. Over 40 per cent of higher court criminal cases were dealt with by resort to a bond or to

Table 3.3   Trends in offences 1979–82: distinct persons found guilty in NSW higher courts

Offence	1979 %	1980 %	1981 %	1982 %
Homicide/assault	12.5	11.2	11.4	11.2
Other offences against the person	0.5	0.6	0.7	0.7
Sexual offences	6.3	7.6	6.6	6.5
Robbery or extortion	10.7	9.0	9.2	9.4
Fraud and misappropriation	12.1	13.5	12.5	11.1
Break enter and steal	18.6	19.1	18.3	20.6
Other offences against property	21.3	21.3	22.1	22.6
Driving	5.9	5.5	7.0	5.9
Drugs	6.2	5.5	6.6	6.6
Other	5.9	6.7	5.5	5.3
	100.0	100.0	100.0	100.0
Total offences, N =	3170	3276	3910	3975

probation, while 36 per cent went to prison for a year or more.

If we turn to look at non-criminal or higher civil courts, far less systematic data is available. In a recent study of delays in the Supreme Courts of New South Wales, Victoria and the Australian Capital Territory the largest classes of civil cases were found to comprise personal injury cases (almost 30 per cent in New South Wales) and debt cases. Table 3.4 contrasts figures from samples from these three courts.

In New South Wales in 1981, a total of 12,910 civil cases were commenced in the Supreme Court but only 4061 were actually listed for hearing. In Victoria, the comparable figures were 11,391 and 2608 respectively, while in the Australian Capital Territory these figures were 1862 and 387 respectively. It is evident from the above state higher court figures that these courts are primarily concerned with fairly narrow types of cases. The great bulk of both civil and criminal cases seem to be concerned with the protection of property rights or are responses to personal injuries of one type or another.

We are now in a better position to turn briefly to examine the structure of Australian state and territory courts. (It may be helpful to refer to Figure 3.1 for the purpose of clarifying the relationship between state and federal courts.)

Table 3.4 Types of matters commenced in higher civil courts in Melbourne, Sydney and Canberra in sample of cases

Matter	Melbourne (N = 704) %	Sydney (N = 690) %	Canberra (N = 320) %
Personal injury	17.7	29.8	26.8
Mortgage default ⎫		18.8	3.8
Landlord & tenant ⎭	18.8	1.9	4.7
Realty	1.0	5.7	0.9
Money owing	33.3	10.4	51.9
Damages	9.2	2.6	2.2
Defamation	0.6	1.6	2.5
Family matters	1.6	0.7	0.6
Estates	1.6	3.6	0.0
Administrative review	0.4	0.9	0.9
Tax	0.0	0.3	0.0
Arbitration	0.6	0.1	0.0
Companies	4.3	10.7	2.5
Industrial property	0.1	0.9	0.0
Other	10.5	11.9	3.1

At the pinnacle of the court system in each of these jurisdictions sits a state or territory Supreme Court. These are courts of general jurisdiction which supervise all courts below them. Unlike federal courts, whose jurisdiction is essentially based upon specific statutes, State Supreme Courts have jurisdiction over all matters arising within their jurisdiction, unless this has been specifically excluded by statute. The jurisdictions of Supreme Courts is modelled upon that of English superior common law courts, although this has been expanded through legislation. All states, apart from the least populous State of Tasmania, have a three tiered system of civil and criminal courts, with the Supreme Court being the superior court, the District or County Court being the intermediate court and the third tier being variously described as Magistrates' Courts, Courts of Petty Sessions, Local Courts or Courts of Summary Jurisdiction. The Territories and the State of Tasmania only have two tiers, without a District or County Court. Elsewhere, intermediate and lower courts generally act as the main trial courts, except in very serious matters which are heard in the Supreme Court. Civil cases are generally allocated between courts by references to the monetary value of the matter in dispute.

In addition to the above broad pattern of state and territory courts,

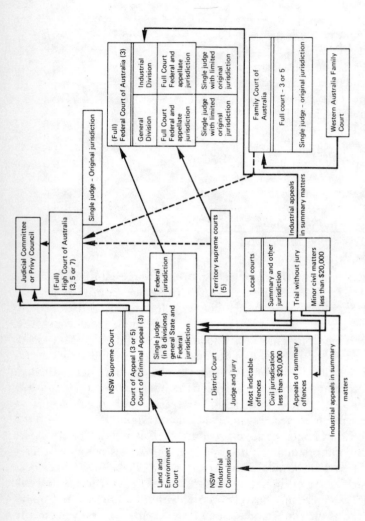

Figure 3.1   Structure of Australian Federal Courts and the State Courts of New South Wales

Note: New South Wales has the most elaborate state system of courts. The other five states have somewhat less elaborate systems. Tribunals have been left out to simplify matters. The broken lines indicate that appeals are only possible in limited circumstances. Adapted from J. Crawford, *Australian Courts of Law* (Melbourne: Oxford University Press, 1982) pp. 230–1.

there are a number of specialist courts in these jurisdictions, dealing with matters such as small claims, industrial disputes, workers compensation, licensing, mining, and land and environment work. One observer of Australian courts has noted that these additional courts are more akin to tribunals than they are to courts of general jurisdiction.[7] This is confirmed by the fact that governments have been far more ready to intervene in these specialist courts than they have in courts of general jurisdiction, apart from those at the lowest level. This is largely due to the fact that these specialist courts are creatures of statute and tend to deal with often quite sensitive administrative issues (as in the area of town planning regulation) or issues involving the allocation of rights and privileges (as in the licensing area). Moreover, these specialist bodies are not protected from governmental intervention by a mantle of common law rights and traditions, such as those which superior court judges are able to call upon. Furthermore, for a long time many specialist adjudicators have also been members of the public services and so, in theory, have been subject to disciplinary proceedings for contravening ministerial directives.

This issue has recently come to a head in relation to members of the magistracy sitting in Courts of Petty Sessions, or their equivalent. Courts of Petty Sessions or local courts are the lowest level of criminal and civil courts and magistrates preside over proceedings in these courts. For some years magistrates have sought to achieve greater independence from executive authority by obtaining tenure akin to that of intermediate and superior court judges in Australia. Judges tend to have security of tenure so long as they are not shown to have misbehaved or have suffered incapacity. In New South Wales and Victoria magistrates have recently achieved a greater degree of security of tenure and independence from public service rules. However, this was not arrived at without a considerable degree of political controversy. Thus, in New South Wales, the government was at last forced to move in this direction after the premature death of the State Labour Party Attorney General and a considerable degree of political embarrassment to the government which arose out of revelations made by the Chief Magistrate concerning the conduct of a former federal Labour Party Attorney General who was then a High Court judge. When these allegations seemed to have been corroborated by an intermediate court state judge, as well as by the majority of a Senate Committee of Inquiry, the State government was forced to proceed with plans to give greater independence to magistrates, who were then to be appointed to the newly created local courts, which replaced the pre-existing Courts of Petty Sessions. This episode is instructive in a number of respects.

First, it illustrates how the tenure of judicial officers can readily be undermined by abolishing a particular court simply by re-naming it and refusing to reappoint members of the old court to the 'new' court. In fact, in New South Wales, the State government refused to reappoint five magistrates, who were to remain as public servants. A similar point can be made from an examination of the recent history of the Land and Environment Court in New South Wales. Its jurisdiction was previously largely covered by the Local Government Appeals Tribunal. In the process of reforming this jurisdiction, the new Land and Environment Court saw its status raised greatly to that of a superior court, akin to the state Supreme Court. However, even this was not sufficient to prevent the kind of political intervention which had characterised the old tribunal. It seems that, like the criminal law, land and environment law is a field which governments perceive to be an integral basis of their authority. It was not surprising therefore that the State government repeatedly turned to the passage of special legislation to overrule the decisions of the court. In view of these events, the Chief Judge of this court was moved to exclaim that: 'Planning and Environment law is an arena in which the cherished democratic principle of independence of the judiciary may well face one of its sternest tests.' After reporting this observation, the *Sydney Morning Herald* went on to add that the special legislation makes nonsense of the principles and procedures of the Government's own Environmental Planning and Assessment Act. Second . . . it raises the question of what value is to be attached by our society to an independent judiciary.'[8]

All of this criticism was to be of no avail for shortly afterwards, the State Attorney General told the Parliament that he had no doubt that the legislature should be free to overrule court decisions. He went on to give a narrow reading of the notion of judicial independence and emphasised that 'Once a [Court] decision is made it is not uncommon for the Government to take particular action in relation to its decision. This is not new, needless to say, it will be done again by Governments of all political persuasions.'[9] The Attorney General justified this by arguing that Parliament was the highest court in the state and so should be free to override decisions of the courts as such. This effectively seems to have blurred any sharp lines between the roles of the executive and of the judiciary. It is hardly surprising, therefore, that subsequently the Chief Judge of this Court chose to leave his Court to head a Royal Commission of Inquiry where he would have greater freedom of action. This episode does illustrate once again, however, the difficulties facing the independence of newer courts and courts which have emerged from a clear tradition of governmental interference or oversight, as in the case of bodies which have emerged out of administrative and regulatory tribunals.

Second, a broader issue can be raised concerning courts of summary justice, which cannot be avoided merely by resorting to the neat expedient of renaming a court. This is the issue of the existence within the judicial process of two tiers of justice, as McBarnet[10] has argued, which each have quite divergent judicial traditions, legal values and styles of processing cases. In other words, the independence of judges is not so much a function of artifacts such as new legal guarantees or arrangements, but rather, it is a product of the type of litigants and legal problems brought before each of these sets of courts. It also reflects different approaches and values of prosecutors in upper and lower tiers. Thus, there is a greater commitment to legalism in upper court proceedings, while in lower court proceedings this commitment is quite ambiguous. In fact, it seems that there is very little real adversariness in the lower courts, whose function seems to be primarily the conviction of defendants. This is illustrated by various empirical evidence from New South Wales and Victoria. A high conviction rate is achieved either by a large proportion of defendants being induced to plead guilty or by a high proportion of defendants being found to be guilty. Thus, for example, in a Victorian lower court study it was found that only 20 per cent of all defendants pleaded not guilty to all counts, with 69 per cent pleading guilty to all charges.[11] It should be noted, however, that 62 per cent of Victorian defendants in higher courts also pleaded guilty. This high rate of guilty pleas is of course a worldwide phenomenon, but, lower courts are especially notable for their low level of adversariness and the capacity of state agencies, such as the police and prosecutors, to construct a high level of convictions. Thus, in New South Wales, for example, for the eight years between 1975 and 1982, the percentage of those in the lower courts found 'not guilty' ranged between 3.6 per cent and 4.9 per cent[12]. In that state's higher criminal courts in 1982, only 7.4 per cent of defendants were acquitted as such, although 42.1 per cent received a fine or were placed on a bond or on probation.[13] The fact is, however, that the higher court figures are somewhat misleading as the vast majority of cases are actually processed by the lower courts. In 1982, for example, New South Wales higher criminal courts dealt with only

5693 cases, while the lower courts of Petty Sessions dealt with 45,813 criminal cases.[14] It could be argued that the lower courts have arisen out of the executive arm of government and quite clearly reflect the needs and priorities of state social control agencies. This has meant that the lower courts are primarily concerned with the political objectives of the maintenance of order and the processing of cases and not with the delivery of legality in terms of the oft-cherished myths of adversariness and due regard for the other ideals of legal formalism. This problem is especially evident in Australia in view of the fact that so much of the machinery of social control was a product of the convict and military society of the first half of the nineteenth century.[15] Executive control of lower courts is therefore far more tolerable in Australia than it is in some other societies, or than it would be in Superior Courts even there, because the latter were established by Imperial legislation (such as the Australian Courts Act of 1828, which set up the Supreme Courts of New South Wales and Tasmania).[16]

Third, and at a more general level, it could be argued that the lower courts play an important part in supporting local political and socially dominant elites. These local power figures often tend to be quite opposed to political and economic elites at the state and national level. This has therefore seen the progressive abolition of the role of justices of the peace in hearing cases in the lower courts. It has also seen more centralised state control of magistrates and their frequent rotation to prevent too close an association with local elites or power holders. This reflects a clear process of seeking to rationalise and routinise magisterial or lower court decision making so as to ensure that the magistracy becomes a more effective agent of centralised legal policy making. This is most apparent in such fields as affirmative action, race relations, drinking-driving and drug control policies. The lower courts play a vital role in these areas of legal policy administration and change. Contemporary debate about the reform of the lower courts and the reappointment of certain magistrates should be seen in the context of these wider political concerns. A similar kind of point can be made in relation to state and federal superior courts in Australia.

THE ROLE OF HIGHER COURT JUDGES

Various suggestions have already been made concerning the relationship between superior or higher courts and their judges on the one hand and political processes on the other. The higher and superior courts comprise State and Territory Supreme Courts, the Federal Court of Australia and the High Court of Australia. State Supreme Courts are essentially local institutions which are courts of general jurisdiction responsible for supervising state law, state legal institutions and the legal professions in their particular jurisdiction. They also act as intermediate courts of appeal in matters of state and federal law, with the High Court usually acting as the final court of appeal, except in the few cases in which appeals to the Privy Council are still available.[17] Supreme Court judges do not have anywhere near the same protection of their tenure as do federal judges. State constitutions only provide for judges holding office during their good behaviour and they could be removed on an address of both State Houses of Parliament (except in Queensland which has only one House). More recently, efforts have begun to be made to 'entrench' the tenure of judges, so as to make their removal more difficult, although this has only occurred in the state of Victoria to date. In theory at least, the integrity or independence of the judiciary is far from guaranteed, although in practice, State Supreme Court judges seem to be just as secure.

In practice, the situation is much the same with federal superior court judges. Although new appointees to the High Court no longer hold office for life, now compulsorily retiring at seventy, the Federal Constitution at least 'entrenchs' their tenure, in that provisions of the Constitution have been notoriously difficult to amend largely due to the fact that referenda require the approval of a majority of electors in a majority of states. Other methods of constitutional change seem to be just as difficult. Nevertheless, Section 72(ii) of the Federal Constitution provides that Justices of the High Court: 'Shall not be removed except by the Governor-General in Council, on an address from both Houses of the Parliament in the same session, praying for such removal, on the ground of proved misbehavior or incapacity.' Opinions vary widely as to what exactly such misbehaviour or incapacity might precisely constitute, as a recent Senate Select Committee of Inquiry discovered.[18] Federal Court judges are protected by an identical provision in the Federal Court of Australia Act.

However, there are more subtle ways in which superior court judges become implicated in the political process, apart from threats of their removal. First, unlike the High Court since 1979, the State and Territory Supreme Courts do not enjoy formal administrative and financial autonomy from the bureaucracy. Court officials in State courts, for example, are public servants, so that their positions are funded out of budgetary allocations to particular government departments. However, despite the High Court's protective legislation, its Chief Justice has nevertheless felt obliged to warn the federal government about limiting the court's annual budgetary allocation.[19] This suggests that policies of financial stringency adopted by the executive can severely curtail the impact and effectiveness of the judiciary. One illustration of this problem arose recently in New South Wales when the Government sought to curtail the availability of court reporters or stenographers in support of judges on circuit. Clearly, as superior courts are Courts of Record, it would have meant that these circuit courts could not function as no record of the proceedings would be available. Consequently, Supreme Court judges threatened a ban on circuit work in rural areas and were moved to resolve that:

> The Attorney-General be informed that in the interests of justice and the litigants, until an adequate court reporting staff is restored for common law sittings of the Supreme Court on circuit, common law civil matters should not be heard on circuit but, during the gazetted period of the circuit, will be heard in Sydney, where proper court reporting facilities are available.[20]

Superior court judges seem to be under a constant fear that they will lose control of their courts due to administrative or political circumstances. An illustration of this was the fear of one senior New South Wales Appeal Court judge that the inordinate delay of up to eighteen months in the hearing of many Supreme Court Cases might well lead to a loss of the control over the court administration by judges.[21] These kinds of fears were even more explicitly spelt out by another New South Wales Appeal Court judge on the occasion of his retirement recently. He pointed to what he saw as the common tendency of governments to pressure the courts, and noted that this takes place 'without a word of protest from professed believers in civil liberties'. He went on to observe that:

> Judicial independence exists to protect the citizen today from the Executive and the greater the power of the Executive and the greater the need for judicial independence and, correspondingly, the temptation for the Executive to try to curb it.
>
> If judicial appointments are made with the objective of getting the right result, the independence of the judiciary is merely wasteful . . . The judiciary are entitled to view with grave scepticism what is said to be the current morality and in any case it may be its responsibility to stand against the current morality.[22]

Inherent in this fairly reactionary position is a strong critique of modernism, reflecting the distaste of common law judges for the legislature and its products. However, while most judges seem still to be fairly co-operative with the executive branch, some are in fact deeply suspicious of its intrusions into the judicial systems. A good illustration of this suspicion arises out of the frequent use of Australian superior court justices to head Royal Commissions of Inquiry into politically sensitive issues. This is a practice which is especially common in Australia, although judges of the Supreme Court of Victoria have long refused to be engaged in such inquiries. The reasoning behind this Victorian position originated in 1923 in the refusal of the then Chief Justice of Victoria, Sir William Irvine, to make his judges available to head such inquiries.

Other judges have not tended to share this view, with the Chief Justice of the New South Wales Supreme Court, Sir Laurence Street, recently heading a Royal Commission of Inquiry into allegations against the leader of the governing political party in this state, Premier Neville Wran. Other judges have gone so far as to argue that the Irvine assessment was 'inaccurate' and 'not justified by the facts'[23] Chief Justice Street has also gone on to express his confidence in judges acting as Royal commissioners, although he did add that 'This necessarily requires a considerable degree of care to avoid pitfalls that underlie the policy in other places of total refusal to accept such office.'[24] However, this approach seems to have encouraged a close relationship between government and the higher judiciary. This prompted the leader of one federal opposition party, Mr Ian Sinclair of the National Party, to severely criticise the impartiality of Royal Commissioner, Mr Justice Cross inquiring into allegations against a Minister in the State Labour Government in New South Wales. Despite criticisms such as these, judges will continue to sit on these kinds of inquiries, if for no other reason than that put by the current President of the New South Wales Court of Appeal, namely that 'it provides interesting relief from the tedium and long grind near the end of a judicial career'.[25] This was a reference to the fact that Royal Commissioners often tend to be nearing retirement when they take on inquiries such as these. This would seem to imply that either there is a fear that younger and less experienced judges may have more to lose from becoming embroiled in political controversy or that older and more experienced judges are better able to cope with overtly political matters.

In any event, there seems to be a tendency to appoint politically

untainted persons to the bench; governments and politicians nevertheless find great appeal in drawing upon the status of the judiciary,
possibly as a legitimating device. We have seen this in the case of Royal
Commissions. It also seems to arise in the appointment of judges to the
largely ceremonial position of the Governor-Generalship. Sir Ninian
Stephen, the present Governor-General was himself a former High
Court judge, as was Sir Isaac Isaacs some years earlier.

Concerns among the judiciary concerning the dangers of extra-legal
roles breaking down the barriers between judicial and executive office
came to a head recently with the federal government's desire to
appoint a New South Wales Supreme Court judge, Mr Justice Donald
Stewart to head the Federal National Crime Authority (NCA).
Previously, Justice Stewart had chaired a wide-ranging Royal Commission of Inquiry into drug trafficking. This had not caused any real
outcry, while his appointment to the NCA did, as this body was to go
beyond merely collecting information and making recommendations.
The NCA would take Justice Stewart's role further by involving him in
the prosecution process. Eventually, Stewart was forced to step down
from the New South Wales Supreme Court and a special position was
made for him on the Supreme Court of the Australian Capital
Territory (ACT). Even this was not done, however, without some
murmurings of discontent in the ACT.[26]

Despite frequent calls for greater independence, Australian superior court judges are well aware of their political roles, even if this is a
covert one. A good illustration of this is in relation to that of lawmaking,
an activity often regarded as being within the exclusive preserve of the
legislative and executive branches of government. Law making seems
to be two broad kinds. First, there are the occasions when judges
remake or discover 'new' common law rules. Secondly, there are those
circumstances when judges strike down legislation or else give it an
interpretation which Parliament simply could not have intended.[27] The
consideration of the law making powers or roles of superior courts and
especially of the High Court is important as considerable legislative
activity is required to overrule judicial decisions. In the case of the
High Court's decisions, it needs seven Acts of Parliament to overrule
one of its decisions (i.e. an Act of the Federal Parliament and of the six
states). Despite frequent assertions by some Australian judges that
they are not law makers, but simply law appliers, there is far from
being a state of judicial unanimity in this regard. One judge has
scorned those who believe 'the fairy tale that judges merely discover,
but do not make the law. [They] yearn . . . for the comfort of the

nursery fire and the protective glow of *stare decisis*'.[28]

Australian judges seem to guard their interpretive function quite jealously. One illustration of this has been the judicial reaction to Parliamentary attempts to lay down specific guidelines for the manner in which judges interpret legislation. For example, at a 1983 federal symposium on statutory interpretation the 'radical' High Court justice and former Labour federal Attorney General, Lionel Murphy, expressed the view that recent efforts by Parliament to instruct the judiciary to resort to the use of extrinsic aids, such as the reports of parliamentary debates and ministerial legislative statements, so as to achieve a purposive rather than literal interpretation represented 'a stern reproof to the judiciary' by the federal Parliament. Murphy went on to suggest that 'Parliament should do nothing at all about it. The matter is progressing in a sensible way [when left to judges]; there are different views, but there's no real need for any legislation'.[29] It seems likely therefore that judges will resist this kind of instrusion into the judicial process, even if it is done with the best of intentions upon the part of the executive.

The recent Australian experience in this area stems from governmental and community concern regarding the inequitable consequences flowing from the High Court's extremely literalist interpretations of federal anti-tax avoidance legislation. This saw a period of massive tax evasion and avoidance by business and professional groups largely as a consequence of the High Court's literalist interpretations of penal and other sections of the Federal Income Tax Assessment Act. Yet, there are important occasions during which the superior courts take over from a willing executive and legislature the task of resolving what has become an insoluble political issue. The most celebrated recent illustration of this powerful political role of the courts arose out of the High Court's decision in the so-called Tasmanian Dams Case. This case arose out of a conflict between a federal government seeking to preserve the wilderness areas of South-West Tasmania around the Franklin River, and the desire of the Government of the State of Tasmania to exploit the hydroelectric potential of this area by building a dam across the Franklin River. The federal government saw itself as having national and international responsibilities in seeking to preserve this wilderness area, in view of the fact that the area was listed as a site worthy of preservation in the World Heritage Convention, to which the Australian government was a signatory. In contrast, the state government saw the issue in terms of the preservation of state rights over its own territory and responsibilities. This constitutional conflict crystallised into possibly the most striking political impasse for almost a decade. Eventually in *The Commonwealth of Australia* v. *The State of Tasmania* (1983, 57 ALJR, 450), the High Court was called upon to resolve this dispute, both parties agreeing to abide by its decision. The Court in due course narrowly came down on the side of the federal government in a confusing 4:3 decision. Despite the political sensitivity of this case it has been argued that the decision fell short of constituting judicial legislation in the 'grand tradition' of judicial decision making, to use Llewellyn's phrase.[30] In other words, while the Court seemed to provide a limited extension of the federal Parliament's foreign affairs power, this controversial decision failed to provide a clear-cut illustration of the High Court as a purposive and deliberate law making authority. The Court in fact seemed to be somewhat reluctant to assume this role and so preferred instead to act within certain fairly limited legalistic constitutional constraints. Perhaps the very essence of the High court's public policy role is shrouded within the ambiguity of the powers of superior court justices which contributes to the continuing belief that they play a (potentially) significant role in the political process. Such ambiguity is certainly not evident in the lower courts, as it is almost always possible to take a case on appeal to a superior court. So it can be said, therefore, that within the judicial system it is the superior courts which have the greatest potential political involvement. Ultimately it seems that the actual role of the superior and appellate courts rests upon the balance between judicial self-restraint and judicial activism which is reached within a particular court.

Inferior courts have also, however, provided their share of the settings for the playing out of political battles. One of the most controversial episodes of this kind involved conspiracy proceedings against four former leading members of the ousted Whitlam Labour government, in the case of *Sankey* v. *Whitlam and others* (1977, 1 NSWLR, 333; 1978, 142 CLR, 1). This case is unusual in that it involved a private prosecution although the defendants were receiving legal aid from the Liberal-National party federal government.

Another illustration of the potential political dimensions of inferior court proceedings arises out of the system whereby the Attorney-General could decide to issue an *ex officio* indictment so as to prosecute his political enemies. This accusation has arisen in a number of recent Australian trials, most notably that involving the then federal deputy leader of the National Party who was prosecuted on forgery charges by a state Labour Attorney-General in New South Wales. The case against Sinclair was eventually dismissed. This led to accusations of political justice and increasing calls for the establishment of an independent Director of Public Prosecutions, as has now happened in the federal sphere and in Victoria. The justification for this was nicely spelt out by a leading Sydney daily newspaper in the following terms.

> The State Attorney-General is the senior law officer in N.S.W.: he is also a practising politician. No matter who the incumbent is, there is always a doubt whether the two roles can be maintained separately. As senior law officer, the Attorney-General is dutybound to prosecute cases in which politics or public affairs are mixed up. But it is inevitable that any decision to prosecute will be seen in a political context.[31]

It is clear that the legitimacy of the courts and their usefulness to government is dependent upon the extent to which they are directly implicated in the political process. Where such implications are too evident, then the courts themselves seem to have acted swiftly to protect themselves by down-playing their political role. Sometimes, this has even been forced upon them by government itself. One longstanding illustration of this has been the virtual removal of Mr Justice Staples from the conciliation and Arbitration Commission by the expedient of refusing to allocate cases for him to hear, at least on his own. Staples had a reputation as a politically forthright judge, which eventually led to much criticism from within government circles. This led the president of the Commission, Sir John Moore, to act to remove him from the hearing of cases. In 1980, Moore removed Mr Justice Staples from his particular duties after he had publicly defended his handling of wage guidelines. Staples had granted the members of a militant union such high pay rises that the full bench was prompted to quash his decision, an action which led to one of the largest strikes in over thirty years.[32] Staples has continued to be paid his full judicial salary but is still prevented from hearing wage cases on his own.

In other instances, courts have wandered into politically sensitive turf – immigration and broadcasting, for example – and provoked government reaction. Problems of this kind have arisen especially in tribunals such as in the Administrative Appeals Tribunal (AAT) and in the Australian Broadcasting Tribunal (ABT). For example, the AAT has lately come into conflict with executive authority by limiting the discretionary powers of the Minister for Immigration to make deportation orders. Although the AAT's view on this public policy issue was later backed up by the Federal Court, one leading judge afterwards speculated that any departure from government policy by the AAT might invite governmental retaliation.[33] Similar public policy dilemmas have arisen in the broadcasting field in the ABT.[34]

SOME CONCLUDING OBSERVATIONS

Many of the major questions concerning the politics of the Australian judiciary remain to be asked, let alone answered. Moreover, we are still some considerable distance from evolving an adequate empirically based set of theories about this area, although this is by no means merely an Australian problem.[35] Such theorising needs to address politics at the local level as well as that of the national state, as courts clearly act politically at all levels. Despite this broader theoretical goal, it needs to be acknowledged that much of what appears in this chapter is largely impressionistic, given the state of our knowledge in Australia. Nevertheless, it is safe to say that Australian courts and judges are a vital element of the democratic order, even if access to the courts, particularly the higher courts, is becoming more difficult. Some judges have argued that the provision of legal aid to many litigants has served to delay and prolong litigation even more and so further serving to limit their accessibility in some areas.[36] At the same time there seems to have been a proliferation of new courts, tribunals and alternative despite processing forums (such as Community Justice Centres) in recent years. All of this suggests that there has been an increasing legalisation of Australian social relations, in a country which already has more professional judges than in the whole of the United Kingdom,[37] despite a considerably lower population. Federalism seems to be largely responsible for this Australian profusion of legalism. Thus, for example, in 1980 there were at least 272 federal administrative tribunals in Australia and as we have seen, since the mid-1970s there has been a massive growth in the number and workload of federal courts such as the Federal Court of Australia and the Family Court. It is most likely that this key role of the Australian courts and their judges in the processes of public policy making and the ordering of democratic society is therefore likely to increase.

NOTES

1. See P. Robertshaw, 'Judicial Politics within the State', *International Journal of the Sociology of Law*, 8 (1980).
2. See generally F. G. Brennan, 'New Growth in the Law – The Judicial Contribution', *Monash Law Review*, 6 (1976); J. Goldring, 'Business, Law and Public Administration', in R. Tomasic (ed.), *Business Regulation in Australia* (Sydney: Commerce Clearing House (Australia) 1984; A. N. Hall, 'Administrative Review before the Administrative Appeals Tribunal – A Fresh Approach to Dispute Resolution?' *Federal Law Review*, 12 (1981); and M. D. Kirby, 'Administrative Law Reform in Action', *University of New South Wales Law Journal*, 2 (1978).
3. M. D. Kirby, 'Administrative Review: Beyond the Frontier marked "Policy – Lawyers Keep Out"', *Federal Law Review*, 12 (1981).
4. High Court of Australia, *Annual Report for 1984*, p. 5.
5. K. A. Ziegert, 'The Limits of Family Law: A Sociolegal Assessment', *Legal Service Bulletin*, 9 (1984).
6. J. Sutton, *Court Statistics 1982* (Sydney: NSW Bureau of Crime Statistics and Research, Department of Attorney General, NSW Government Printing Office, 1983), p. 55.
7. J. Crawford, *Australian Courts of Law* (Melbourne: Oxford University Press, 1982), p. 258.
8. *Sydney Morning Herald*, 15 March 1983.
9. *Sydney Morning Herald*, 16 March 1983.
10. D. J. McBarnet, *Conviction: Law, the State and the Construction of Justice* (London: Macmillan, 1981).
11. R. Douglas, *et al.*, *Guilty, Your Worship: A Study of Victoria's Magistrates' Courts* (Melbourne: Legal Studies Department of La Trobe University, 1980), p. 40.
12. Sutton, *Court Statistics 1978*, p. 12 and *1982*, p. 11.
13. Sutton, *Court Statistics* 1982, p. 56.
14. Skutton, *Court Statistics*, pp. 10 and 55.
15. J. B. Hirst, *Convict Society and its Enemies – A History of Early New South Wales* (Sydney: George Allen and Unwin, 1983).
16. J. M. Bennett, *A History of the Supreme Court of New South Wales* (Sydney: The Law Book Co., 1974), p. 218.
17. Crawford, *Australian Courts*, pp. 107–8.
18. Parliament of Australia, Senate, *Report to the Senate from the Senate Select Committee on the Conduct of a Judge* (M. C. Tate, Chairman), Parliamentary Paper No. 168, 1984 (Canberra: Commonweatlh Government Printer, 1984), Appendix 4 and 6 (ii).
19. Sir H. Gibbs, 'The State of the Australian Judicature', *The Australian Law Journal*, 55 (1981).
20. J. Slee, 'Judges threaten us to ban circuit work in Country', *Sydney Morning Herald*, 2 December 1981, p. 3.
21. J. Slee, 'Judge says long court delays must stop', *Sydney Morning Herald*, 16 August 1982, p. 3.
22. Quoted in T. Storey, 'Political pressure on courts worries a retiring judge', *Sydney Morning Herald*, 30 October, 1984, p. 2. Also see J. Falvey, 'Judge

slams erosion of independence', *The Weekend Australian*, 20–21 October 1984.

23. P. B. Toose, 'The Appointment of Judges to Commissions of Enquiry and other Extra-Judicial Duties', in *Judicial Essays* (Sydney: The Law Foundation of New South Wales, 1975), p. 57.

24. Quoted in J. Slee, 'Judges' role questioned after Sinclair attack', *Sydney Morning Herald*, 3 March 1984, p. 4.

25. Quoted in J. Slee, 'Judges' role questioned after Sinclair attack'.

26. There are always exceptions, one here being the appointment of Mr Justice Dixon of the High Court as Ambassador to Washington during the Second World War. See his *Jesting Pilate: And Other Papers and Addresses* (Sydney: The Law Book Co., 1965).

27. See generally A. E.-S. Tay and E. Kamenka (eds), *Law-Making in Australia* (Melbourne: Edward Arnold, 1980).

28. G. J. Samuels, Review of Tay and Kamenka, *Law-Making* in *Bulletin of the Australian Society of Legal Philosophy*, 17 (1980), p. 33.

29. Attorney General's Department, *Symposium on Statutory Interpretation* (Canberra: Australian Government Printing Office, 1983), 39–40.

30. J. Goldring, 'Initial Reactions to the Dam Case: Dam or Floodgates?' *Legal Services Bulletin*, 8 (1983), p. 158.

31. *Sydney Morning Herald*, 18 August 1981, p. 6.

32. J. Dargaville, 'Staples makes bitter attack', *The Weekend Australian*, February 14–15, 1981, p. 3.

33. See M. Jacobs, 'Kirby calls for ratification of Appeals Tribunal's role', *Australian Financial Review*, 20 July 1981 and V. Blunden, 'Immigration case to High Court', *Sydney Morning Herald*, 25 July 1981, p. 5.

34. See further M. Armstrong, *Broadcasting Law and Policy in Australia* (Sydney: Butterworths, 1982) and G. Walsh, 'Broadcasting tribunal in a bind', *The Bulletin*, 25 September 1984.

35. See, for example, K. D. Boyum and L. Mather, *Empirical Theories about Courts* (New York: Longman, 1983).

36. See, for example, D. A. Yeldman, 'Delays in Criminal Trials', paper presented to Criminal Law Committee, Sydney University Law Graduates Association, 13 March 1984.

37. Crawford, *Australian Courts*, p. 276.

4 The Courts in Canada
Carl Baar

Canada is a federal parliamentary system. Its constitution has, since 1867, distributed legislative power between the federal parliament and the provincial parliaments (now ten in number). The Supreme Court of Canada has for over a century decided constitutional cases concerning the distribution of power between federal and provincial governments. The Canadian legal system as a whole is built on a British common law heritage with the exception of Quebec, which is governed by civil law on matters within its jurisdiction.

These basic statements suggest that the Canadian judiciary would play an important role in the development and maintenance of democratic institutions in that country. Yet the popularly accepted view of Canadian courts is that they have had a narrow and restricted role. What elements of the country's political and legal culture have combined to render relatively unimportant a court system that could potentially exercise the power associated with British and United States courts?

Some of the factors that have led to the limited role of the Canadian courts include:

(1) Their ambiguous constitutional status. The Canadian courts are not clearly defined as a third branch of government, as are their United States federal counterparts. The Supreme Court of Canada did not exist at the time of confederation in 1867, but was created by an act of parliament in 1875. By the time of its centenary in 1975, it could still have been altered or perhaps even abolished by another statute of the federal parliament.

(2) Their historic lack of finality in constitutional matters. Until 1949, a constitutional decision of the Canadian courts could be appealed to the Judicial Committee of the Privy Council in England. On a number of occasions – some highly controversial – a constitutional decision by the Supreme Court of Canada on the proper limits of the authority of the federal or provincial governments was overruled by that panel of law lords. The Judicial Committee even heard *per saltum* appeals, which are those taken directly from the highest court of a province without prior consideration by the Supreme Court of Canada.[1]

(3) A narrow positivism in constitutional and statutory interpretation. Reading John Austin's definition of law as the command of the sovereign, and seeing parliament as the sovereign legislative body, Canadian courts have shied away from creative or principled interpretations of statute law, preferring a literal reading of statutes (and no use of extrinsic legislative materials) even when that results in approving a wide range of discretionary administrative power delegated by parliament to the cabinet and executive officials.

(4) Ideological conservatism. In general, Canadian courts have tended to be more conservative than the country's legislatures or administrative tribunals. In practice, this has meant that the courts are unlikely to read criminal laws narrowly or labour law broadly; and they are unlikely to place limits on the discretion of public officials in general and law enforcement officers in particular.[2]

(5) The absence of entrenched constitutional rights. Until 1982, the Canadian constitution included no bill of rights. Thus, the Supreme Court of Canada had no authority to hold federal or provincial action unconstitutional if it violated fundamental rights. The 1960 Canadian Bill of Rights was a federal statute, applicable only to federal action – and then only as a guide to interpretation.

(6) The use of federal-provincial conferences to supercede constitutional interpretation of the distribution of legislative powers. In the one major area of constitutional law where the judiciary has played an active role – the division of powers between federal and provincial governments – politicians from both levels (or 'orders') of government have questioned the wisdom and legitimacy of particular decisions. As a result, these governments met frequently for half a century at formal conferences in which consensus arrangements were negotiated to divide responsibility and share costs for jointly-operated programmes.[3]

These six factors have led, both individually and in combination, to a limited role for the Canadian courts. Historically these factors have reinforced one another. For example, the Judicial Committee, treating the Canadian constitution as an ordinary statute (until 1982 it was, in fact and form, a statute of the British – 'Imperial' – Parliament), narrowly construed federal authority. The Supreme Court of Canada, bound by precedent and unwilling to develop a more creative interpretation of Judicial Committee decisions, applied the precedents. Federal and provincial governments have negotiated their way around the decisions, and the courts have remained silent. In another example, a conservative Supreme Court, cautious to avoid overextending itself under its 1875 enabling act, refused to invalidate federal laws which appeared to conflict with provisions of the Canadian Bill of Rights.[4]

The most notorious examples of how the courts' role has been narrowly conceived and construed go back half a century. In 1928, the Supreme Court of Canada told five women that they could not be appointed to the Canadian Senate because the constitutional provision allowing 'persons' to be appointed did not authorise the appointment of women. Common law precedents defining the word 'person' did not include woman, the Court ruled unanimously. In that case, the Judicial Committee of the Privy Council abandoned its positivistic mode of reasoning (by which the Supreme Court had felt itself bound), declared the constitution to be 'a living tree capable of growth within its natural limits', and extended the definition of persons to include women.[5]

In contrast, during the depression years, the Judicial Committee invalidated a series of federal laws designed to deal with the economic hardships of the time, enunciating the theory that federal and provincial governments constituted 'watertight compartments' on the Canadian ship of state, hardly a flexible let alone realistic view of how federal states are governed.[6] But then, as Canadian critics said at the time, how familiar could the English be with the operation of a federal state?

Since 1949, the Judicial Committee is no longer Canada's highest appellate court. During the 1950s, the Supreme Court of Canada marked its independence in a series of constitutional decisions that limited provincial power in matters affecting individual rights.[7] However, by the 1970s, that same court, reflecting a more conservative and cautious majority, was making decisions marked by a more positivist and restrained approach reminiscent of the Judicial Committee era.[8]

Peter Russell, one of Canada's most respected constitutional scholars, has argued that the outward restraint displayed by the Canadian courts obscures their real power, thus fortifying their ability to exercise judicial power.[9] In particular, the Supreme Court of Canada has had an increased role since 1975 in litigation involving the division of powers between federal and provincial governments.

Russell attributes this newly-emerging role to both 'a general increase in litigitiousness' and the court's tendency to balance the claims of the two levels of government.[10]

This development is a prelude to more fundamental changes facing a legal culture within which Canadian courts have defined their historically limited role. On 17 April 1982, Canada's constitution was 'patriated' – brought home in a new form, no longer the British North America (BNA) Act of 1867, but a constitution that included the Canadian Charter of Rights and Freedoms, setting out express limitations on both federal and provincial governments enforceable in the courts. Before considering what changes may be in store under this new constitutional framework, it is necessary to present basic background information about the Canadian court system: its structure, personnel, jurisdiction, and decision making processes.

STRUCTURE OF THE CANADIAN COURT SYSTEM

The Canadian court system was conceived as a unitary system, in explicit contrast to the dual system of courts in the United States. Thus, while the United States has both a federal court system (for federal law and diversity of citizenship matters) and fifty state court systems, Canada's constitution envisaged a national court of last resort, limited specialised federal courts, and fully-developed provincial court systems. What makes the Canadian system unitary is the provision in Section 96 of the original British North America Act that judges of the provincial superior, county and district courts would be appointed by the federal government. Section 96 thus contemplated a system of provincially organised and administered courts staffed by federally appointed judges.

This constitutional scheme is still the basis of contemporary Canadian court structure (see Figure 4.1).[11] The Supreme Court of Canada sits atop the national judicial pyramid. Directly below are the provincial courts of appeal. In nine out of ten provinces, the highest court is named the Court of Appeal. The only current exception is tiny Prince Edward Island, whose Supreme Court has both trial and appellate jurisdiction; after one judge tries a case, it is appealed to a three-judge panel drawn from the remaining members of the same court. Below the courts of appeal are the superior courts of each province. Names vary: Court of Queen's Bench (Alberta, Saskatchewan, Manitoba and New Brunswick), Supreme Court (British Columbia, Prince Edward Island, Nova Scotia and Newfoundland),

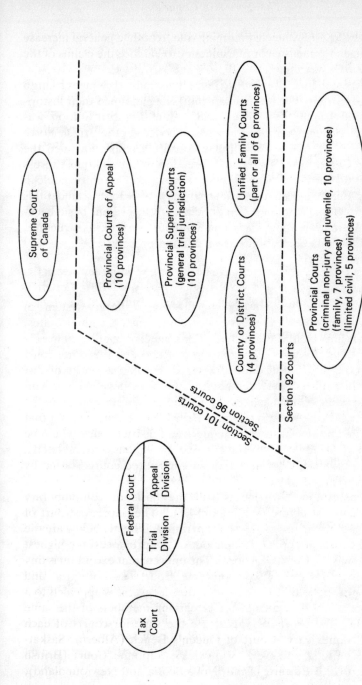

Figure 4.1 The structure of the courts in Canada

Note: For a more detailed diagram see Canadian Centre for Justice Statistics, *Manpower Resources and Costs of Courts and Criminal Prosecutions in Canada 1980–82*, Catalogue 85–212E, p. 23.

High Court of Justice (Ontario) and *cour supérieure* (Quebec). The ten superior courts function as central trial courts for their provinces, following the English model of the High Court of Justice whose members sit centrally and travel on circuit to various county towns and trial centres. Ontario is the most extreme example; all 50 High Court Justices reside in Toronto, spending half their time sitting in some 50 different trial centres in a province whose western boundary adjoins Minnesota and whose eastern boundary is within fifty miles of the state of Vermont. In other provinces, resident superior court judges may be located in one, two or three major cities.

At the next level in the trial court hierarchy are the county or district courts, originally conceptualised once again on the English scheme, as a set of local courts which would 'bring justice to every man's door'. Throughout the past century, every province except Quebec had a system of county or district courts. However, since 1973, the county or district courts of five provinces have been merged with their respective superior courts, so that county courts survive only in British Columbia and Nova Scotia, and district courts only in Ontario and Newfoundland.

The merger of county courts with superior courts has not altered the basic constitutional scheme of provincially organised courts staffed by federally appointed judges. However, other recent developments have multiplied the exceptions to the original design. At the federal level, a Federal Court of Canada, with trial and appeal divisions, was created in 1971. It took over the specialised financial jurisdiction of the long-established Exchequer Court, and added jurisdiction over appeals from federal administrative agencies, long a responsibility of provincial superior courts. In 1983, a Tax Court was created by upgrading the status of a pre-existing federal tax appeal tribunal. More fundamental evolutionary changes have occurred in the provinces, where courts have grown up staffed by provincially appointed judges. In the late nineteenth and early twentieth centuries, these were the minor courts staffed by lay magistrates and justices of the peace, with authority to hear minor civil matters, violations of local by-laws, and preliminary matters in criminal cases (authorising warrants, setting bail, hearing first appearances). By the mid-twentieth century, a number of provinces had devolved jurisdiction over family and juvenile matters to provincial appointees, along with growing responsibility for criminal cases. Lawyers began being appointed to replace lay magistrates. By the 1960s, first Quebec, then Ontario renamed the magistrates judges, and magistrates courts Provincial Courts.

Throughout the 1970s, other provinces followed suit. Today, only Newfoundland still appoints lay judges to its Provincial Court, and in those cases sends an appointee to law school after a period of three years on the bench.

The evolution of Provincial Courts has added a substantial layer to the court systems of every province. Quebec is the most elaborate: it has a *cour de sessions de la paix* (the Sessions Court) with jurisdiction over all criminal cases not tried by a jury; the *tribunal de la jeunesse* (Youth Court) for juvenile matters; a Provincial Court with civil jurisdiction that now extends well beyond small claims to an upper limit of $10,000; and numerous Municipal Courts with by-law jurisdiction. Ontario has a Provincial Court with three divisions: criminal, civil and family. Every other province also vests all juvenile and substantial criminal jurisdiction in its Provincial Court; seven provincial courts have extensive family law jurisdiction, and five have civil jurisdiction, usually up to between one to three thousand dollars. The growth of these courts represents the major change in Canadian court structure since confederation, and can be accounted for by a number of factors:

(1) Pressure to upgrade the status and professionalism of lower court judges.

(2) Willingness of federally appointed judges to give up jurisdiction over 'minor' matters.

(3) Willingness of the federal parliament to enlarge the jurisdiction of provincial courts in criminal matters.

(4) Federal–provincial conflict over appointments. It is not unusual for different parties to be in power at different levels of government, encouraging a province to appoint 'its judges' rather than having the courts staffed by members of that province's bar chosen by the party in power in Ottawa. Some provinces have magnified the issue still further; thus one reason for Quebec having expanded the jurisdiction of its provincially appointed judges to the greatest extent is the desire of nationalist and later separatist governments to minimise the impact of Ottawa on institutions within the province.

(5) A traditionally liberal interpretation of the BNA Act by the Supreme Court of Canada and the Judicial Committee to allow the devolution of jurisdiction, particularly in family matters. This factor has been minimised in recent years, as the Supreme Court has restricted the devolution of jurisdiction in a number of cases involving criminal, family and administrative law matters.[12]

A court structure paralleling that of the ten provinces has also been established in each of the two territories in Canada: the Yukon and the North-West Territories (NWT). Each has a Supreme Court staffed by federally appointed judges (one for the Yukon, two for the NWT). Each has a Territorial Court analogous to the Provincial Courts south of the 54th parallel, with judges appointed by the territorial government. There is also a Yukon Court of Appeal, along with a North-West Territories Court of Appeal, but these are 'foreign' courts: the British Columbia Court of Appeal serves that function for the Yukon, the Alberta Court of Appeal for the NWT.

The growth of Provincial Courts staffed by provincially appointed judges has also altered the purely hierarchical nature of the court systems of the provinces. Traditionally, a serious criminal case would begin in a magistrates court and then move to a county court or a superior court for trial. Now, while that path would still be followed in a jury trial, the overwhelming majority of serious criminal cases are dealt with in the Provincial Court. In practice, in criminal as well as family matters, the Provincial Courts have become identified as subject-matter specialists rather than merely the lowest layer in a hierarchical system.

While trial courts have evolved a division of labour based on subject matter, appeals courts continue to hear a full range of issues. More important for comparative purposes, constitutional matters are not segregated from other legal issues. Any of the courts described in this section can rule on a constitutional question arising in litigation validly before it. At the same time, constitutional issues were rare prior to enactment of the Charter of Rights in 1982. While the Supreme Court of Canada might hear a half-dozen constitutional matters per term in the 1970s, it averaged one or two annually for most of its history.

JUDICIAL PERSONNEL

Canadian judgeships are appointed positions. No Canadian judge is elected, nor do Canadian judges (even in Quebec's civil law system) follow the career model of continental Europe. Judges are appointed by the cabinet (either federal or provincial), with the major role played by the Minister of Justice/Attorney General. Federally appointed judges must be members of the bar of the province for which they are appointed (under sections 97 and 98 of the Constitution Act, 1867), and in addition 'a barrister or advocate of at least ten years standing at the bar of any province' (under section 3 of the Judges Act, a federal law that establishes the number of and salaries for federally appointed judges). Provincially appointed judges have similar minimum qualifications, as lay judges have been phased out of all provinces save Newfoundland over the past decade.

Since the late 1960s, a variety of efforts have been made to constrain the discretion of cabinets over judicial appointments, on the grounds that partisan political considerations have reduced the overall quality of persons appointed to the bench. Thus federal Ministers of Justice, beginning with the then Justice Minister Pierre Trudeau, established consultative arrangements with a committee of the Canadian Bar Association (paralleling arrangements established by the American Bar Association in the United States) which could review the names of potential nominees submitted by the minister but could not nominate others. Some provincial governments, notably British Columbia and Quebec, went further in the 1970s, establishing councils and committees that included judges, lawyers and lay persons to recruit, screen and submit names of potential nominees to the Attorney-General of the province. (The systems in those provinces parallel the nomination processes in merit-selection states in the United States.)

Despite these trends, the importance, even if not dominance, of partisan considerations in judicial appointments has been a fact of Canadian political life. It is reflected in the oft-repeated maxim that 'to become a judge in the United States, you must be elected; to become a judge in Canada, you must be defeated'. Efforts to improve the quality of judicial appointments have had some effect, but have rarely led to the appointment of a Conservative by a Liberal government, a Liberal by a Conservative government, or a New Democratic Party member by either one. The issue of patronage in judicial appointments reached a new level of public concern in the summer of 1984, when the federal Liberal government on the eve of an election call appointed a number of party faithful (including the Minister of Justice himself) to judgeships and other long-term appointments. The appointments became an election issue and the opposition Conservatives swept to power, giving added visibility to the work of a Canadian Bar Association study committee on judicial appointments. That committee's recommendations are likely to go in the direction of the nominating council model in British Columbia (or Quebec), but the federal government is likely to greet any such recommendation with scepticism and reticence.

The most formalised and best known constraints on judicial

appointments affect the Supreme Court of Canada. By law and convention, the nine members of the court must represent the various regions of the country. The fundamental difference between Quebec and the nine common law provinces is reflected in the requirement that three of the nine justices come from the bar of 'the civil law province'. This one-third representation was incorporated in the original Supreme Court Act of 1875, and is now included in language in the patriated 1982 constitution.[13] The other six justices are by convention distributed geographically by region. The four less-populated Atlantic provinces are entitled to one justice. Thus when the justice from Nova Scotia retired in the fall of 1984, no one contemplated appointing a replacement from outside the region. The four western provinces have normally had two justices, and Ontario (with 40 per cent of the country's population) had three. The two western justices normally rotate among the four provinces, so it has been unlikely that a justice from one western province will be succeeded by a justice from the same province. Deviations are minimal. For example, in the early 1980s, an Ontario vacancy was filled by an appointee from British Columbia, in anticipation of the retirement the following year of an Alberta appointee, who was in turn replaced by a person from Ontario.

Regional representation is the most clearly established pattern in appointments to the Supreme Court of Canada. It also serves partially as a proxy for other forms of representation. Thus linguistic differences have been traditionally reflected by the 6–3 division between common law provinces and Quebec, producing three French-Canadian justices. At certain points in the court's history, one of the three civil law appointees has been an anglophone (someone whose first language is English), but the current pattern of all three Quebec justices being francophones is likely to hold. No francophone appointments from outside Quebec had ever been made until 1984, when an Ontario appointment went to Quebec-born Gerard LeDain, and the recent Atlantic province appointment went to an Acadian from New Brunswick. However, only one justice has ever been appointed from outside the British Isles or French ethnic communities. That justice, Bora Laskin, of Russian-Jewish heritage, was replaced after his death in 1984 by LeDain, and no other 'multicultural' appointment has been discussed in spite of the high percentage of the general Canadian population of non-British and non-French background. One woman has sat on the Supreme Court of Canada; she was appointed to the first vacancy that occurred after Justice Sandra Day O'Connor was appointed to the United States Supreme Court.

The other major constraint on Supreme Court appointments beyond regional representation is the convention that appointees have been superior court judges, and normally judges of the courts of appeal of the provinces. All nine of the current justices had been appeal judges at the time of their appointments (LeDain on the Appeal Division of the Federal Court of Canada). All but one of the individuals whose names were suggested in the media as possible appointees to the recent Atlantic province vacancy were justices of a provincial appeals court or superior trial court; the one exception was a prominent New Brunswick lawyer who was a past president of the Canadian Bar Association. Justices have occasionally been appointed directly from the ranks of the bar, but only once in the last eighty years was a cabinet minster or member of parliament named directly to the Supreme Court.[14] Canadian practice thus diverges sharply from United States practice, where justices of the Supreme Court of the United States have been more commonly drawn from legal and political rather than judicial careers. While this Canadian practice may remove the Supreme Court of Canada further from the centre of political debate, it may also have reinforced the more legalistic and restrained approach to constitutional issues that has contrasted the Canadian and the United States Supreme Court.

Recruitment and representational patterns are more varied among judges appointed to provincial courts by the federal government. Court of appeal judges are commonly appointed from the superior trial courts, but often directly from the senior ranks of the legal profession, and sometimes from among legal academics or high-ranking officials in provincial or federal ministries of justice. Representation of particular areas or communities within a province may figure in an appointment, but the most important explicit factors may be the need for an individual with a particular subject-matter competence (e.g. criminal law).

Section 96 (i.e. federally appointed) trial judges are sometimes drawn from the provincially appointed judiciary, but this pattern is not common. The most common internal judicial 'promotion' is probably from a superior trial court to a court of appeal. Members of the bar chosen for section 96 judgeships are typically drawn from the litigation bar, and range from 45–60 years of age. Women and ethnic minorities are increasingly being appointed (no woman held a superior court judgeship until 1969). At the provincial court level, judges are more frequently appointed before reaching age forty, and are typically drawn from specialised criminal law or family law practices.

All federally appointed judges and almost all provincially appointed judges serve during good behaviour – i.e. they hold lifetime appointments and are removable only for cause or upon reaching a mandatory retirement age. Every judicial appointment made in Canada is now subject to mandatory retirement: age 75 for the Supreme Court of Canada and for provincial appeal and superior trial courts, age 70 for county and district courts, and age 65 for most provincially appointed judges. Most provinces also provide for continued service between age 65 and 70 at the discretion of the provincial cabinet.[15] Federally appointed judges can opt for supernumerary (semi-retired) status, with reduced salary before mandatory retirement, but may not be continued after age 70 or 75.

Tenure during good behaviour begs the question of how misbehaviour is defined. There is no written code of ethics for judges; even unofficial attempts to develop such a code have been discouraged. At the same time, the norms of judicial conduct that have developed have been relatively rigid, in keeping with the caution and conservatism of Canadian judges. Judges may but rarely do write books, give public speeches or testify before public bodies on judicial needs. Federally appointed judges are prohibited by the federal Elections Act from even voting, lest their impartiality be questioned in litigation over a contested election. Thus controversial judicial conduct could be deemed misbehaviour in Canada even when it may be acceptable within some other legal cultures.

Discussions of removal of judges focus primarily on the methods for removal. Thus superior court judges (and justices of the Supreme Court and Federal Court of Canada) may be removed only by joint address – a procedure akin to impeachment in which the Governor-General, acting on behalf of the cabinet, presents a bill of particulars to the Senate and House of Commons which is then subject to debate and vote. No Canadian judge has ever been removed by joint address, although three attempts at removal were made in the 1800s and one in 1967. County and district court judges may be removed by order-in-council – i.e. a cabinet directive made without reference to Parliament, and that procedure was used on two occasions in the 1930s.[16]

In the early 1970s, the Canadian Judicial Council (consisting entirely of federally appointed judges) was created and given authority to investigate complaints against Section 96 judges and make recommendations to the cabinet. Legally, a Council recommendation is not required for the pre-existing removal procedures to be invoked, but it is likely that such a recommendation will be required as a matter of practice. No judge has been removed under the new provisions; however, more than one judge has resigned pending or following a Council investigation.[17]

Provincial removal mechanisms are more diverse. Councils exist to consider removal or censure in a majority of provinces, but responsibility generally has remained in the hands of provincial cabinets ('live by the OC [Order-in-council], die by the OC', summarised one judge), sometimes operating under vague or broad mandates. A number of provincially appointed judges have been removed in recent years, while for most of Canadian history, provincially appointed judges have held office at pleasure. Thus security of tenure is a relatively new concept at this level of the court system.

One set of judicial officials still hold office at pleasure, or for carefully circumscribed terms: the justices of the peace appointed by the various provinces. JPs generally carry out quasi-judicial administrative functions (e.g. signing arrest warrants), but they have increasingly taken on the minor functions associated with the provincial police magistrates of the early twentieth century. JPs in many provinces do bail hearings and handle parking tickets; in Ontario, they deal with a wide range of provincial offences such as liquor violations, traffic violations, and trespass. Justices of the peace have generally not been viewed or studied as judicial officers, but as Provincial Court Judges have grown in status, JPs have come to take on an increasing volume and variety of routine judicial tasks, and their uncertain status has become the object of public debate and well-publicised court battle.[18]

No formal training is required of any judicial appointee; however, an increasing range of in-service training progammes have been developed across the country. Most visible has been the work of the Canadian Judicial Council in its annual seminars for superior and county court judges, as well as its seminars for newly appointed (Section 96) judges. Training programmes for provincially appointed judges vary considerably, from national workshops funded by the federal Department of Justice to provincial seminars focusing on the specific details of new legislation.

The wide range of Canadian courts suggests that Canadian judges range equally widely across the status hierarchy. Thus provincially appointed judges may be drawn from practitioners in small towns and in criminal and family practices – hardly the legal elite of Canada or most other countries. On the other hand, superior court judges at both trial and appeal level are commonly drawn from among high-prestige members of the bar of various provinces. Prominent counsel have rejected judicial appointments – usually because of the difficulty of moving to another community, taking a cut in salary, or enduring the travel associated with the circuit systems in some superior courts. However, despite the narrowness sometimes bred by considerations of political patronage, the judiciary has been drawn from members of the legal profession active in their own communities and equal in status to other professionals and community leaders

JURISDICTION OF THE COURTS

The jurisdiction of Canadian courts is established by a combination of statute law and common law. Federal statutes not only spell out the jurisdiction of the Supreme Court and Federal Court of Canada, but also establish jurisdictional boundaries of provincial courts on matters within federal jurisdiction – for example, the Criminal Code and the Divorce Act. Provincial statutes spell out the jurisdiction of their courts, subject to constitutional and federal statutory limitations. At the same time, the Supreme Court of Canada is established under section 101 of the Constitution Act,1867 as 'a general court of appeal for Canada' suggesting that its jurisdiction is inherent and complete unless otherwise specified. Similarly, most superior courts are set out in provincial law as successors to English superior courts and therefore possessing inherent jurisdiction to issue a full range of orders traditionally within the authority of its predecessor courts in the United Kingdom. The broad authority of the Supreme Court of Canada and the superior courts of the provinces has bred important political controversies over the role of the courts in Canada.

As a general court of appeal for Canada, the Supreme Court can hear appeals touching not only on federal matters but also on purely provincial matters. It can therefore hear and rule on appeals regarding the common law of any province or the civil law in Quebec. In United States terms, Canadian courts can develop a federal common law in the same manner as the United States Supreme Court before *Erie Railroad* v. *Tompkins* in 1938. In Canadian terms, the major point of controversy has involved the authority of a court dominated by common law judges to establish precedents on the operation of civil law doctrine. For decades, Quebec lawyers have argued for abolition of civil law appeals to the Supreme Court of Canada, or for a Civil Law Section of the Supreme Court, but the present system persists.

In practice, the Supreme Court's emphasis has shifted in the past decade. A 1973 statute expanded the discretionary appellate jurisdiction of the Supreme Court so that private law appeals come by leave (i.e. by the granting of a motion for leave to appeal, the Canadian equivalent to the United States Supreme Court's writ of certiorari). As a result, the Supreme Court of Canada has increasingly specialised in federal statute law matters (which include the entire body of criminal law and procedure), causing some scholars to note with regret the steadily decreasing role of the court in private law.[19]

The jurisdiction of the provincial superior courts has become the most important constitutional standard for upholding the independence of the judiciary. The Supreme Court of Canada has for many years – and increasingly in the past decade – held that legislatures cannot remove from the jurisdiction of the superior courts matters that came within its authority at the time of confederation (1867). The courts have reasoned that to allow such a shift in jurisdiction – principally to provincial administrative tribunals as well as courts staffed by provincially appointed judges – would shift controversies from a court whose independence is constitutionally entrenched to other bodies which lack the same degree of independence. By this reasoning, the Supreme Court of Canada has limited the powers of rent review tribunals (Alberta and Ontario) and tribunals to regulate professions (Quebec),[20] and prevented provincially appointed judges from hearing criminal jury trials (New Brunswick),[21] certain property matters in family law (British Columbia)[22] or certain administrative appeals (Quebec).[23] The superior trial courts in Canada have not traditionally had a greater range of authority than their British or United States counterparts, but they have been more vigorous in preserving what they have from legislative encroachment.

Canadian courts have the same depth of authority as other common law courts. They can punish contempts of court, and they have at hand a wide range of remedies to effect compliance with court orders (including injunctions in labour disputes). At the same time, the caution and conservatism of the Supreme Court and the superior courts pervades the judicial system. No Canadian court would presume to have the judicial capacity to remake a school system or reform the country's jails.[24] Yet ironically, superior courts, to the extent that they carry over the authority of English courts, retain a 'writ of general gaol delivery' which allows the circuit judge to order a local sheriff to bring from the gaol (jail) all prisoners therein to satisfy the court that they are being held according to the law of the land.[25] Yet no Canadian judge would conceive of using this authority to exercise superintending control over the operation of a segment of the criminal justice system. A particular abuse of the process might lead to the dismissal of pending criminal charges in an individual case, but is not likely to generate a more broadly applicable rule to govern the conduct of police or corrections officials.

JUDICIAL DECISION MAKING PROCESSES

In the stereotypical Canadian trial court – the superior, county or district court staffed by a federally appointed judge – a single judge presides over an adversary proceeding. The judge is a full-time appointee, precluded by statute from holding extra-judicial employment. The lawyers dominate the proceedings, not only in the courtroom but throughout the entire process: in civil proceedings, counsel determine the pace of litigation; criminal cases proceed on the initiative of the prosecution. Jury trials are available in major civil and serious criminal matters (required only in murder cases), but juries are in use in a smaller range of cases in Canada than in the United States.

In the lower courts – the Provincial Courts staffed by provincially appointed judges – the pattern is less clearly established. In most provinces, judges are now full-time. However, part-time and fee judges still remain, though it has been over a decade since the last stipendiary magistrate was paid on the basis of the number of convictions he registered. Provincial Court proceedings are in theory adversarial, and legal aid (even in the form of rotating 'duty counsel' drawn from the private bar and sitting in the courtroom) is available in criminal and youth court proceedings, but day-to-day practice is often reminiscent of the scenes described by many students of lower courts. Large numbers of private individuals appear without counsel; defendants in criminal cases usually plead guilty; matters are dealt with summarily in noisy and busy courtrooms.

A key actor in criminal trial courts is the crown attorney. The office is conceived as more than that of a prosecutor. Crown attorneys are provincially appointed officials, in contrast to the locally elected or appointed prosecutors in most United States states; along with a staff of assistant crown attorneys, they handle prosecutions in each local trial court. But crown attorneys are also conceived of as 'local ministers of justice', so that their formal role obligates them to screen charges brought by the police – not only in terms of the strength of the evidence and the congestion of the court but also in terms of the public interest in carrying forward a particular prosecution. The crown's role is to present the evidence to the court, not to act as a purely partisan advocate of one side of an adversary proceeding. In practice, this role definition is not uniformly (or even generally) followed. Screening of charges varies so widely that while only 10 per cent of criminal charges are dismissed by New Brunswick courts, 40 per cent of criminal charges are dismissed by Ontario courts.[26] While many crown attorneys may adopt a dispassionate style of argumentation in the courtroom, defence counsel would challenge the view that crowns are somehow more objective. The role of the crown as part of a province-wide agency has been further undermined in the past decade by the use of federal prosecutors (often private attorneys on contract) in drug prosecutions under the federal Narcotics Control Act.[27]

Courts of appeal in each province operate in panels. For most cases, panels of three are used; in major cases, panels may be enlarged to five. Trial judges from the superior court sit from time to time on appeal court panels in some provinces. The Chief Justice of the province, who sits as the Chief Justice of the court of appeal, selects the panel, presides on any panel of which he is a member, and designates cases as sufficiently important to warrant five-judge rather than three-judge panels. Beyond that, the Chief Justice's influence is that of a colleague on the bench: it increases by the persuasive force of legal argument and personality, not by official position.

While some provincial appellate jurisdiction is discretionary, the principle that the losing party at a trial is entitled to one appeal is observed in practice. In most provinces, the largest single category of appeals are sentencing appeals in criminal cases. While appeals on sentence are virtually non-existent in the United States, they are allowed in every province in Canada (under federal legislation) and are available to the crown as well as the defence. While sentences that are altered by appellate courts are more likely to be reduced than to be increased, crown appeals are not unusual, and convicted defendants have found themselves with years added to their sentences after a successful crown appeal. Even with sentence appeals, the workload of the provincial courts of appeal is low enough that no intermediate appellate courts have been created in any Canadian provinces (in contrast to the intermediate appellate courts in two-thirds of the United States states). Ontario, however, has shifted a portion of its civil appeals to another superior court, the Divisional Court, which consists of three-judge panels of High Court justices who sit on appeals from provincial administrative tribunals.

A substantial proportion of the decisions of provincial courts of appeal are pronounced from the bench, with reasons for decision given orally. If members of a panel cannot agree on an oral decision in a brief conference following the close of formal arguments, or if the case is sufficiently important, the decision will be reserved and presented later along with written reasons. The written reasons may be presented by a single judge on behalf of the majority; in some cases seriatim opinions may be presented, so that the panel reaches a collective decision, but the reasons for decision may not be shared by a majority of the panel's members.

The Supreme Court of Canada's decision making process varies both from the provincial courts of appeal and from the process that characterises the Supreme Court of the United States. In many important cases, all nine justices sit. However, seven-judge and even five-judge panels have more frequently been used. No case is decided by a panel smaller than five judges (even a civil law appeal from Quebec). Since the Supreme Court acquired a larger scope for discretionary jurisdiction a decade ago, the five-judge panels so common in the first hundred years of its operation have grown increasingly rare. Seven-judge panels remain common however, even in constitutional matters; in only one of the first five cases under the new Charter of Rights did all nine justices sit. Again, it is the Chief Justice who determines the size and composition of the panels – and again his influence as Chief extends no further. Bora Laskin, the Chief Justice throughout the 1970s and considered to have a brilliant legal mind and an energetic personality, was frequently in dissent in some of the most controversial cases heard by the court.

The internal decision making process of the Supreme Court of Canada has been shrouded in secrecy. Historians have been unable to uncover any written memoranda or draft opinions similar to those that have helped United States scholars reconstruct the decision making process of the United States Supreme Court.[28] In the past, no formal conferences were held to discuss cases or assign opinions; as a result, seratim opinions were common, opinions of the court rare. Oral argument is held in open court, and may go on for days in major cases, since the strict time limits of the United States Supreme Court are unknown in Canada. However, oral argument is not recorded or transcribed in any way, so no historical record exists beyond sketchy press reports in a handful of newsworthy cases.

Available evidence indicates that changes in the Supreme Court's internal processes are under way. The press of business, along with the increasing number of major cases arising since the constitutional entrenchment of a Charter of Rights in 1982, has seen a continued decrease in the use of seratim opinions; a single justice is much more likely to speak for a majority, and the number of concurring opinions has declined. Furthermore, recent major cases have presented extended reasons of the court, with no individual justice's named attached. A series of early Charter decisions that were reserved for longer than normal periods of time have emerged with unanimous decisions. All of this evidence suggests that the justices are conferring more frequently and systematically, and are dividing work in ways not done in the past.

In spite of an increase in the number of motions for leave to appeal, the Supreme Court continues to accept the same number of cases per year as in the past (approximately 125), and continues to hear leave motions argued before panels of three justices. Rather than shift to the use of written materials only (as in the United States Supreme Court), the Canadian Supreme Court is now experimenting with the use of video for leave hearings, reducing the travel costs for counsel far away from Ottawa but not affecting the time of the justices themselves. The leave process reflects the reluctance of Canadian judges to use personal law clerks or staff attorneys to screen applications.

One of the distinctive features of the Supreme Court of Canada is that it operates as a bilingual institution. Attorneys may file briefs (termed factums) and other documents in either French or English, and may make administrative inquiries or present oral arguments in either French or English. Simultaneous translation is available in the courtroom for justices, counsel and spectators. The court's official reports are published simultaneously in both languages. At the same time, the justices may find themselves working with legal material in a language in which they are not fluent, compounding court delay. It is not surprising, therefore, that the two most recent Supreme Court appointees from outside Quebec are fluent in both official languages (replacing two appointees fluent only in English).

Canadian courts are governed by precedent. A provincial court of appeal is governed by a decision of the Supreme Court of Canada, the trial courts of a province are governed by the decisions of the provincial court of appeal, and the Provincial Courts of a province are governed by the decisions of the province's superior court. It is now possible for a court to overrule one of its own past precedents, but this is recent and uncommon. Does the use of precedent suggest a rigid system? If so, it oversimplifies the complexities of legal reasoning. A precedent governs a similar case arising in the future. But when is a case similar? The answer is often easy in routine cases in trial courts, but the answer is more difficult as cases grow more complex. Thus most appellate judges and many trial judges are in a position to distinguish potentially applicable precedents from the facts of the case before them. The Supreme Court of Canada, rather than overrule a past precedent, has been known to confine that precedent to its facts, narrowing its impact by preventing it from being elevated to a more general rule. Through this process, precedents proliferate. An appellate court judgment becomes increasingly unpredictable, since one first has to figure out how the judges will categorise the facts of the case before knowing which of the available precedents will be used.

INSTITUTIONAL LINKS

The complexity of judicial decision making processes may obscure the political role of the courts. The mechanical application of a line of precedents can still result in the invalidating of a piece of federal or provincial legislation. The distinguishing of previous precedents may result in a judicial decision upholding federal or provincial law, and reinforcing political authorities, even though the apparent weight of precedent would seem to go against the government. In either case, the courts have played a political role. In political terms, they have been more active and independent in the former case; in legal terms, they have been more innovative in the latter case.

Thus the Canadian courts play a political role whenever they review a statute or a government action, whether they find that action *intra vires* (within the authority of) or *ultra vires* (beyond the authority of) the government or official in question. Before the 1982 Charter of Rights, the authority of Canadian courts to review government action on constitutional grounds was limited largely to whether a particular statute fell within the authority of the federal parliament (under Section 91 of the 1867 Constitution Act) or the provincial parliaments (under Section 92). The Canadian courts could review and invalidate government action on other grounds as well: actions of law enforcement officials in criminal cases could be held to violate statutory standards or common law standards; actions of administrative bodies could be invalidated if they violated administrative law standards of fairness, bias, or natural justice (whether embodied in statutes or precedent).

What generalisations could be made about the political impact of the Canadian courts' exercise of judicial review? Have they challenged governments? In constitutional matters, the answer is simple. Since questions arising under Sections 91 and 92 inevitably involve conflicts between governments, one government wins while another loses. Some critics of the Supreme Court of Canada perceive that it has a pro-federal government bias, and provincial governments have long sought a role in the appointment of Supreme Court justices (a power now wielded by Ottawa, generally without consultation with the provinces). At the same time, the Judicial Committee's historic role was seen as favouring provincial power. The current pattern reflects a certain balance: provincial legislation is held *ultra vires* more frequently than federal legislation, but the limits on federal power are significantly greater in Canada than under the post-1937 United States Constitution. Thus while the Canadian parliament has a broader legislative power over commerce than does the United States congress, narrow interpretation of the commerce power by the Judicial Committee has meant that even today labour legislation is handled by the provinces, and the Supreme Court of Canada in 1980 placed tight restrictions on federal authority over labelling of consumer products.[29] Judicial Committee principles are still very much alive.

To the extent that the Supreme Court of Canada has invalidated acts of the federal parliament or the provincial legislatures, or actions of officials of either order of government, it has been an occasional source of inconvenience or frustration or delay, it has altered the form that governmental response to public issues has taken, but it has not fundamentally altered the nature or direction of public policy. That is perhaps the most that a court can do or should do to shape the policies and institutions of a democracy. Whether it is enough to make those institutions survive, let alone grow or flourish, depends on forces external to the courts, over which the courts have little or no effective control.

The delicate and important role the Canadian courts can play is most graphically illustrated by a unique case that was perhaps the most important one decided by the Supreme Court of Canada in its entire history: the Constitutional Reference of 1981.[30] The case centred on the question of whether an amendment to the Canadian constitution (which was at that time still a statute of the United Kingdom parliament) altering the powers of provincial governments could be

submitted to the British parliament by the Canadian federal government without approval of the provinces. A federal government
proposal to patriate the Canadian constitution in a form that included
an amending formula and an entrenched charter of rights had secured
the consent of only two out of ten provinces, but the federal
government vowed to submit it unilaterally. Provincial governments
opposed to the action brought suit in their provinces. The Manitoba
Court of Appeal supported the federal position, arguing that while
provincial approval of constitutional changes had been sought and
secured in the past, this was not a formal constitutional requirement,
and therefore beyond the power of the courts to enforce. The
Newfoundland Court of Appeal supported the provincial position,
concluding that the federal government was acting beyond its constitutional authority. The issue was brought to the Supreme Court of
Canada, where a majority ruled that the federal government was
within its formal constitutional authority, but had violated a convention requiring substantial (but not necessarily unanimous) provincial
approval of constitutional changes affecting provincial authority.

Any Supreme Court of Canada decision in this case would have been
controversial, and this one was. From a United States perspective, the
Canadian court had decided a 'political question', one more appropriate for resolution by 'the political branches'. From a Canadian
perspective, it had supported a provincial government position and at
least temporarily frustrated federal government plans. But the court
had also defined a convention that had not been clear; the eleven
governments had previously sought unanimous agreement, and the
court had not made that a requirement for a constitutional accord. As a
result, federal-provincial negotiations began anew, and an agreement
was reached that won the support of nine out of ten provinces – all but
Quebec. A key to the agreement was a provision allowing federal and
provincial governments to opt out of major sections of the Charter of
Rights: passage of a legislative resolution would allow laws to operate
for five years 'notwithstanding' provisions guaranteeing equality,
freedom of thought and expression, or fundamental justice (due
process).

The Supreme Court's decision was seen as having regenerated a
process of constitutional change whose outcome would be seen as
more legitimate. Its long-run impact on the operation of the newly-
entrenched Charter, and the place of Quebec in confederation, is more
difficult to predict. That the Supreme Court of Canada played an
historic and interventionist role in the political process is undeniable.[31]

One characteristic of this case was one that it had in common with many major constitutional decisions: it was a reference case. That is, it came to the Supreme Court of Canada in the form of a request by the federal government for a decision on particular constitutional questions involving the validity of pending government action. Reference cases are in form and principle similar to the advisory opinion requested two centuries ago of the United States Supreme Court, and refused by that court as not constituting a case or controversy under Article III of the United States Constitution. No similar constraint exists in Canada, and the Supreme Court Act of 1875 gave the federal cabinet authority to refer questions, an authority it has used on a number of occasions. Similar authority exists in the various provinces, whereby a provincial cabinet can refer a question of the validity of one of its statutes to the highest court of the province.

The reference case has been an important linkage between court and government. It has by definition given the courts a political role to play. However, since no court has held that it possesses the authority to reject a reference (though individual judges have refused to answer some questions on grounds of vagueness), and the cabinet can control both the wording of the question and the timing of its submission, a court hearing a reference case could be manipulated into a position where it is more likely to support the government that has submitted the case. The United States Supreme Court feared that an advisory opinion would become a precedent binding the court in a later case in which a concrete fact situation might engender a different response. It is difficult to conclude that this has in fact happened in Canada. The most that could be said is that the reference procedure has tended to reinforce the more co-operative, reticent and ideologically conservative stance often attributed to the Supreme Court of Canada.

Institutional links below the Supreme Court of Canada reinforce the view of Canadian courts and judges as co-operative, reticent and ideologically conservative. To the extent that lawyers control the flow of cases in Canadian trial courts, crown attorneys can direct the flow of criminal cases from first appearance to trial and appeal. On routine matters, this means that judges need not deal with cases that the crown attorney anticipates will result in an acquittal. In non-routine matters, it means the crown may decline to appeal a trial judge's ruling that police action violated the Charter of Rights, avoiding a higher court precedent that could impede police discretion.

Section 96 judges frequently take on special assignments as royal commissioners or chairmen of commissions of inquiry. Provincial governments are even more likely to make these appointments than is the federal government. The commissions operate under statutes that provide subpoena power, and may last from a few months to a few years. The published reports of an inquiry are often quite extensive, and some have had major public policy and even historical impact. Both the expertise and the prestige of the judiciary are harnessed by these inquiries, but the political benefits seem to flow exclusively to the government that sets up the inquiry. Once a judge submits a report and returns to the bench, he or she is no longer free to comment on the matters covered in the report – or to comment on whether subsequent government legislation is in harmony with the report's recommendations or not. Thus the requirement of judicial impartiality enhances government's freedom of action in dealing with the report of a judicial commission of inquiry. Some judges have suggested that impartiality means no judge should be asked to serve, or should agree to serve, on such inquiries.

The use of judges on inquiries is well known to the public because of the publicity these inquiries generate. Judges may also take on extra-judicial activities in the localities in which they sit. One example is in Ontario, where district court judges sit as members of local police commissions. Ontario law for many years required that a judge sit on every police commission, and many judges also served as commission chairmen. Even after repeal of the Ontario law, local judges remain on police commissions, even though the police officers whom a commission governs may appear before the judge as witnesses in criminal cases.

Another category of institutional links that have long been routine for Canadian courts focus on the administration of court services. Court administration is a responsibility of the provinces (except for the Supreme, Federal and Tax Courts of Canada), and in every province that responsibility has been delegated to the provincial attorney general/minister of justice. Therefore all court administrators are employed by an executive department; budgets, staffing levels and personnel policy are set according to standards developed for executive departments; even rules of courts in most provinces require cabinet approval.

Provincial attorneys-general, all of whom are elected members of their provincial legislature and appointed members of their provincial cabinet, are unanimous in justifying their role in court administration. They argue that someone must be held accountable for the expenditure of public funds to operate the courts, and only they as ministers can be called to account before the legislature; judges as independent officials cannot be. Furthermore, the attorneys-general argue, executive control over court administration does not compromise the independence of the judiciary, because judicial independence extends only to the adjudicative function, not to the provision of administrative support services. The court clerk who is appointed, paid and promoted by the attorney general's department is none the less under the direction of the judge while in the courtroom.

Members of the judiciary have grown increasingly apprehensive about this administrative system even though it has been the norm for a century. Critics have continually pointed out the anomaly of the department responsible for prosecution of criminal cases also being responsible for administrators in managing the flow of cases, and the key part played by officials outside the courtroom in ensuring the effectiveness of the judicial role. A major 1981 study called for the independent judicial administration of the courts,[32] but the reticence of a number of provincial chief justices has combined with the scepticism and opposition of attorneys-general to discourage any change in the existing pattern of court administrative relations.

To many Canadian officials, the contrast between executive control of court administration in the provinces and judicial control of court administration in the United States illustrates a difference in constitutional systems: a parliamentary system requires ministerial responsibility and hence executive control, while a system based on the separation of powers leads to judicial control over court administration within a separate third branch of government.[33] However, this constitutional contrast ignores history, for before 1939 the United States federal courts were administered by the Attorney General, who ceded control when the United States federal judiciary showed its willingness to take responsibility. In 1977, initial steps in the same direction were taken by the Supreme Court of Canada. Thus the present pattern of executive-judicial links in Canadian court administration may be less a matter of constitutional necessity than of the same legal culture that has sustained a co-operative, reticent and ideologically conservative judiciary for the past century.

PROSPECTS FOR CHANGE

Every current discussion of the future role of the courts in Canada focuses on the impact of the newly-entrenched Canadian Charter of

Rights and Freedoms. That document covers a full range of civil liberties protections, from freedom of belief and expression to a wide range of legal procedural guarantees, from linguistic and mobility rights to equality provisions that proscribe 'discrimination based on race, national or ethnic origin, colour, religion, sex, age or mental or physical disability' without precluding affirmative action programmes. The Charter also comes with built-in limitations. Not only are many provisions subject to legislative override by the 'notwithstanding' clause, but the very first section provides – in a style similar to European human rights documents – limits on Charter rights. They are guaranteed 'subject only to such reasonable limits prescribed by law as can be demonstrably justified in a free and democratic society'.

Many students of the courts were doubtful that public excitement about the Charter would be reflected in much new law. Yet within the first twelve months, over 500 court cases raised Charter issues.[34] Trial judges throughout Canada, called on to interpret a new constitutional document free from any binding appellate court precedents, sustained Charter arguments in dozens of cases. Some Provincial Court judges even went so far as to declare that they were not independent tribunals as required by the Charter, and therefore could not enter convictions in criminal cases, because of their administrative dependence on the executive.[35] Appellate courts quickly dampened the enthusiasm of the more zealous trial judges, but even those courts sustained Charter arguments against a wide range of federal and provincial laws and law enforcement practices. A frequently-used reverse onus provision in the federal Narcotics Control Act was found to violate the Charter by three provincial courts of appeal.[36] The federal Lord's Day Act was invalidated by the Alberta Court of Appeal.[37] Ontario's film censorship board was invalidated by that province's Court of Appeal.[38]

The Supreme Court of Canada has been slower and more cautious in Charter cases, but even it had granted leave to appeal in over twenty Charter cases within eighteen months after entrenchment. Quebec court decisions invalidating a provision of that province's language laws limiting access to English language schools were unanimously sustained.[39] An Ontario decision invalidating citizenship requirements for admission to the bar was overturned, as the Supreme Court preferred a more limited interpretation of Charter protections of mobility rights.[40] The Alberta court's 3–2 decision on the Lord's Day Act was sustained by a unanimous Supreme Court that defined freedom of religion more broadly than it had a generation before.

What can be concluded thus far about the impact of the Charter? It has had measurable effects on courts at every level, even having an impact on the internal decision making processes of the Supreme Court of Canada, which has faced growing delays but has brought forth unanimous decisions on cases where unanimity would have been unlikely if not unthinkable a decade ago. Courts and judges at every level have stated that their role is different from that in pre-Charter days. Critics of the courts' expanded role see Canadian law and politics becoming less British and more American.

The role of the Canadian courts in constitutional issues has clearly changed. Where the courts for a century have been called upon to decide how the constitution distributes legislative power between the central government and the provinces, constitutional law has already shifted its emphasis to questions about the limitations imposed on all levels of government by a set of constitutionally-entrenched rights. With this change in emphasis goes a change in perspective. In their past efforts to preserve parliamentary supremacy by not invalidating government actions, the courts on many occasions sustained an exercise of power by government officials never contemplated (or at least never debated) by parliament. To the extent that officials exceeded their authority, the remedy was seen to be with parliament and not the courts. By placing an emphasis on the limits of government action, the Charter requires judicial action. Even cabinet directives never previously subject to judicial review could be questioned in Charter litigation.[41] In short, the Canadian courts will have a new role in the development of democratic government in Canada. To the extent that the courts vigorously pursue that role, the nature of Canada's democratic government will not be the same. Those who see parliamentary institutions as a stronger basis for preservation of democracy than judicial protection of individual rights will lament the change, as many have already done.[42]

How likely are the courts to pursue this new role? The thesis of this chapter has been that Canadian courts have had a narrow and restricted role – partly due to their constitutional status, but partly due to their own legal and political approach. The absence of constitutionally-entrenched rights was only one of half a dozen factors that led to the courts' limited role. The abolition of appeals to the Judicial Committee of the Privy Council in 1949 gave rise to a spurt of constitutional activity by the Supreme Court of Canada in the 1950s, but after a decade the courts returned to more traditional patterns. Will the Charter provide the basis for a more sustained change, one that will alter the traditions of positivist interpretation and ideological conservatism, and thus produce a change in legal culture that will suffuse the full range of Canadian trial and appellate courts with a broader definition of their role? It is too early to answer this question, but not too early to watch with a sense of anticipation unmatched in the history of the Canadian judiciary.

NOTES

I am indebted to Professor Peter H. Russell for reading and criticising an earlier draft of this chapter.

1. For a constitutional law casebook designed for non-law students, see Peter H. Russell, *Leading Constitutional Decisions*, 3rd edn (Ottawa: Carleton University Press, 1982); for the definitive treatise in the field, see Peter W. Hogg, *Constitutional Law of Canada*, 2nd edn (Toronto: Carswell, 1985).
2. See generally Paul Weiler, *In the Last Resort: A Critical Study of the Supreme Court of Canada* (Toronto: Carswell, 1974).
3. See J. A. Corry, 'Constitutional Trends and Federalism', in A. R. M. Lower, *et al.*, *Evolving Canadian Federalism* (Durham, NC: Duke University Press, 1958).
4. See for example, *Robertson and Rosetanni* v. *The Queen* (1963) SCR 651, and *Attorney General of Canada* v. *Lavell* (1974) SCR 1349.
5. *Henrietta Muir Edwards* v. *Attorney General for Canada* (1930) AC 124.
6. *Attorney General of Canada* v. *Attorney General of Ontario* (Employment and Social Insurance Act Reference) (1937) AC 355; *Attorney General of British Columbia* v. *Attorney General of Canada* (Natural Products Marketing Act Reference) (1937) AC 377; *Attorney General of Canada* v. *Attorney General of Ontario* (Labour Conventions Case) (1937) AC 327. The 'watertight compartments' metaphor is at the close of the Labour Conventions Case.
7. *Saumur* v. *Quebec and Attorney General of Quebec* (1953) 2 SCR 299; *Switzman* v. *Elbling and Attorney General of Quebec* (1957) SCR 285; *Roncarelli* v. *Duplessis* (1959) SCR 121.
8. *Attorney General of Canada and Dupond* v. *Montreal* (1978) 2 SCR 770; *Nova Scotia Board of Censors* v. *McNeil* (1978) 2 SCR 662.
9. Peter Russell, 'Judicial Power in Canada's Political Culture', in *Courts and Trials: A Multidisciplinary Approach*, Martin L. Friedland (ed.), (Toronto: University of Toronto Press, 1975).
10. Peter H. Russell, 'The Supreme Court and Federal-Provincial Relations: The Political Use of Legal Resources', *Canadian Public Policy*, XI: 161 (June 1985), pp. 168–9.
11. Material in this section is drawn largely from chapter 4 of Perry S. Millar and Carl Baar, *Judicial Administration in Canada* (Montreal: McGill–Queens University Press, 1981) and Canadian Centre for Justice Statistics, *Manpower, Resources and Costs of Courts and Criminal Prosecutions in Canada 1980–82* (Ottawa: Statistics Canada, 1983).

12. Compare Reference re Adoption Act (1938) SCR 398, with more recent cases cited in notes 20–3 below.
13. Constitution Act, 1982, sections 41(d) and 42(1)(d). Constitutional scholars disagree on whether this language effectively entrenches the 1875 statutory provisions in the constitution. Contrast William R. Lederman, 'Constitutional Procedure and the Reform of the Supreme Court of Canada', *Les Cahiers de Droit* XXVI: 195 (March 1985), with Peter W. Hogg, *Canada Act 1982 Annotated* (Toronto: Carswell, 1982), pp. 92–4.
14. I am indebted to Professor Ian Bushnell for historical information on appointments to the Supreme Court of Canada.
15. Jules Deschênes with the collaboration of Carl Baar, *Maîtres chez eux/ Masters in Their Own House* (Ottawa: Canadian Judicial Council, 1981), pp. 112–14.
16. Gerald L. Gall, *The Canadian Legal System* (Toronto: Carswell, 1977), pp. 155–6.
17. Gall, *The Canadian Legal System*. Note in particular the well-publicised controversy over off-the-bench statements by Justice Thomas R. Berger of the British Columbia Supreme Court. Relevant material may be found in F. L. Morton (ed.), *Law, Politics and the Judicial Process in Canada* (Calgary: University of Calgary Press, 1984), pp. 108–20. Morton's book is an excellent current source of material on the Canadian judicial process. For a history of civil liberties in Canada, see Thomas R. Berger's book, *Fragile Freedoms: Human Rights and Dissent in Canada* (Toronto: Clarke Irwin, 1981).
18. Re Currie and Niagara Escarpment Commission, 13 CCC (3d) 35 (Ontario High Court of Justice, 1984), overruled on appeal (Ontario Court of Appeal, 1984).
19. See the symposium on 'The Future of the Supreme Court of Canada as the Final Appellate Tribunal in Private Law Litigation', in *Canadian Business Law Journal*, VII: 389 (1983).
20. Re Residential Tenancies Act (1981) 1 SCR 714; *Crevier* v. *Attorney General of Quebec* (1981) 2 SCR 220.
21. *McEvoy* v. *Attorney General of New Brunswick* (1983) 1 SCR 705.
22. Re B.C. Family Relations Act (1982) 1 SCR 129.
23. *Seminaire de Chicoutimi* v. *City of Chicoutimi* (1973) SCR 681.
24. For the best-known critique of United States judicial activism, see Donald L. Horowitz, *The Courts and Social Policy* (Washington, DC: Brookings, 1977).
25. See H. R. Poultney, 'The Criminal Courts of the Province of Ontario and Their Process', *Law Society of Upper Canada Gazette*, IX: 192 (September 1975).
26. Estimates provided by the Canadian Centre for Justice Statistics.
27. A constitutional challenge of the practice was unsuccessful; see *The Queen* v. *Hauser* (1979) 1 SCR 984.
28. See for example David Ricardo Williams, *Duff: A Life in the Law* (Vancouver: University of British Columbia Press, 1984), and the forthcoming history of the Supreme Court of Canada by James Snell and Frederick Vaughan.
29. *Labatt* v. *Attorney General of Canada* (1980) 1 SCR 914.

30. *Attorney General of Manitoba, et al.* v. *Attorney General of Canada, et al.* (Reference Re Amendment of the Constitution of Canada) (1981) 1 SCR 753.
31. See Peter Russell's commentary on the case in *The Court and the Constitution* (Kingston: Institute of Intergovernmental Relations, 1982).
32. Jules Deschênes, *Maîtres chez eux*, note 15 above. See also chapter 3 of Millar and Baar, *Judicial Administration in Canada*, note 11 above.
33. Carl Baar, 'Patterns and Strategies of Court Administration in Canada and the United States', *Canadian Public Administration*, XX: 242 (Summer 1977).
34. For a full analysis, see F. L. Morton, 'Charting the Charter–Year One: A Statistical Analysis', in *Canadian Human Rights Yearbook 1984–85*.
35. For the best known case, see the Ontario Court of Appeal's reasons in *The Queen* v. *Valente* (No. 2), 41 OR (2d) 187, 2 CCC (3d) 417, 145 DLR (3d) 452 (1983).
36. *The Queen* v. *Oakes* (Ont. Ct. of Apl., 1983), 2 CCC (3d) 339; *The Queen* v. *Stanger* (Alta. Ct. of Apl., 1983), 2 DLR (4th) 124; *The Queen* v. *Landry* (Que. Ct. of Apl., 1983), 2 DLR (4th) 518.
37. *The Queen* v. *Big M. Drug Mart Ltd.*, 5 DLR (4th) 121 (1983).
38. Re Ontario Film and Video Appreciation Society and Ontario Board of Censors, 5 DLR (4th) 766 (1984).
39. *Attorney General of Quebec* v. *Quebec Association of Protestant School Boards*, (1984) 2 SCR 66.
40. *Law Society of Upper Canada* v. *Skapinker*, (1984) 1 SCR 357.
41. *The Queen* v. *Operation Dismantle* (Fed. Ct. of Apl., 1983), 3 DLR (4th) 193.
42. See for example Donald Smiley, *The Canadian Charter of Rights and Freedoms, 1981* (Toronto: Ontario Economic Council, Discussion Paper Series, 1981), and generally Keith Banting and Richard Simeon (eds), *And No One Cheered* (Toronto: Methuen, 1983), and Peter H. Russell, 'The Effect of the Charter of Rights on the Policy-Making Role of Canadian Courts', *Canadian Public Administration*, XXV: 1 (1982).

5 The Courts in the Federal Republic of Germany
Kenneth M. Holland

INTRODUCTION

The framers of the 1949 West German Constitution, or Basic Law (*Grundgesetz*) (GG), sought above all to prevent the re-emergence of tyranny. They expected to preserve a liberal regime by correcting the faults that led to the collapse of the Weimar Republic. The constitution thus has four primary goals: to give effect to majority rule, to protect individual liberty, to guarantee equality of means as well as of opportunity, and to maintain federalism. Awaiting the reunification of Germany, a nation divided into two states after the Second World War, the founders of the Federal Republic 'desir[ed] to give a new order to political life for a transitional period' (Preamble, *Grundgesetz*) and thus eschewed the term 'constitution' in favour of 'basic law'.

During the past forty years, as Germans have ceased to hope for reunification in the near future, the 1949 polity has achieved its ends and surpassed all expectations. Blessed with able statesmen at the helm, West Germany has overcome external political difficulties and assumed a leading position in the North Atlantic Treaty Organisation and the European Community. Accompanying political integration with the West has been the economic reconstruction of the destroyed country, followed by economic growth sufficient to establish West Germany as the fourth wealthiest state, outranked only by the United States, the Soviet Union and Japan. The federal system has become a model for other nations. Social welfare is extensive, and the West German people are among the most free in the world. A significant share of the credit for these successes belongs to the courts.

Not only have the post-war courts resolved a myriad of civil and criminal disputes, they have resolved them in accordance with the law. By supporting the *Rechtsstaat* (a state governed by law and justice), the judges have provided an atmosphere of predictability and stability conducive to capital risk and investment and, therefore, economic development. Although the constitution is neutral in economic matters and favours neither capitalism nor socialism, the judges have supported the development of a free market system which has produced 'the economic miracle'.[1] By forcing the government and individuals to respect the rights guaranteed by the Basic Law, judges have enhanced the legitimacy of the fledgling regime and greatly contributed to internal stability. New constitutions are quite vulnerable, for they lack 'that veneration which time bestows on everything, and without which perhpas the wisest and freest governments would not possess the requisite stability'.[2] In particular, the Federal Constitutional Court (*Bundesverfassungsgericht*) has helped win popular acceptance of the liberal democratic order. More successful than either its Austrian or Italian counterparts,[3] the German Constitutional Court has come 'to serve as an excellent object lesson for students of jurisprudence in other countries'.[4]

The most important lesson the framers learned from the failure of Weimar was that a democracy guaranteeing civil liberties carries within its principles the seed of its own destruction. The constitution thus frames a 'militant democracy', equipped to overcome any individuals or groups that would use constitutional freedoms to overthrow the republic and destroy freedom.

LEGAL CULTURE

To understand the contribution courts make to the maintenance of democratic institutions it is necessary to comprehend the nature of the legal system within which they operate. West Germany, unlike Britain, Canada, Australia, and the United States, derives its legal system heavily from Roman law, as do France, Sweden, Italy, and Japan. In Roman or civil law countries, the source of law is not previous judicial decisions but a set of legislative codes. The function of the Roman law judge is to apply whatever part of the code, considered clear and complete, that is relevant to the conflict at hand.[5] The civil law judge may not add to or subtract from the corpus of law. In English-speaking, common law countries, on the other hand, a primary source of law is judicial decisions rendered in concrete cases. Judges must observe the rule of precedents, or *stare decisis*. They must judge present cases as similar cases were decided in the past. Under the civil law, the decisions of judges are not law and do not bind other judges. An exception is that German Constitutional Court interpretations of the Basic Law are binding on all judges.

There are other differences between the two legal systems. 'The pluralistic American notion of law resulting from bargaining and compromising among politicians and competing interest groups is alien to the German idea of law that triumphed in the codes'.[6] Similarly, dissenting opinions historically have been prohibited in civil law countries, for they would violate the 'secrecy of consultation' among the judges prior to announcement of the decision and would indicate that the codes were unclear and that judges possessed discretion in their application.[7] Since 1970, judges of the Constitutional Court have been permitted to file dissenting opinions, and precedent has become increasingly important for German courts. The Constitutional Court especially appears to be 'coming close to case-law-techniques'.[8] The increasing importance of statutory law in common law jurisdictions and of precedent in civil law jurisdictions, however, suggests a convergence of the two systems.[9] Moreover, the notion that courts possess the authority to review the constitutionality of statutes and to invalidate laws repugnant to the constitution is alien to the Roman law system.[10]

Anglo-American legal procedures are *adversarial* in nature. The aggrieved party is responsible for initiating the lawsuit or prosecution. The disputing parties present evidence before the trier of fact and control the pace of the proceedings. The judge's function, if he sits with a jury, is to enforce the rules of evidence and due process, when called upon by one of the parties who believes his opponent has committed an infraction. The jury, who cannot ask questions or take notes, must determine guilt and innocence entirely on the basis of what they have seen and heard in the courtroom. In an adversarial contest, the judge, who cannot call witnesses or introduce evidence, is basically a passive referee.

By contrast, civil law procedure accords with an *inquisitorial* model. Under the principle of inquisition the judge controls the pace and scope of the proceedings, calling and examining witnesses, and assumes responsibility for discovering the truth. The judicial inquisition principle frees the court from dependence on the parties.[11] The judge is an active inquirer, not a passive umpire. In Germany, the 'inquisition maxim' is more operative in criminal than in civil proceedings.[12] Under the inquisitorial system, there are fewer restrictions upon the police, especially in the interrogation of witnesses and suspects and in the conduct of searches and seizures. Justice is equated with substance – punishing the guilty and absolving the innocent – whereas adversarial proceedings equate justice with adherence to correct procedure. If the defendant received a fair trial, the verdict is just, even if the jury convicts an innocent man or acquits a guilty one.[13]

Another distinction is that on the continent of Europe, 'prosecutors are legally bound to prosecute all serious crimes that come to their attention'.[14] In the English-speaking nations, however, prosecutors enjoy wide discretion and frequently refuse to prosecute suspects arrested by the police. Germans regard mandatory prosecution as required by the principle of legality (*Legalitaetsprinzip*).

In fact, one of the striking features of German legal culture is the extent to which legalism has penetrated German society. West Germany, like the United States, is a highly rights conscious society. West Germans display a marked tendency to 'resort to formal legal rules to solve many of the problems of ordinary human existence'.[15] Serving a population of 62 million are 3593 public prosecutors, 39,075 attorneys-at-law, 7269 notaries,[16] and 16,657 professional judges – proportionally eight times the number of judges in the United States. West Germans prefer adjudication to less legalistic modes of dispute resolution such as negotiation, mediation, and arbitration. Also contributing to this disposition to seek adjudication of conflicts are the particularity of West German code law and the relative speed and cheapness of German justice.[17] Where many countries rely upon administrative bodies to settle conflicts between the individual and government, such as a challenge to denial of social security benefits, West Germany refers such disputes to independent courts. Even cases of military discipline in Germany are tried by civilian courts rather than courts martial, as in most countries.

The experience of Nazi totalitarianism led to a major change in German legal culture. Prior to 1949, the dominant philosophy of law in Germany was positivism, the belief that the will of the legislator is the ultimate source of law. Constitutions were regarded as exhortatory and admonitory and could certainly not limit the lawmaker's discretion.[18] Statutes controlled all cases brought before the courts.

The Nazi era, however, shook the people's faith in the legislature and led to a discrediting of legal positivism.[19] The framers of the Basic Law acted on the basis of the natural law school of jurisprudence, according to which man-made law in order to be binding must be consistent with immutable standards of morality. *Rechtsstaat* was reinterpreted to mean the just state, not the legal state. The constitution thus contains protections for two kinds of 'basic rights':

'human rights' enjoyed by all people in all places at all times (Article 2*GG*) and 'civil rights' enjoyed by Germans since 1949 (Article 8 *GG*). Certain constitutional principles are inviolable. There is a 'constitutional minimum' which even the sovereign people of Germany must perpetually honour.[20] The framers instituted judicial review, in part, in order to check legislative and executive violations of the higher law.

Consistent with this emphasis on natural rights, the Federal Republic ratified the European Convention for the Protection of Human Rights and Fundamental Freedoms in 1953. In 1973 West Germany also ratified the International Conventions on Civil and Political as well as Economic, Social, and Cultural Rights. Over 2500 complaints have been filed against West Germany before the Commission of Human Rights in Strasbourg and the European Court of Human Rights. Only four of the complaints, dealing with excessively long court proceedings, resulted in the establishment of a violation. Consistent with natural rights theory, Article 20(4) of the Basic Law recognises the right of the German people to resist and overthrow an unjust regime.

The Basic Law, nevertheless, does not regard individual rights as absolute. Article 18 states that whoever abuses freedom of expression, of press, of assembly in order to combat democracy and freedom shall forfeit his basic rights. Similarly, Article 21 says that political parties that seek to abolish liberal democracy shall be unconstitutional and proscribed by the Federal Constitutional Court. The Court has upheld the secret execution of wiretaps with the reasoning that the protection of some rights requires restriction of other basic rights, such as the right to privacy and to judicial review of warrant requests.[21] As memories of the Nazi tyranny have faded, natural law arguments have become less common in German judicial opinions.[22]

STRUCTURE OF THE COURTS

Federal regimes may employ two types of court systems: dual and integrated. In dual systems, such as that of the United States, there are two parallel hierarchies of courts. Federal trial and appellate courts exist beside state trial and appellate courts. These separate systems merge only at the top. West Germany employs the integrated structure, under which all the trial courts are provincial courts and the only federal courts are appellate tribunals. In Germany, there is no separate system of federal courts to administer federal law. Most proceedings, therefore, are conducted by the state (*Land*) courts.

Far-reaching specialisation marks the German Federal court system. It consists of five branches, each with a federal supreme court. The ordinary courts are competent for all criminal and civil proceedings. The county court (*Amtsgericht*) is a single-judge court of first instance in petty civil and criminal cases. In the case of more serious crimes, where the maximum penalty is three years imprisonment, the professional judge is assisted by two lay judges. When certain serious crimes are involved, two professional and two lay judges sit in judgment.

The district courts (*Landgerichte*), though, are the normal trial courts for major criminal and civil cases. Panels of three professional judges decide most civil cases. Suits dealing with trade matters are heard by one professional and two lay judges. Panels consisting of three professional judges and two lay assessors try criminal cases. The district courts also act as courts of second instance for appeals from the county court.

German procedural law distinguishes between appeals and revisions. The appellate court reviews not only the legal aspects of the case but also the facts and may call for new evidence. A court of revision, however, must confine itself to correcting errors in points of law.

Where the district courts are courts of first instance in civil suits, appeals are possible to the regional courts (*Oberlandesgerichte*). The regional court works in panels of three professional judges. The Federal Court of Justice (*Bundesgerichtshof*) hears revisions from both the district and regional courts. It consists of ten civil and criminal senates. It must hear all cases that come to it from the lower courts for review.

In criminal matters where the district court is the court of first instance, revision is the only possible avenue, bringing the case before either the regional court (three professional judges) or the Federal Court of Justice (five professional judges). The latter in addition entertains criminal revisions from the regional courts. Regional courts also act as courts of first instance when there is an alleged violation of state interests, e.g. high treason. Panels of five professional judges try these cases, and revision is possible to the Federal Court of Justice. Revision permits either prosecutor or defendant to appeal against a criminal court judgment on a point of law.[23] The labour courts resolve disputes arising from collective bargaining or questions relating to application of the worker participation law. As Figure 1 indicates, there is a three-tiered system of courts, allowing for appeals on more complex cases.

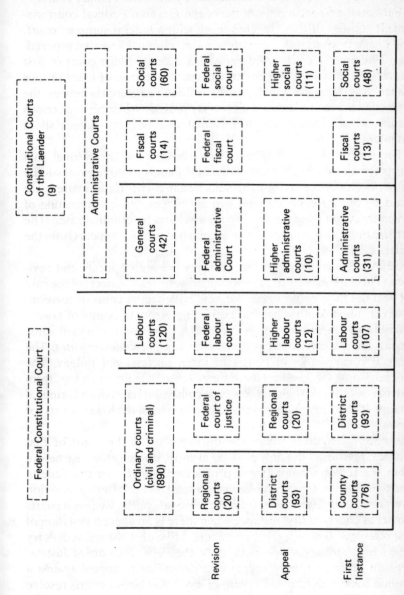

Figure 5.1 Court structure in the Federal Republic of Germany

In Germany, unlike Italy, the network of courts does not ramify merely into ordinary and administrative courts. The Basic Law (Article 95) establishes fiscal, or tax, and social courts alongside the administrative courts, labour courts, and the ordinary courts for civil and criminal matters. The intention behind specialisation is threefold: to provide speedy justice, technically correct justice, and justice that takes into account the opinion of the relevant public.[24] On these courts traditional judges frequently sit beside lay judges who are technical experts in a given subject matter or who represent groups affected by rulings of the court. these 'honorary' judges enjoy full voting rights. Trade union members, e.g. sit on labour courts. This practice has the important effect of enhancing the legitimacy of the court's decisions and of enlisting the co-operation of the interest groups represented on the bench. Lay judge 'corporatism', however, is in tension with the ideal of judicial neutrality and underscores the political function of the courts.

The general administrative courts handle all administrative law proceedings except those falling under the jurisdiction of the social and fiscal courts. Examples of the kinds of cases heard by these courts are proceedings instituted by individual citizens against public authorities to secure planning permission or the reversal of a closure of commercial premises and actions by civil servants against their employers.

The fiscal courts decide disputes between individuals and the state over taxes, while the social courts rule on disputes involving social insurance, unemployment insurance, war victims' benefits, and compulsory medical insurance. Each of the five federal supreme courts hears cases in senates of five judges, one of whom serves as chairman. The Federal Court of Justice is composed of 104 judges, the Federal Labour Court 17, the Federal Administrative Court 66, the Federal Fiscal Court 40, and the Federal Social Court 40.

One of the innovations of the 1949 constitution was the establishment of the Federal Constitutional Court. It is the guardian of the Basic Law, with the power of judicial review over all state and federal government officials. The Constitutional Court is unique among West German courts. It is one of the co-equal branches of the federal government, equal in dignity to and independent of the states, Federal President, Federal Parliament (*Bundestag*), Federal Chancellor, and Federal Council (*Bundesrat*). It is non-adjudicatory in that its function is not to resolve disputes but to act as the final interpreter of the constitution. It is yet another manifestation of the German penchant for specialisation. It does not, therefore, act as an appellate court with general supervisory authority over the lower courts. It has, in fact, no jurisdiction over non-constitutional questions. The Constitutional Court, therefore, is not analogous to the Supreme Court of the United States. For ordinary civil and criminal cases, the Federal Court of Justice is the supreme court and is the ultimate judicial authority for all questions other than consitutional ones. The Constitutional Court is the only court that can exercise judicial review of legislation and that is its singular role.

The confinement of the power of constitutional review to a single judicial organ is known as 'centralised' judicial review. Although German judges are bound by the law, if they believe that a law is incompatible with the constitution they must suspend the trial in progress and express their doubts to the Constitutional Court. German judges, however, especially members of the five federal supreme courts, are most reluctant to refer constitutional issues to the Constitutional Court. They prefer dispelling doubts of constitutionality by interpreting statutes so that they conform with the Constitution. These judges are thus engaging in 'a kind of cryptic judicial review to overcome the requirements' of the Basic Law.[25] Rank and file judges, in fact, regard the Court as an 'appurtenance' to the judicial system, are not very familiar with its decisions, and regard it as under the control of the political parties.[26]

The Federal Constitutional Court sits in Karlsruhe and consists of two chambers, or senates, of eight judges each. An Act of Parliament designates the jurisdiction of each senate. The Court's president presides over the First Senate and its vice-president over the Second Senate. In cases of disagreement between the panels over the constitution's meaning, the plenum of the Court (all sixteen judges) has the final word. Consistent with the natural law mode of thinking that became popular after the collapse of Nazism, each state has its own constitution and, except Schleswig–Holstein and Berlin, a constitutional court to enforce it.

PERSONNEL

All judges, public prosecutors, lawyers and notaries receive a standard professional training. It begins with a four-year law curriculum at a university which is followed by a two-and-a-half years' practical apprenticeship, especially in the courts. Those who afterwards pass the second state law examination have the qualifications of a judge. The successful examinee must then choose to become either a lawyer or a judge. Historically, the brightest law students have aspired to be judges. Today, however, higher financial rewards are attracting many into the private practice of law who in the past would have chosen the more prestigious judicial career. Unlike in Britain and the United States, in Germany lawyers and judges pursue separate careers and belong to distinct professions. Judges maintain closer social relationships with civil servants than with attorneys.[27]

German judges are not elected but appointed by the state. Article 97(1) of the Basic Law guarantees that 'the judges are independent and subject only to the law'. Judges may not be dismissed or transferred against their will. After a probationary period of at least three years, they are given lifetime appointments (i.e. until age sixty-eight). German judges are considerably more independent of executive officials and ruling political parties than they were during the Nazi period. In the *Laender*, ministers of justice appoint the judges and the recommendation of higher ranking judges is usually necessary for promotion.[28] Federal judges, however, are much less susceptible to executive and legislative influence.

Article 95(2) of the Basic Law requires that election to a federal court be by a Judicial Election Committee. The committee is composed of one representative from each *Land* and an equal number of persons elected by the *Bundestag* (the lower house of Parliament), usually *Bundestag* deputies chosen on the basis of proportional representation of political parties.[29] Voting in the Judicial Election Committee is by simple majority. All appointments require the approval of the federal minister who heads the ministry which supervises the court with the vacancy. The Federal Minister of Justice, e.g. must approve appointments to the Federal Court of Justice. The Federal President makes the actual appointment of federal judges and may refuse to appoint someone nominated by the Judicial Election Committee. Lay judges on the Federal Labour and Social Courts are appointed by the Federal Minister of Labour from a list of candidates drawn up by the groups concerned. They serve four-year terms.

Judges named to the Federal Constitutional Court serve twelve years. They are ineligible for reappointment and must retire at age sixty-eight. Three members of each senate must be selected from the body of judges on other federal courts. A majority of the appointees to the Constitutional Court are not career judges (although they could be) but are civil servants, law professors, or, most commonly, politicians (especially *Bundestag* deputies), all of whom have passed the second state law examination.[30] This unique composition of the Constitutional Court emphasises its political role.

The *Bundestag* and *Bundesrat* each select one half of the Constitutional Court judges. The *Bundestag* plenum selects an electoral college of twelve deputies. Political parties are represented on the electoral college in proportion to their strength in the *Bundestag*. Election of a judge requires a two-thirds majority of the electoral college. The *Bundesrat* directly chooses its Constitutional Court judges by a two-thirds vote. The two-thirds requirement guarantees intensive bargaining between the two major political parties and insures that the parties play the decisive role in the selection of Constitutional Court justices.[31] The Federal President makes the actual appointments but he must follow the advice of the electoral organs.

Edmund Burke observed that if one seeks to understand the behaviour of a policitical institution knowing who staffs it is much more enlightening than familiarity with its formal constitution, for 'the [human] materials of which in a great measure it is composed . . . is of ten thousand times greater consequence than all the formalities in the world'.[32] Analyses of the sociological make-up of judges reveal that approximately half the members of the West German judiciary stem from the families of civil servants and judges. Far fewer judges are children of judges than of civil servants. Background is significant because

> German civil servants have long had a reputation for traditional values, and evidence exists that they value public discussion and democratic conflict less, place greater value on duty to the state, and are more conservative on social issues than the average citizen.[33]

During the Weimar period, many judges joined the army and the wealthy landowners and industrialists in opposing liberal democracy.[34] In general German judges still share similar attitudes and backgrounds, i.e. conservative. In contrast, most Constitutional Court justices (58.7 per cent) are not career judges and, accordingly, value authoritarianism somewhat less.

Federal Constitutional Court justices must be at least forty years old. Nearly all the justices have middle- or upper-middle-class backgrounds. The various West German states are represented on the Court roughly in proportion to their population. Catholics are underrepresented on the Court. The two major parties, CDU/CSU (Christian Democrats) and SPD (Social Democrats) are about equally

Table 5.1   Federal Constitutional Court:* judicial background characteristics

Characteristic	%
Age	
40–49	32.61
50–59	34.78
60–65	21.74
Over 65	10.87
Parental occupation	
Civil servant	23.91
Teacher or Professor	15.22
Judge or Lawyer	6.52
Other professional	17.39
Businessman	17.39
Landowner	6.52
Worker	4.35
Unknown	8.70
Prior occupation	
Civil Service	28.26
Judge	41.30
Professor	10.87
Legislator	17.39
Lawyer	2.17
Religion	
Protestant	54.35
Catholic	36.96
Other	8.70
Party identification	
CDU/CSU	50.00
SPD	43.48
FDP	4.35
DP	2.17

* These are the background characteristics of the 46 justices who served 1951–72. From Donald P. Kommers, *Judicial Politics in West Germany: A Study of the Federal Constitutional Court* (Beverly Hills: Sage, 1976) pp. 144–6.

represented, this apportionment reflecting their relative strength in the Parliament. What is the relationship between these background characteristics and personal values? 'Ideologically, they evince little or no tendency toward dogmatism; juristically, they seem rather pragmatic and, almost universally, are aware of and sensitive to the political nature of their work as Constitutional Court Justices.'[35]

Two Constitutional Court justices have been disqualified from participating in cases when, by off-the-bench remarks, the justices had cast doubt on their impartiality. Each senate has the authority to disqualify, a power that departs from the practice of most constitutional courts where recusal is left to the discretion of the individual justice.[36]

The increased involvement in policy making of judges in democratic nations since the Second World War has led to greater attention to the problem of judicial responsibility, i.e. the issue of 'who guards the guardians'. The removal power was abused in Nazi Germany where the executive disciplined judges who failed to consider 'the will of the Fuehrer' as their supreme rule.[37] To protect judicial independence, the framers of the Basic Law devised a far more cumbersome procedure. The Federal Parliament can initiate proceedings against any federal judge thought to be guilty of 'infring[ing] the principles of th[e] Basic Law'.[38] The Constitutional Court, however, tries the accusation, and a two-thirds vote of the Court is required to convict. The Court may give the offending magistrate a different function, retire him, or dismiss him. So far this power of impeachment has had only symbolic significance; no case has been brought to the Constitutional Court. It is ill adapted, certainly, for the punishment of minor transgressions.

An Act of 8 September 1961 established special judicial service courts. These are not independent bodies but are formed from existing courts. In addition to disciplining erring judges by issuing reprimands, reducing salary, or dismissing from the service, these courts can retire a judge who, because of serious illness of long duration, is unable to continue his duties.[39] These courts do not have jurisdiction, however, over the Constitutional Court. Even Parliament may not impeach a justice of the Constitutional Court – only the Federal President can dismiss a justice and then only on a motion of the Court itself.

In 1981 Parliament followed France and enacted further legislation on judicial responsibility. Unique among the advanced democracies, Germany and France have extended to judges acting in their official capacity the notion that the state must compensate for damages caused to its citizens by violation of the law. To shield judges from harassing litigation, the injured party cannot sue the judge but can initiate an action against the state. In both countries the state retains the right to sue the judge at fault to recover any damages paid to the victim. The latter proceeding, however, is relatively rare.[40]

SCOPE OF AUTHORITY

Since 1969 German judges have enjoyed a more narrow scope of authority in criminal proceedings. Prior to that date, the decision about whether there is sufficient evidence to justify going to trial was in the hands of an investigatory judge. The examining magistrate determined whether a case went to the presiding judge. In that year, however, Parliament abolished the institution of judicial investigation. Public prosecutors now handle criminal investigations and judges are restricted to determining guilt and imposing sentence.[41] On the civil side, the scope of judicial authority remains wide. Although non-judicial bodies possess adjudicatory functions in Anglo-American and socialist nations, because of the experience with executive abuse of power, adjudication is the sole province of courts in Germany, as well as in Japan and Italy. The 'right of action', or the right to have legal disputes resolved by a court including the right to judicial review of administrative action, is accordingly quite broad in West Germany. The Constitution (Article 19) guarantees a judicial remedy for every violation of right, and 'if no other court has jurisdiction, recourse shall be to the ordinary courts'.

Originally the Constitutional Court had authority from Parliament to issue advisory opinions. The political branches requested such opinions twice, once with regard to a pending tax bill and once with regard to a pending treaty. In 1952 the Constitutional Court expressed the view that advisory opinions were alien to the judicial function and in 1956 Parliament removed the Court's jurisdiction to give such opinions. Principally motivating the government was the fear of a judicial check on its power to make treaties.[42] This law is the only instance of parliamentary withdrawal of authority from the Constitutional Court.

Like other courts, the Federal Constitutional Court may not originate a case on its own initiative but must wait for a party to bring unconstitutional acts to its attention. Unlike the United States Supreme Court, the West German Constitutional Court is a court of original jurisdiction. The lower West German courts decide concrete cases; the Constitutional Court rules on the constitutionality of laws. There are three basic ways constitutional questions come before the Court, as authorised by Articles 93 and 100 of the Basic Law. First, the Federal Government, a *Land* Government, or one third of the *Bundestag* members may seek *abstract judicial review* of statutes before they actually take effect. Abstract judicial review is almost always a last resort by a political party to defeat a controversial statute.[43] Secondly, if a court has constitutional doubts concerning a law whose validity is relevant to the decision of a case before it, it must stay the proceedings and seek *concrete judicial review* from the Constitutional Court.

Thirdly, the Court also fulfils part of the function of the French *Conseil d'Etat*. Since 1951 any individual whose basic rights have been directly denied by a statute, judicial decision, or administrative act can file a *constitutional complaint* with the Constitutional Court. About one-third of the complaints are filed by criminal defendants alleging that their trial was unfair. Most of the non-criminal complaints allege violations of the right to property. There are relatively few complaints against violations of personal freedoms such as freedom of religion, expression, and association.[44] Filing such complaints is free of charge and the Constitutional Court processes them with relative rapidity.[45] The Court may suspend the application of the challenged action pending decision on its constitutionality. A committee of three Constitutional Court judges determines whether the complaint is substantial enough to merit a full hearing. The committees dismiss more than 97 per cent of these individual complaints.[46]

Although politically important, abstract judicial reviews account for less than 1 per cent of cases filed with the Court. Concrete judicial reviews contribute 5 per cent, and constitutional complaints account for 93 per cent of the Court's docket.[47] The Court is busy, as evidenced by the fact that it receives about 2000 petitions for review annually.

The justices consider almost all cases on the basis of written briefs. Oral argument is held only once or twice a year. After the case is accepted, the presiding officer of the senate, with jurisdiction over the subject matter involved, assigns it to a justice on the basis of his particular interest or specialisation. The justice receiving the case, known as the reporter, is responsible for preparing the case for discussion and for recommending a decision. The reporter will draft the opinion in the case even if his colleagues reject his recommendation. The reporter's recommendation is carried about 75 per cent of the time.[48] Most cases are unanimously decided.

Since 1951, the Constitutional Court has passed judgment on in excess of 30,000 cases. Some of those attracted intense public interest. The Court has overturned about one hundred state and federal laws and restrictfully interpreted several treaties. In its first argued case, *The Southwest Case*,[49] the Court carved out a broad authority. It asserted that it could find implicit, natural law norms in the Basic Law that took precedence over specific, positive law norms stated in the same document. It declared that not only its specific rulings but its reasoning were binding upon the federal government, and it claimed the authority to answer constitutional questions not raised by the litigants themselves if the case presented them.

The Court, nevertheless, is very much aware of its political character. Conscious of the potential danger to itself and to the legislative process represented by judicial review, the Court 'imposes on itself . . . the principle of judicial self-restraint'.[50] Its sensitivity to the consequences of exercising its jurisdiction has led, however, to criticism. 'Observers find a far-reaching lack of orientation and arbitrariness in the interpretative efforts of the Court whose procedure on the whole is labelled as "pragmatic, flexible and undogmatic".'[51] The Court prefers decisions that are politically feasible to those that are technically sound.

LINKS WITH OTHER POLITICAL INSTITUTIONS

To assess the power of courts it is necessary to detail their relationships with other political actors, viz. the executive, the legislature, political parties, the states, interest groups, and supra-national organisations. West Germany is unusual in the extent to which it formalises the links among institutions. This tendency is a function of the corporatist strain in West German political culture. For example, the federal government, the *Laender*, the supervising ministries, the *Bundestag*, and certain interest groups all have been assigned formal roles in the selection of judges on the federal courts.[52]

The Executive Branch

The Federal Constitutional Court insists that the standard of judicial independence requires separation of the judicial function from the public administration and prohibits mayors, municipal council members, and other officials from serving in courts.[53] In order to reduce bureaucratic pressure over the Federal Administrative and Fiscal Courts, Parliament in 1969 shifted supervisory authority from the Ministries of the Interior and Finance, respectively, to the Ministry of Justice, over whose policies the courts would not be sitting in judgment.[54] Because the Constitutional Court is a co-equal constitutional organ, it draws up its own budget and receives appropriations directly from Parliament, bypassing the Justice Ministry. The most famous confrontation between a ministry and the Constitutional Court culminated in 1966 when a divided Court upheld a nocturnal search of the offices and detention of sixty employees of *Der Spiegel*, a magazine which had published an article critical of the Minister of Defence. The political opposition had likened the raid to tactics used by Hitler's Gestapo.[55]

One of the most sensitive areas of conflict between the courts and the executive is the constitutional validity of treaties. The Constitutional Court has been reluctant to nullify treaties for fear of embarrassing the nation in its foreign relations. Thus, it found the Saarland treaty unconstitutional *per se* but did not declare it void.[56] The strictures of the Basic Law notwithstanding, as far as the Court is concerned, a treaty negotiated by the government is a *fait accompli*.

The Legislative Branch

Alexis de Tocqueville's observation that scarcely any political issue arises under the United States Constitution that is not resolved into a judicial question applies to the Bonn Republic.[57] Because the losing side in Parliament frequently challenges, through abstract judicial review, a measure it initially opposed on political grounds, the Constitutional Court effectively has become a participant in the legislative process.[58] The court thus acts as a safety valve, relieving political pressure by redefining partisan issues as legal ones. Most importantly, government and the opposition regard whatever decision the Court lays down as final and incontestable.[59] The Court in fact enhances the legitimacy of parliamentary democracy because the vast majority of its decisions uphold the constitutionality of challenged statutes. The reluctance of the justices to oppose the will of Parliament is reflected in the rather dubious practice of distinguishing between two kinds of unconstitutional statutes: those which are 'void' and those which are 'only unconstitutional'. The Court for instance held the law governing admissions to the universities repugnant to the Basic Law but declined to invalidate it on the ground that universities would be left with no legal basis in the selection of applicants.[60] Indeed, the cultural ministers in the various states have not responded to the Court's call for reform.[61]

The Constitutional Court is unusual among constitutional courts generally in the extent to which it directs Parliament to enact legislation. Legislatures typically offend against the constitution by positive action of some kind. The West German Constitutional Court, however, has held that in some situations the failure of the legislative department to act violated individuals' constitutional rights.[62] For example, in 1958 the Court ruled that Article 6(5) of the Basic Law required Parliament to enact legislation protecting illegitimate children and that the failure to act violated that provision. Nevertheless, Parliament did not pass such legislation until 1969. Again, the Court upheld the penalty of life imprisonment for murder but notified Parliament that it must pass a law establishing precisely when someone serving a life sentence would be eligible for parole.[63] The best known instance of a ruling that the state has a constitutional obligation to take positive action occurred in 1975 when the Constitutional Court declared unconstitutional and void the *Bundestag*'s legalisation of abortion on the grounds that the fetus is a person and that West Germany, especially during the Nazi period, had shown insufficient respect for the dignity of human life. The Court did not stop at invalidating the statute but went on to declare that the state had a duty under Article 2 of the Basic Law to protect unborn human life against attacks from the state and others, including the mother. It concluded that the Constitution requires Parliament to enact both penal and non-penal legislation to protect the unborn.[64] Polls showed that 50 per cent of West Germans opposed the decision, 32 per cent supported it, and 18 per cent had no opinion.[65] As an act of protest against the decision, the 'Revolutionary Women's Group' bombed the Constitutional Court building in Karlsruhe. Faced with this opposition to the Court's decision, Parliament responded in 1976 by enacting a new law authorising abortions to protect the pregnant woman's 'health'.[66] Showing weakness, the Court upheld the new, obviously evasive, statute by pointing out that its 1975 opinion recognised medical, eugenic, and ethical 'indications' that if present justify abortion. However, largely satisfied on the whole with the Court's functioning, Parliament has continued over the past thirty-five years to expand its jurisdiction into new areas such as electoral disputes and the participation of splinter parties.[67]

Political Parties

The Constitutional Court, in fact, has had a major impact on the place allotted to political parties in the German political system. Citing the rationale that the multiplicity of parties in parliament contributed to the feebleness of the Weimar Republic, in 1957 the Court upheld the right of Parliament to exclude splinter parties (parties that gather less than 5 per cent of the national vote) from the allocation of seats in proportional representation elections.[68] Invoking Article 21's requirement that political parties conform to democratic principles in their organisation and support 'the free democratic basic order', the court has banned both the neo-Nazi and Communist parties.[69] These essentially non-judicial proceedings highlight the political nature of the Constitutional Court. With the increase in internal stability, however, the Court has permitted both parties to re-emerge under different labels.

In two other major rulings, the Court severely limited public funding of political parties and disallowed tax deductions to corporations for their contributions to parties.[70] The Court's decisions thus reveal little evidence of party influence. This independence is somewhat surprising given the role of parties in the judicial selection process. The CDU/CSU, SPD, and FPD have agreed to a quota system 'in which each party allows the other to name whomever it pleases to its quota of posts, retaining, however, the right to veto the selection of candidates with extreme views or poor qualifications'.[71]

The States

With regard to appointments to the Federal Court of Justice, geographic origin is more important than party quotas. The *Laender* are allotted quotas in proportion to their population.[72] The Constitutional Court's attitude toward the German states has undergone a gradual change since 1951. Mindful of the abuse of centralised power during the Nazi period, the Constitutional Court initially viewed itself as a guardian of federalism. In its first case the court invalidated a Federation statute interfering with local elections and declared that 'as members of the Federation, *Laender* are states with their own sovereign power which, even if limited as to subject matter, is not derived from the Federation, but recognised by it'.[73] In seven of nine direct federal-state conflicts, the Constitutional Court ruled against the federal government.[74] The Court became uncomfortable with the role of arbiter of the constitution's division of powers between the Federation and the states and in 1957 called upon 'the Federation and the *Laender* to negotiate, on an equal basis, a suitable compromise when their interests are in tension'.[75] It even took a strongly pro-centralised power position the following year when it prohibited two states from holding popular referenda on the acquisition of atomic weaponry by the West German military.[76] In general, however, the

Court refuses to give clear-cut decisions in state-federal disputes.[77] Because the opposition party always controls some of the *Land* governments, the right of *Laender* to request abstract judicial review under Article 93(1) of the Basic Law leads the parties to attempt to disguise party opposition in the cloak of a concern for states' rights. Indeed, most state-federal cases are actually conflicts between the Social Democrats and the Christian Democrats.[78]

Interest Groups

German political culture holds parties in much higher esteem than interest groups.[79] According to Article 21 of the Basic Law, 'the political parties shall participate in the forming of the political will of the people'. In the context of West German political culture, this means that interest groups are expected to direct their efforts to influence government through a political party, which moderates the demands of disparate interests through coalition building and consensus forming.[80] The Party Contribution Tax Cases (1958) were based in part on the Constitutional Court's fear of interest group intrusion into the legislative process.

Opposing the culture's negative sanction of interest group pressure, especially when applied to the courts, is the positive sanction of corporatism, the doctrine that government authority should be exercised through bodies based on occupational or trade interests.[81] There is evidence, however, that direct interest group pressure on the courts is becoming more accepted. Parliament recently established a right to collective litigation, similar to the class action suit common in the United States, that enables associations, such as civic action groups opposed to the location of an industry in a certain area, to take action in administrative courts.[82] Such actions (*Verbandsklagen*) are now common in Germany as well as in France.[83] Groups opposed to nuclear power employed a judicial strategy and filed an eventually unsuccessful suit in a Higher Administrative Court to stop the licensing of nuclear power plants.[84]

Supra-National Organisations

The Federal Republic's membership in the European Community has led to conflicts between European and German courts. In 1974 the second senate of the German Constitutional Court validated a Community requirement that national firms desiring to carry on trade within the Common Market make a security deposit. In its opinion, however, the Court, following the lead of the Italian Constitutional Court, insisted that the German Basic Law was superior to any regulation of the European Economic Community.[85] This ruling led to strong protests from the European Court of Justice and judges from other EEC member states and the charge that the Federal Constitutional Court had violated Article 164 of the EEC Treaty.[86] The following year two German women challenged the Constitutional Court's abortion decision before the European Commission of Human Rights. Another national/supra-national conflict was avoided, however, when the Commission and the Committee of Ministers decided that there was no violation of the European Convention.[87]

CONTEMPORARY TRENDS AND DEMOCRACY

German civic culture does not place as high a value on unrestrained freedom of speech and press and on political dissidence as does the civic culture of the United States. The Federal Constitutional Court, in fact, has been more protective of minority political interests and political dissidence than legislative, executive, and other judicial bodies in Germany.[88]

The two great challenges facing the German judiciary today, however, are terrorism and the demand for extension of the welfare state. Since the 1960s violence against the state has become commonplace. A perceived inability of the legal system to deal effectively with political kidnapping, assassinations, and other forms of terrorist violence led to a major amendment of the Basic Law in 1968 (Articles 35, 53a, 80a, 91, and 115). The Constitution now makes elaborate provisions for governmental action in emergencies. Although Article 115g provides that during a state of emergency 'the constitutional status and the exercise of the constitutional functions of the Federal Constitutional Court and its judges must not be impaired', it is unclear how effective the courts would be in protecting civil rights and liberties during such periods.

Article 20(1) of the Basic Law proclaims the Federal Republic to be 'a democratic and social federal state'. The Parliament has fulfilled its obligations under this provision by erecting an elaborate scheme of public subsidies, services, and entitlements. In 1978, 17.7 million of the total 22.1 million households in the Federal Republic drew some form of financial support from public funds, especially in the categories of unemployment insurance, child benefits, pensions, housing allowances, and social welfare for the neediest.[89] The Federal Constitutional Court has encouraged and contributed to this development.[90] Since 1974, however, the number of German unemployed has grown to a worrying degree. The parliament, disappointed in its expectations of lasting economic growth, has been cutting back on social welfare benefits. These problems led in 1982 to the defeat of the SPD government and its replacement by a government led by the more conservative Christian Democrats. The Constitutional Court has hinted that it might interpret 'the objective duties' of the state under Article 20 to provide housing, jobs, and education, as 'actionable rights'.[91] It is unclear how the federal government would respond to such a ruling, but given the scarcity of resources and doubts about the role of courts in the allocation of public revenue, it is likely that there would result a major clash between constitutional organs, in which the Court would be forced to draw upon the considerable political capital it has accumulated over the past thirty-five years. It is feared that a parliamentary refusal to comply with a judicial order to effect the promises implicit in Article 20's 'welfare state clause' could even destroy the precedence of the Constitution over legislation.[92]

NOTES

1. See Investment Aid Case, 4 BVerfGE 7 (1954). 'BVerfGE' is the name given to the published opinions of the Federal Constitutional Court.
2. Alexander Hamilton, James Madison, and John Jay, *The Federalist Papers* (New York: The New American Library, 1961 [1788]), no. 49, p. 314.
3. Henry J. Abraham, *The Judicial Process*, 4th edn (New York: Oxford University Press, 1980), p. 316.
4. Fritz Nova, 'Political Innovation of the West German Federal Constitutional Court: The State of Discussion on Judicial Review', *The American Political Science Review*, LXX (1976), p. 125.
5. John D. Gorby, 'West German Abortion Decision: A Contrast to *Roe* v. *Wade*', *The John Marshall Journal of Practice and Procedure*, IX (1976), p. 563.
6. Walter F. Murphy and Joseph Tanenhaus, *Comparative Constitutional Law: Cases and Commentaries* (New York: St Martin's, 1977), p. 27.
7. Wolfgang Heyde, *The Administration of Justice in the Federal Republic of Germany* (Bonn, West Germany: The Federal Government of Germany, 1971), p. 52.
8. Ulrich Karpen, 'Application of the Basic Law', in Christian Starck (ed.),

Main Principles of the German Basic Law (Baden-Baden, West Germany: Nomos Verlagsgessellschaft, 1983), p. 80.

9. John H. Herz, *The Government of Germany* (New York: Harcourt, Brace & World, 1967), p. 111.
10. Joern Ipsen, 'Constitutional Review of Laws', in Christian Starck (ed.), *Main Principles of the German Basic Law* (Baden-Baden, West Germany: Nomos Verlagsgesellschaft, 1983), p. 112.
11. Otwin Massing, 'The Federal Constitutional Court as an Instrument of Social Control: Propaedeutic Sketches for a Critical Functional Form-analysis of Constitutional Jurisdiction', in Klaus von Beyme, *German Political Studies* (Beverly Hills, CA: Sage, 1974), p. 31.
12. Heyde, *Administration of Justice*, 147; Peter Gottwald, 'Simplified Civil Procedure in West Germany', *The American Journal of Comparative Law*, XXXI (1983), p. 689.
13. James G. Carr, 'Wiretapping in West Germany', *The American Journal of Comparative Law*, XXIX (1981), p. 612.
14. Mirjan Damaska, 'The Reality of Prosecutorial Discretion: Coments on a German Monograph', *The American Journal of Comparative Law*, XXIX (1981), p. 119.
15. Murphy and Tanenhaus, *Comparative Constitutional Law*, pp. 27–8.
16. Found in Civil law countries, notaries hold public appointments to issue and authenticate legal documents in non-contentious proceedings, such as real estate transactions, and to counsel the parties concerned.
17. Donald P. Kommers, *Judicial Politics in West Germany: A Study of the Federal Constitutional Court* (Beverly Hills, CA: SAGE, 1976), pp. 50–1.
18. Ipsen, 'Constitutional Review', p. 109.
19. Mauro Cappelletti, *Judicial Review in the Contemporary World* (Indiana-polis: Bobbs-Merrill, 1971), p. viii.
20. Siegfried Magiera, 'The Interpretation of the Basic Law', in Christian Starck (ed.), *Main Principles of the German Basic Law* (Baden-Baden, West Germany: Nomos Verlagsgesellschaft, 1983), p. 89.
21. Privacy of Communications Case, 30 BVerfGE 1, 18 (1970).
22. Gunnar Folke Schuppert, 'The Constituent Power', in Christian Starck (ed.), *Main Principles of the German Basic Law* (Baden-Baden, West Germany: Nomos Verlagsgesellschaft, 1983), p. 41.
23. Mauro Cappelletti and William Cohen, *Comparative Constitutional Law: Cases and Materials* (Indianapolis: Bobbs-Merrill, 1979), p. 363.
24. Cappelletti and Cohen, *Comparative Constitutional Law*, p. 207.
25. Ipsen, 'Constitutional Review', p. 132.
26. Glen N. Schram, 'The Recruitment of Judges for the West German Federal Courts', *The American Journal of Comparative Law*, XXI (1973), p. 699.
27. Kommers, *Judicial Politics*, p. 53.
28. Kommers, *Judicial Politics*, p. 53.
29. Schram, 'Recruitment of Judges', p. 694.
30. Cappelletti, *Judicial Review*, p. 66.
31. Kommers, *Judicial Politics*, p. 114.
32. Edmund Burke, *Reflections on the Revolution in France* (New York: Penguin Books, 1982 [1790]), p. 127.

33. Schram, 'Recruitment of Judges', p. 710.
34. Daniel C. Kramer, *Comparative Civil Rights and Liberties* (Washington, DC: University Press of America, 1982), p. 5.
35. Kommers, *Judicial Politics*, pp. 156-7.
36. Murphy and Tanenhaus, *Comparative Constitutional Law*, p. 586.
37. Mauro Cappelletti, '"Who Watches the Watchmen?" A Comparative Study on Judicial Responsibility', *The American Journal of Comparative Law*, XXXI (1983), p. 55.
38. Article 98 (*Grundgesetz*).
39. Heyde, *Administration of Justice*, p. 26.
40. Cappelletti, '"Who Watches the Watchmen?"' p. 34.
41. Cappelletti and Cohen, *Comparative Constitutional Law*, pp. 370-1.
42. Kommers, *Judicial Politics*, p. 101.
43. Ipsen, 'Constitutional Review', p. 122.
44. Kommers, *Judicial Politics*, p. 171-4.
45. Cappelletti, *Judicial Review*, p. 99.
46. Ipsen, 'Constitutional Review', p. 127.
47. Kommers, *Judicial Politics*, p. 163.
48. Kommers, *Judicial Politics*, p. 192.
49. 1 BVerfGE 14 (1951).
50. Basic East-West Treaty Case, 36 BVerfGE 1 (1973).
51. Magiera, 'Interpretation of the Basic Law', p. 93.
52. Schram, 'Recruitment of Judges', p. 711.
53. Cappelletti and Cohen, *Comparative Constitutional Law*, p. 340.
54. Schram, 'Recruitment of Judges', p. 692.
55. Ronald F. Bunn, *German Politics and the Spiegel Affair: A Case Study of the Bonn System* (Baton Rouge: Louisiana State University Press, 1968).
56. Nova, 'Political Innovation', p. 122.
57. Karpen, 'Application of the Basic Law', p. 80.
58. Hans G. Rupp, 'Judicial Review in the Federal Republic of Germany', *The American Journal of Comparative Law*, IX (1960), pp. 43-4.
59. Ipsen, 'Constitutional Review', p. 134.
60. The Numerus Clausus Case, 33 BVerfGE 303 (1972).
61. Kommers, *Judicial Politics* p. 277.
62. Rupp, 'Judicial Review', pp. 38-9.
63. 45 BVerfGE 187 (1979).
64. Abortion Reform Law Case, 39 BVerfGE 1 (1975).
65. Edmund C. Jann, *The Abortion Decision of February 25, 1975 of the Federal Constitutional Court, Federal Republic of Germany* (Washington, DC: Library of Congress Law Library, 1975) p. 131.
66. Murphy and Tanenhaus, *Comparative Constitutional Law*, p. 428.
67. Nova, 'Political Innovation', p. 124.
68. Bavarian Party Case, 6 BVerfGE 84 (1957).
69. Socialist Reich Party Case, 2 BVerfGE 1 (1952); Communist Party Case, 5 BVerfGE 85 (1956).
70. Party Finance Cases, 20 BVerfGE 56 (1966); Party Contribution Tax Cases, 8 BVerfGE 51 (1958).
71. Schram, 'Recruitment of Judges', p. 700.
72. Schram, 'Recruitment of Judges', p. 706.

73. Southwest Case, 1 BVerfGE 14 (1951).
74. Kommers, *Judicial Politics*, p. 234.
75. Concordat Case, BVerfGE 309 (1957).
76. Atomic Weapons Referenda Case, 8 BVerfGE 105 (1958).
77. Karpen, 'Application of the Basic Law', p. 71.
78. Murphy and Tanenhaus, *Comparative Constitutional Law*, p. 24.
79. Kommers, *Judicial Politics*, pp. 240–1.
80. Not finding a suitable welcome from the established parties, the environmentalists formed several new parties, the most successful of which is 'the Greens'. This party has recently won a number of seats in both the *Laender* and Federal parliaments.
81. Schram, 'Recruitment of Judges', p. 695.
82. *Facts About Germany* (Guetersloh, West Germany: Lexikothek Verlag, 1982), p. 106.
83. Cappelletti, *Judicial Review*, p. 8.
84. Ipsen, 'Constitutional Review', p. 117.
85. *Internationale Handelsgesellschaft* Case, 37 BVerfGE 271 (1974).
86. Murphy and Tanenhaus, *Comparative Constitutional Law*, p. 239.
87. Cappelletti and Cohen, *Comparative Constitutional Law*, pp. 610–11.
88. Kommers, *Judicial Politics*, p. 301.
89. *Facts About Germany*, p. 265.
90. Karpen, 'Application of the Basic Law', p. 58.
91. Eckart Klein, 'The Concept of the Basic Law', in Christian Starck (ed.), *Main Principles of the German Basic Law* (Baden-Baden, West Germany: Nomos Verlagsgesellschaft, 1983), pp. 27–8.
92. Christian Starck, 'Introduction', in Christian Starck (ed.), *Main Principles of the German Basic Law* (Baden-Baden, West Germany: Nomos Verlagsgesellschaft, 1983), p. 12.

6 The Courts in England

Jerold L. Waltman

Any analysis of the judicial institutions of the United Kingdom must begin by differentiating England and Wales from Scotland and Northern Ireland. The latter two have their own systems of courts, and while joined at the apex, they do not overlap with the English–Welsh system, which for convenience we will henceforth simply call English.[1]

Courts occupy an ambiguous position in English constitutional theory and tradition. On the one hand, there is a strong tradition of the rule of law. The law was used as a sharp philosophical tool to limit the power of the monarchy in the seventeenth century. Though the political fortunes of the judges and kings waxed and waned, the idea of the law as a check on the exercise of royal power was never completely surrendered by the judiciary. As recently as 1974 Lord Scarman wrote 'the rule of law is . . . a curb on power – irrespective of the person or institution who wields it'.[2]

Instead, the erasing of the rule of law as the first principle of English government derived from that other institutional instrument used by royal opponents – Parliament. With the Glorious Revolution of 1688, Parliament established itself as supreme. From that point forward the unbridled sovereignty of Parliament has been the touchstone of the constitution. The sovereignty of Parliament carries two meanings. First, Parliament may legislate on any subject whatsoever; and second, no other public body may move to nullify an Act of Parliament. In logic, this leaves no room at all for the rule of law.

By and large, the dilemma was solved by the courts simply deferring to Parliament. When cases arose in grey areas, Parliamentary statutes were interpreted expansively, as were administrative actions taken under their aegis.[3] This is not to say that even in their nadir beginning in the nineteenth century courts did not exercise influence over public policy. Parliament, in company with all legislatures, passed statutes full of ambiguous language, language the courts had to apply in specific cases.

However, in the last decade there has been a resurgence of interest among judges and others in exactly what the role of the courts and the rule of law is in basic constitutional questions. Since virtually every commentator agrees that the British constitutional system is undergoing fundamental change,[4] it is inevitable that the courts are caught up in it. After a survey of the judicial institutions, we shall return to these questions.

THE LEGAL CULTURE

England is the country which gave birth to the common law. After the Norman conquest (1066) the new monarch used the royal courts as instruments of political legitimation as well as for the administration of criminal justice.[5] Since the Norman overlords had little direct contact with the Saxons, offering the populace a forum for dispute settlement hastened the institutional penetration of Norman rule. The practice of having the royal judges 'ride circuit', holding court in various locales, led to the law becoming 'common' to all of England.

But the concept of common law now embraces much more than a set of rules to be followed throughout the kingdom. It is rather, according to Roscoe Pound, 'essentially a mode of judicial thinking'.[6] The stress on *judicial* thinking is important, for the common law puts the accent on the power of judges to be the developers and transmitters of the law. Yet judges are bound by the decision rule of *stare decisis*, 'stand by the decision'. When cases are brought to court, the judge is obligated to decide them in the same way as previous cases involving the same or similar circumstances. If the case presents novel questions, as cases will as there are social and economic changes, then the judge must fashion a modification of the older rules. What results, in theory, is an organic system of laws, always stable, but always evolving to meet new conditions. Incremental change is, therefore, built into the system.

The common law seems to be highly congruent with British political culture. Its roots are deep in a shadowy past; it has no 'break' in its development; it is stable yet always open to change; and it has a mechanism to keep it in pace with social change.

Two further points need to be made concerning the legal philosophy of the English. One is that the law's development has put the emphasis on wrongs rather than rights. Remedies, therefore, are of vital importance. Often, for instance, a plaintiff must first request a certain remedy and then demonstrate why his case's facts justify that remedy. In short, if there is no remedy, he may have no case. Secondly, in the nineteenth century the legal philosophy of John Austin came to dominate English jurisprudence, and its effects linger.[7] Austin held that the analysis of law can be distinguished from the study of legislation. In the former, the fundamental point was that the jurist took what was as a 'given' and extrapolated from there. This legal positivism detached law from transcendent values and thereby circumscribed the judicial role even further than a due emphasis on following precedent dictated. Judicial creativity was discouraged and a rigid adherence to the letter of rules became axiomatic.

STRUCTURE OF THE COURTS

The structure of the legal system is found in the Courts Act 1971, although it only marginally modified a system that has been in effect for over a hundred years.[8] A simplified diagram is presented in Figure 6.1.

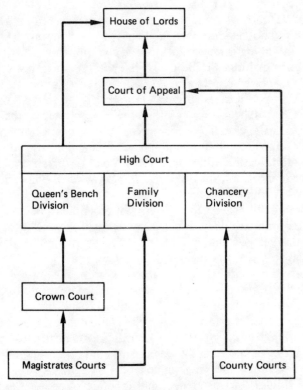

Figure 6.1   The courts of England and Wales

At the bottom of the hierarchy are the Magistrates' Courts, which originate all criminal cases and a few civil actions (mostly matrimonial cases). Actually, about 95 per cent of all criminal cases are tried here and most go no further.[9] The magistracy is the modern outgrowth of the Justice of the Peace system, established in the same century as Parliament, the thirteenth.[10] The kings appointed these unpaid officials to handle all matters concerning local government. Trying small cases and binding more serious criminals over to the royal courts were duties performed alongside administering roads, bridges and other public works and enforcing the poor law. In 1888 Parliament established locally elected councils to take over most of the magistrates' administrative functions, although a remnant remains. Magistrates, for example, still license pubs, allow for variances in liquor serving hours, and control local betting and gaming.

Their current judicial powers are still extensive. In addition to being a juvenile court and having authority to issue warrants and summonses, all criminal offences must originate before a magistrate. If the crime is serious, the defendant will be bound over to the Crown Court. (Even if it is not the accused may elect to go to the Crown Court.) In cases they try magistrates may impose sentences of up to six months in prison and fines of up to £1000.[11] At times, when a person is found guilty the magistrate may feel his maximums inadequate and send the party to the Crown Court for sentencing.

The most remarkable aspect of the magistracy is that except for a handful of people it is still composed of unpaid laypersons. Before 1966 they were not even given any training; now a few brief lectures are thought to suffice. When they take up their duties, magistrates sit in panels of three, but occasionally two are used.[12] In London and a few other large cities, paid magistrates who are lawyers do sit alone. A route of appeal from magistrates' decision is available to the Crown Court.

On the civil side, the lower courts of original jurisdiction are County Courts, of which there are about 340. These courts are staffed by regularly appointed judges who try cases alone. Controversies ranging up to £1000 may be adjudicated here, although the bulk involve sums falling under £200. The judges are entitled circuit judges after the old practice of circuit riding. If needed, High Court judges and Court of Appeals judges may also be pressed into service in County Courts. Under certain conditions Recorders (explained below) are also used.

Circuit judges also sit in the Crown Court, but here again Recorders and High Court judges participate on the bench. The case load consists, as noted, of appeals from Magistrates' Courts and trials of those accused of serious crimes. Ordinarily, a criminal trial in Crown Court occurs before a judge with the participation of a jury of twelve. Unlike some jurisdictions, particularly the United States, juries are impanelled quickly and drawn from the nearly universal Electoral Register.

The major civil cases in England are heard at the High Court, most of whose work is done at the stately Royal Courts of Justice in the Strand, London. Although pictured as one court, its seventy judges sit in three distinct divisions.[13] The Queen's Bench Division is the busiest of the three since it hears all types of common law civil actions, especially tort and breach of contract cases. Moreover, appeals from Crown Courts in certain instances go to the Queen's Bench. Original trials are conducted by a single judge, but appeals are heard by three or five judges. The head of the Division is the Lord Chief Justice, an ancient and prestigious office. The Chancery Division grew out of a court that handled matters of equity, that is issues where the common law did not provide an equitable remedy. Today, its work consists of trusts, estates, mortgage foreclosures and the like. The Lord Chancellor is the official head of this Division, but he delegates effective power to a Vice-Chancellor. The third division is the Family Division, dealing with such matters as marriage, divorce, child custody, and the distribution of property in a marriage. Its presiding officer is labelled President.

Appeals from the High Court (with a few exceptions), Crown Courts, and County Courts go to the Court of Appeal, in which there are separate Civil and Criminal Divisions, composed together of sixteen Lord Justices of Appeal. Three justices are the usual number hearing a case, but five or even seven are employed occasionally. The Master of the Rolls heads the Civil Division while the Lord Chief Justice has responsibility for the Criminal Division. If leave is given by the Court of Appeal or permission granted by the House of Lords, a case may go to the nation's highest tribunal.

Utilising the House of Lords as a final court of appeal creates confusion because it is also the upper house of Parliament. Actually, the judicial function is exercised by twelve specially appointed Law Lords, who have only a tenuous connection with the House's legislative business. By convention, for example, they do not speak or vote on any matter except one directly related to the law. Moreover, no other Lord may inject himself into the Judicial Committee's business.[14] For practical purposes, then, the Law Lords are a separate institution. In contrast to the pomp and ceremony of most English courts, replete with the wigs and robes depicted in countless movies, the Lords' proceedings appear quite informal. A panel of five is the norm, sitting in business suits in a rather (by British standards) unpretentious room.

The chief judicial officer in Britain is the Lord Chancellor.[15] Not only does he chair the Law Lords, but he also appoints judges and supervises the work of the entire judiciary. Furthermore, he is a political officer with a seat in the Cabinet.[16] Consequently, each incoming Government appoints its own Lord Chancellor; yet the prestige of the office and the deference to legal norms have come together to keep the office from falling into the hands of overt political partisans. While certainly the parties have appointed Lord Chancellors with slightly different outlooks, each has been an eminently qualified jurist.

THE PERSONNEL OF THE JUDICIARY

Magistrates[17]

There are about 25,000 active magistrates and another 9000 supplementals, a status one must assume at age seventy. About sixty are full time paid officials, called stipendiary magistrates, who serve in London and other metropolitan areas. Virtually any adult citizen is eligible to become a magistrate, but in spite of repeated attempts they do not really represent a cross section of society.

The Lord Chancellor appoints magistrates and may remove them for cause. His office is advised by a structure of secret committees who forward the actual nominations. Although this procedure keeps many details hidden, as secrecy is taken more seriously in Britain than elsewhere, the local committees are usually made up of five magistrates. The role of political parties is by most accounts the most significant factor. In some areas the parties forward names to the committees; in all they have a veto over the selectees. There is, moreover, a deliberate policy of mirroring the partisan makeup of each jurisdiction, a goal usually met.[18]

Conditions, of course, vary from one region to another but some regularities are discernible. There is an attempt to balance, for example, such demographic factors as sex and religion. Occupational diversity is also a goal, but one imperfectly realised. Middle-class people predominate; manual wage earners constitute only 15.9 per cent of all magistrates. Within the middle class certain occupations such as teachers are vastly over-represented since they can more easily arrange their schedules to accommodate the workload. Moreover, wives of upper middle-class professionals are common choices for magistrates. Magistrates under forty are rare because few can be convinced to sacrifice the time. The most important attribute shared by magistrates is their involvement with voluntary organisations of a charitable, civic, religious, youth, or athletic type. One factor surely is that these are the sorts of people willing to devote themselves to public services. In addition, though, these bodies commonly are the ones that send the most names to the local selection committees; and, further, according to Burney, it was this qualification that several ex-members of selection committees said they looked for above all others.

While, therefore, the magistrates are neither a professionally trained elite nor a cross-section of the community, there is little complaining about their work, apparently indicating that on the whole they do a creditable job. Elizabeth Burney concluded after her thorough study of six benches that 'Lay justice is administered by people who, in the main, are moderate, fair and conscientious: decent people picked for their ability to get on with other decent people'.[19]

Judges

England's professional judiciary is composed of people who have demonstrated their legal capabilities over years of private practice of law. A judgeship is viewed by the legal fraternity as a capstone to a successful career. Appointments are never given to those under forty, and it is not typical before around fifty.

Technically, the Law Lords, the Court of Appeals judges, the Lord Chief Justice, the Master of the Rolls, and the President of the Family Division are appointed by the Prime Minister and all other judges by the Lord Chancellor. However, in making his appointments, the Prime Minister relies on the Lord Chancellor to submit a name: 'The likelihood is that a modern Prime Minister would depart from the recommendations of his Lord Chancellor only in the most exceptional case'.[20]

Judges are normally appointed to a certain level and seldom promoted.[21] They must retire at seventy-two or seventy-five (circuit judges at the former; superior judges, those on the High Court and above, at the latter), and leaving the bench for a private career is frowned upon.[22] Removal power is vested in the Lord Chancellor for circuit judges and both houses of Parliament for superior judges, but may only be exercised on the grounds of misbehaviour or 'persistent neglect of duties'. In practice, all judges are virtually immune from removal, as not a single English judge has been relieved of his duties since 1701.[23] There was some intermittent sniping by Labour MPs in the early 1970s at judges serving on the special Industrial Relations Court, but nothing serious came of it.

The bench is drawn almost exclusively from the ranks of barristers, the courtroom branch of the legal profession.[24] Solicitors are the lawyers who actually consult with clients and draft most legal documents. If there is a need to go to court, the solicitor will select a barrister, for only they have a 'right of audience' in most courts.[25] Barristers are trained exclusively at one of the four Inns of Court – one of the few self-governing bodies established in the Middle Ages that have kept their powers almost intact.[26] After completing his education, the young barrister opens an office alone since he is forbidden to practice in partnership. Normally, it requires several years before enough income is earned to enable him to become self-sustaining. If he achieves a degree of eminence, in mid-career he will be made a Queen's Counsellor (QC).

There are about 5000 barristers in England and Wales. However, when a judgeship becomes open the Lord Chancellor has only a limited number of choices. Barristers now have the option of serving as recorders, which is in essence a part-time circuit judge. This experience gives them the opportunity to see if they like judging and gives the judges a chance to observe their work. When an opening occurs, the Lord Chancellor will make soundings among judges and other barristers and normally select someone with service as a recorder. If it is a superior judgeship that is open, the search is much more confined. 'Effectively', Professor Griffith notes, 'the group consists of experienced barristers between the ages of 45 and 60 and the number of genuine possibilities – the short list – may be as small as half a dozen.'[27] The reasons are that of those qualified, some will be known not to want an appointment, although some 'don't mind being asked',[28] and others will be screened out because of personality or some other eccentricity.

The one element that plays almost no role is partisan politics. Until early in this century party activity was an important path to the bench. However, the practice declined before the First World War and especially since the Second World War there has been no hint of party politics. 'Today, being an active member of a political party seems to be neither a qualification nor a disqualification for appointment.'[29]

The judiciary that these procedures produce is heavily weighted with an upper-class and upper midle-class bias. Of course, judiciaries always comprise an elite, but in England it is even more pronounced than elsewhere. One study of superior judges found, for example, that 70 per cent attended Oxford or Cambridge (the two most prestigious universities) and 56 per cent were products of one of the elite 'public' (private) schools.[30] Fully one-fifth had fathers who were knighted or titled. Furthermore, as Table 6.1 shows, there is a layering effect even within the upper judiciary. The traits that speak of upper-class England increase noticeably as one moves from the High Court to the Law Lords. The reasons are embedded in the class structure, especially as it was in the years when today's judicial recruits were beginning their careers. At the base, while the Inns of Court no longer practice overt class discrimination, the path is eased by public school and 'Oxbridge'. Furthermore, the length of study and the necessity for independent means in the early years of practice limit barristers almost entirely to sons and daughters of wealthy families. The procedure of non-promotion also tends to sort out candidates for judicial office. That is, to reach the upper levels of the profession that constitute the recruiting ground for superior judges, one needs not only good but excellent contacts among other segments of the elite.

Table 6.1   Some background characteristics of judges

Characteristic	Percentage appointed to:		
	Law Lords	Court of Appeal	High Court
Father in *Who's Who*	22	21	2
Oxford/Cambridge	77	75	64
Held administrative office	60	46	35
Made QC under 41	33	23	9

Note: The universe is the 317 judges appointed between 1876 and 1972.
Source: Adapted from C. Neal Tate, 'Paths to the Bench in Britain: A Quasi-Experimental Study of the Recruitment of a Judicial Elite', *Western Political Quarterly*, XXVIII (March, 1975) pp. 108–29.

It would be difficult to find a more technically competent judiciary anywhere. But it is a competency based in the private practice of law, the intricacies of criminal procedure, property transfers, agency arrangements, business contracts, and tort action. Neither law nor its practice regularly confronts the major questions of public policy. Since judges lack experience in politics and administration, they lack a political 'feel'.

Moreover, there is a legal conservatism built into the English judicial mind. In part, this reflects the general political culture. In part, though, it results from appointing as judges middle-aged men and women who have already had a successful career. It is not an age at which great innovation is expected, nor has the range of their private practices led them to a creative bent of mind. On the contrary, it produces a preference for stability, for the known.

To the extent that judges' political ideologies are known, they are mostly conservative and usually Conservative. Class background, income, peer group, and a career defending the status quo all conspire to yield this unsurprising result. Yet, it is not a monolith, as judges span the range of 'respectable' political ideas, 'from that part of the centre which is shared by right-wing Labour, Liberal and "progressive" Conservative opinion to that part of the right which is associated with traditional Toryism – but not beyond into the reaches of the far right'.[31] None the less, the rightward slant of the bulk of the judiciary is pronounced.

It was a combination of all these factors – background, habits of thought, career patterns, political opinions – which led Professor Griffith to conclude:

> It is as difficult to imagine the judiciary of the United Kingdom handing down judgments like those sometimes handed down by the Supreme Court of the United States, based on radical and reformist principles, as it would to imagine such judgments being handed down by the Supreme Court of the Soviet Union.[32]

The British judiciary prides itself on its independence, as judges take oaths to administer the law 'without fear or favour, affection or ill-will'. Their salaries are assured in that they are paid out of a non-Parliamentary approved account, the Consolidated Fund. This fact also insulates them from irate MPs during the annual debates over the budget.

But the independence has been part of a tacit agreement between judges and politicians. Politicians normally do not meddle with the judiciary even when they could. Ministers do not pressure the Lord Chancellor to award judgeships to the party faithful. Party leaders never remove judges and only alter any statute dealing with the courts after extensive consultations. For their part the judges restrict their scope of authority to private law matters, avoiding the 'political thicket'. Most judges have seemed aware that treading too closely to questions of public policy could propel them into an unwinnable battle with the majority at Westminster. English judges traded range of authority for degree of authority in a narrow field, independence for a reduced role on the public stage. Until recently it was a bargain that was taken as given by both sides.

This is not to say that judges were ever entirely divorced from the political process broadly defined. Service on important investigative bodies such as Royal Commissions and Departmental Committees has been continually requested by all Governments.[33] Since 1945 only academics have served on more of these than judges, while judges have chaired more than twice as many as any other group. Some investigations dealt with clearly legal matters, justices of the peace, legal procedures to deal with terrorists, and jury service, for example. Others have ranged far afield, covering topics as diverse as Scottish inshore fisheries, pay for dock workers, and taxation. Among the most important were those considering highly political and controversial matters – the constitution, riots, police conduct.

In addition, questions of civil liberties, though defined by statute, have often ended up in court. When dealing with the results of demonstrations or freedom of the press, fundamental political decisions are always being made, regardless of what they are called.[34]

Finally, the field of administrative law has always been most vexing. When Parliament enacts a law it normally empowers administrators to carry it out. When they do so they are therefore applying the law. What happens, though, if an administrator misreads the law? As a matter of fact, the courts have always held that they have the right to rule such actions *ultra vires*, that is outside the law and therefore void.[35] This is judicial review English style, granting Parliament the power to pass any law it chooses but retaining for the courts the right to determine if administrative actions fall within the law's scope.

The doctrine of 'natural justice', rooted in the common law, is often brought forth by the courts.[36] While it shares a historical and philosophical lineage with natural rights, it is only an interpretive yardstick. Its ambiguity makes it difficult to define, especially as regards substantive issues, as will be seen in the Government Communication Headquarters (GCHQ) case below. However, courts have repeatedly held that there are at least two procedural requirements deriving from natural justice: (1) no one should be denied a fair hearing and (2) no one should be a judge in his own case.

When dealing with petitions requesting that administrative actions be ruled *ultra vires* judges may, of course, adopt one of two strategies. One is to simply take refuge in a restrained role, almost closing the procedural door to the courts and upholding administrators when cases are heard. The other is more activist, making appeals to the courts easier and holding administrators closely to the judicial reading of the statute.

THE COURTS, DEMOCRACY AND POLITICAL CHANGE

A recent change of approach in administrative law is symptomatic of the more deep-seated changes occurring in the institutional fabric of British government. Moreover, these changes are wedded to profound changes in the political culture.

Until twenty years ago judges took an extremely restrained position *vis-à-vis* administrative agencies. For example, they held that only judicial actions, as opposed to administrative ones, were reviewable at all by the courts. Then, they held virtually every action to be administrative. In the name of deferring to Parliament courts exhibited a stony silence when faced with almost any type of administrative malfeasance.

Change was rooted in several sources. One was that the left began to share some of the doubts about bureaucratic pathologies expressed earlier by the right.[37] Too, growing evidence of administrative high-handedness in the treatment of individuals made the issue more and more salient. Then, law reform became an 'in' topic, especially under Lord Gardiner's Chancellorship (1964–70). Lastly, the role of certain individuals, especially Lord Denning, must be noted. From his post as Master of the Rolls, he used his speeches (opinions) to argue for a more activist role in overseeing administrative actions. His sharp dissents became a rallying point for advocates of reform.[38]

The first case to signal a change in orientation was *Ridge* v. *Baldwin* (1964).[39] A chief constable had been charged with a crime but acquitted, an episode thoroughly reported in the newspapers. He was none the less dismissed by his overseeing committee without a hearing. The trial judge concluded that the newspapers had contained enough information to enable the committee to make a fair decision, thus meeting the test of natural justice. After the case followed a labyrinthine route through the courts the House of Lords held that since he had not had a chance to defend himself the action dismissing the constable was *ultra vires*.

Since then several other cases have nurtured an embryonic move toward judicial activism. Some involved individuals' and companies' dealings with administrative agencies. A television owner, an airline entrepreneur, and a chemical company all had adverse administrative actions overturned by the courts.[40] The last case was especially noteworthy because the statute setting up the public body which made the decision explicitly said that its determinations 'shall not be called into question in any court of law'.

As the courts have become more sympathetic to losers in administrative determinations, naturally more litigants are coming to court, including important political groups. An interesting case arose in the spring of 1983 as the nation prepared for the June general election.[41] Parliament some years ago established a Boundary Commission to redraw constituencies for MPs every ten to fifteen years.[42] In the statute are a set of guidelines for the Commission to follow. When a report was issued soon before the 1983 election which was detrimental to the Labour Party, its leaders filed a suit contending that the Commission had not ranked the instructions in the proper order. Although the party lost its case, the Court of Appeal went to some lengths to reiterate that the courts can hear these types of cases whether the statute says so or not. Heavy proof would be needed to justify overturning the decision on the merits but it could be done the court said, refusing it seems to retreat from a reservoir of potential power.

Of equal if not greater import in the administrative area is what seems to be an increasing tendency for public officials to choose the courts as a forum to settle their disputes. For example, when a Minister ordered a local education authority to adopt the controversial comprehensive plan for organising its secondary schools, the authority went to court.[43] To the surprise of a number of observers the court voided the Minister's action because there was no explicit statutory authority to take the particular action even though several statutes gave her vast powers over local schools. Then in 1981, Thatcher Government allies took the Greater London Council (GLC) to court over its policy of running London Transport at a loss and making up the difference with property taxes.[44] All the relevant statute demanded was that GLC maintain an 'efficient and economic' transport system. The political overtones were important inasmuch as the GLC was controlled by a Labour majority which used it as a forum for outspoken opposition to a whole range of Thatcher policies.

Another case from 1981–82 demonstrates the British adoption of the age-old United States tactic of using the courts to delay decision making, the plaintiff hoping to either wear the adversary down or that events will intervene in the meantime.[45] The Housing Act 1980 contained an extremely controversial section mandating the sale of council houses to qualified tenants. Council housing had been a cornerstone of Labour policy for decades and selling them piecemeal to occupiers struck at the heart of its communitarian ideology. The Norwich City Council adopted stalling tactics, not processing applications swiftly and refusing to use Inland Revenue officials designated for the purpose. The Secretary of the Environment, who oversees housing, took over the project – after several skirmishes – together with central civil servants. The council filed a suit and obtained an injunction. A High Court judge dryly noted that the court's inquiry was solely into the Secretary's exercise of his powers, not the wisdom of his policy. By statute he had to have reasons for the action and the court could, the judge stressed, inquire into whether he asked the proper questions or considered all relevant factors. Here, it was said, he had obvious reasons and was therefore upheld. The council appealed to the Court of Appeal, losing again. In this instance, the adversary did not flag and nothing happened in the time Norwich bought, but if the courts will issue an injunction and then hear a case, it is a tactic that undoubtedly will be employed with increasing frequency.

The realm of civil liberties has also been in evolution. Since the rights of English citizens are protected only by Parliamentary statute they are not legally beyond the reach of a simple majority in the House of Commons. Traditionally, a faith in a genteel political style has sufficed to cause no alarm over this state of affairs. However, as political stress has surfaced, not only in Northern Ireland but in the 1981 Brixton and Toxteth riots and disturbing evidence of police corruption, the faith has ebbed. Serious political discussion of a bill of rights can now be found in any respectable corner.[46] Naturally, any type of written bill of rights would have to be actionable in the courts to have any practical impact, and only a few seem hesitant to take the step for that reason. At the same time, the courts have had a decided increase in civil liberties cases and have flirted with the use of natural justice as a substantive tool to limit governmental actions – even in highly sensitive areas of policy.

The Government Communications Headquarters (GCHQ) is a highly secret intelligence centre devoted to breaking foreign codes.[47] Workers at GCHQ had organised a union and on seven occasions between 1979 and 1981 had engaged in work stoppages. In late 1983 the Prime Minister as Head of the Civil Service and acting on the royal prerogative[48] banned the union, substituting a staff association under employer control. The High Court held that the ban violated natural justice in that it abridged the right of association, carefully pointing out that the court was not challenging the royal prerogative, only the exercise of it. On appeal, the Court of Appeal agreed that there are areas in which the exercise of the prerogative is subject to judicial scrutiny; however, national security was not one of them and the judge below was held not to have given enough weight to national security. While the Prime Minister's action was thereby made legal, what was left unsaid was that the court might reserve for itself in the future the right to define 'national security'.

Another field that has been the subject of intense debate, but no action, is decentralisation, especially the type known as 'devolution'.[49] A resurgence of Scottish and Welsh nationalism in the 1970s led to the near adoption of special elected assemblies in those two nations. A Parliamentary statute would have granted certain powers to these assemblies with, of course, a right to revoke any or all of them at any time. If they had been established though and began functioning it is likely political disputes of an intermediate character, important but not vital enough to force the majority at Westminster to suspend the enabling statute, would have ended up in court. Also, it would have been inevitable that cases involving conflicting commercial regulations would have sometimes posed knotty questions of constitutional interpretation, raising the stakes and political scrutiny of judicial decisions.[50] While the demise of this devolution proposal stilled these waters for a time, there is no evidence that sentiment for devolution has died out.

Lastly, the courts have been drawn into one of the most contro- versial areas of recent British politics – industrial relations. Most likely, judges would have preferred not to be involved in this policy area, but the actions of both governments and private bodies have forced their entry. In many ways the difficulties stem from historical reasons. During the early years of industrialisation, the courts were decidedly anti-union, leaving a residue of mistrust and bitterness among trade unionists that extends to the present. In 1971, however, the administration of Edward Heath decided to pursue its thinly veiled plan to curtail trade union power by setting up a National Industrial Relations Court, the membership of which was drawn only partly from the judiciary. The unions boycotted the court and vowed to defeat it, adding to the tumultuous labour unrest in the early 1970s. When it came to power in 1974, the Labour Party immediately repealed the act establishing this court. None the less, the labour battles have gone on and so has the involvement of judges in the disputes. In the recent strike by coal miners, the most bitter and violent in British history, the courts were often near centre stage. A group of dissident miners, for instance, went to court charging that the National Union of Mineworkers had violated its own rules in not holding a vote before the strike. When union pickets interfered with a firm making deliveries at the struck mines, the contractor obtained an injunction. Its being disobeyed resulted in the union being held in contempt and its assets placed in receivership. Then, after the strike criminal charges were pursued against a number of pickets accused of violent behaviour, all amid threats that the union would strike again over the issue. In sum, there was more use of the civil and criminal power of the courts in this strike than ever before and it would appear it is a tactic that will be employed again by those who have the legal upper hand. Given the structure of the British economy, with its declining base of old industries that are heavily unionised, it is hard not to foresee other stikes and other parades to the courts.

From what factors does the increasing politicisation of the courts derive? Are there uniting threads to the upsurge of activism in administrative law, the tendency of politicians to fight their battles at least partially in court, a resurgence of concern over basic civil liberties, continuing discussion of decentralisation, and attempts to settle industrial disputes outside collective bargaining?

One element has to be the failure of Parliament, the Cabinet, and the Civil Service to respond to the political demands of the last two decades. It seems that both elites and masses consider the Westminster–Whitehall nexus to be a cumbersome machine increasingly removed from the concerns of the citizenry. While in many ways the economic malaise, which most point to as failure number one, is beyond the control of any British government, at the same time the decline in public confidence has been noticeable.[51]

The ordinary political process in fact is well geared for two types of issues: the minutiae and the grand matters of state. As any visitor to Britain will attest the garbage is collected as well as anywhere, the trains usually run on time, the mail is delivered expertly, and the parks are well maintained. At the other extreme, during the Second World War there were marvels worked. However, in that great intermediate range of public issues the highly centralised political institutions are unwilling or unable to overcome the power of entrenched interests of one type or another. What results is political and policy stalemate in areas of importance to many people. The stalemate sends these people to the courtroom where at least something may be decided. In one sense, the increased use of courts is the institutional parallel of the renewed interest in geographical decentralisation.

A second and overlapping cause is the drift toward a post-industrial society. Although the move is slower and more painful than elsewhere, the transition from an economic system based on heavy industry to one based on information and high technology is occurring. The political system in consequence becomes enormously more complex as new services and regulatory activities multiply. If central government ever could control government, it surely cannot now. The sheer volume of contacts the ordinary citizen now has with the state was bound to increase the conflicts between governors and governed, but it brought with it no new participatory mechanism. In the same vein, the institutional complexity creates a need for a neutral site at which their inevitable disputes can be resolved.

Finally, merging with these two factors but also contributing its own independent effect is the growth of populism in British political culture.[52] One must be careful not to transport North American models across the Atlantic without qualifications, making Britons into potential supporters of a William Jennings Bryan. Nevertheless, surveys and other evidence point to a rather significant shift in public attitudes in a populist direction.

As a minimum, populism entails mistrust of government and demands for greater participation. Almost by definition populists distrust elites and those institutions manned by them. It might seem ironic, therefore, that populism in Britain could lead to a march to the courts. However, if one receives a more sympathetic hearing than from a distant bureaucrat and more action than from a powerless politician, the courts may not seem so elitist. Populist activists therefore could naturally be expected to press their cases there.

Political participation has been defined in Britain since before the First World War as the exercise of the franchise, most importantly for the House of Commons. This system has been praised as allowing citizens maximum input and assuring that those in power could be held accountable. Yet, if democracy means somehow making citizens' preferences effective in the outcomes of public policy a national election may not be the only, nor perhaps even the best, route to the achievement of that end.

In fact, under yesterday's two party model of the British constitution, with the voters choosing a party and MPs being rigidly controlled by the party leaders, the effect was to transfer power to party elites. This adversarialism and bifurcation of policy choices could have very undemocratic outcomes.[53] Indeed, there may be a link between the growing dissension on the Commons floor and the politicisation of the courts.[54] Both could be read as signs that the British constitution is in a period of transition.

It is this contention that underlies the whole panoply of contemporary British political life. The constitution has been in evolution for at least 650 years, and longer according to some authorities. Its principles have changed even as much as the outward institutional apparatus has remained. There is no reason to suppose that the evolution has ceased, that the next stage of Western political development will not comfortably fit into British robes, medieval buildings, and quaint titles. It is likely, I would think, that the judiciary will play a significant role in the new polity.

However, change will not come rapidly in Britain and the courts will probably never be central political actors. Judges now in office were schooled in an earlier era; moreover, the political arena is decidedly distasteful to many.[55] The courts will not rush headlong into politics even if that is where the populace wants them. Most importantly, the English judiciary is embedded in a political culture and institutional structure that prizes gradual change. Whatever their role in the emerging British political system, radical departures by the courts are most unlikely.

NOTES

1. The United Kingdom consists of England, Wales, Scotland, and Northern Ireland. Wales was politically and administratively absorbed by England in 1536. Scotland and England signed a treaty in 1707 merging the two nations, the terms of which left law, religion, and education separate in Scotland. When Britain divested herself of Ireland in 1922, it retained Protestant-majority Ulster. It was given a separate Parliament as well as judicial system, and while the former has been suspended, the latter remains.
2. Sir Leslie Scarman, *English Law: The New Dimension* (London: Stevens, 1974), p. 68.
3. The most extreme statement can be found in *Liversidge* v. *Anderson* (1942) AC 206. An excellent general discussion can be found in S. A. de

Smith and J. M. Evans, *Judicial Review of Administrative Action*, 4th edn (London: Stevens, 1980).

4. See, *inter alia*, Philip Norton, *The Constitution in Flux* (Oxford: Martin Robertson, 1982); Nevil Johnson, *In Search of the Constitution* (New York: Pergamon Press, 1977); and Anthony H. Birch, 'Britain's Impending Constitutional Dilemmas', *Parliamentary Affairs*, XXXVII (Winter, 1984), pp. 97–101.

5. See Lief Carter, *Reason in Law*, 2nd edn (Boston, Mass.: Little, Brown, 1984), pp. 152–7.

6. Roscoe Pound, *The Spirit of the Common Law* (Boston, Mass.: Beacon Press, 1966; originally published 1921), .p. 1.

7. See John Austin, *Lectures on Jurisprudence*, 3 vols (New York: Burt Franklin, 1970; originally published, 1861).

8. A complete discussion of court structure can be found in R. M. Jackson, *The Machinery of Justice in England*, 7th edn (Cambridge: Cambridge University Press, 1977).

9. Data on cases, convictions, etc., are available in *Civil Judicial Statistics* (London: HMSO, Cmnd., annually).

10. A good overview of the history of magistrates courts is Elizabeth Burney, *J.P.: Magistrate, Court and Community* (London: Hutchinson, 1979), ch. 3.

11. A bill now pending in Parliament would increase these to one year and £2000.

12. Magistrates are also advised by a clerk who is a lawyer. But this clerk may not retire with them and may only answer legal questions.

13. Reference is sometimes made to the Divisional Court. This is the label attached to a High Court judge sitting in original jurisdiction in any of the three divisions.

14. There is an exception to this. Former judges and some other legally trained peers have authorisation to sit, but they rarely do.

15. The Lord Chancellor's role is discussed in the following: Allan Paterson, *The Law Lords* (London: Macmillan, 1982); Robert Stevens, *Law and Politics: The House of Lords as a Judicial Body, 1800–1976* (Chapel Hill: University of North Carolina Press, 1978); Louis Blom-Cooper and Gavin Drewry, *Final Appeal: A Study of the House of Lords in its Judicial Capacity* (Oxford: Clarendon Press, 1972); and R. F. V. Heuston, *Lives of the Lord Chancellors, 1885–1940* (Oxford: Oxford University Press, 1964).

16. He also presides over the entire Lords' proceedings and has several other disparate duties, such as supervision of the Public Records Office.

17. Elizabeth Burney, *J.P.*, is the best available work on magistrates. Pat Carlen, *Magistrates Courts* (London: Martin Robertson, 1976) and Roger Hood, *Sentencing in Magistrates' Courts* (London: Stevens and Son, 1962) should also be consulted.

18. The party breakdown nationally hovers around Conservative 35 per cent, Labour 30 per cent, Liberals 10 per cent, and uncommitted 25 per cent.

19. Burney, *J.P.*, p. 212.

20. John A. G. Griffith, *The Politics of the Judiciary* (London: Fontana, 1977), p. 18.

21. Jackson, *Machinery*, p. 471.
22. One judge resigned in 1970 to take a position with a bank. His action provoked several severe rebukes. Jackson, *Machinery*, pp. 466–7.
23. Harry Street and Rodney Brazier, *de Smith's Constitutional and Administrative Law*, 4th edn (London: Penguin, 1981), p. 377. One Irish judge was removed in 1830 after he embezzled money and neglected his bench duties for several years. Philip Norton, *The British Polity* (New York: Longman, 1984), p. 314.
24. On the legal profession see Michael Zander, *Lawyers and the Public Interest: A Study in Restrictive Practices* (London: Weidenfeld and Nicolson, 1968) and Brian Abel-Smith and Robert Stevens, *Lawyers and Courts: A Sociological Study of the English Legal System, 1750–1965* (Cambridge: Harvard University Press, 1967).
25. Solicitors may appear in Magistrates Courts and in certain instances in County Courts.
26. Anthony Sampson, *The Changing Anatomy of Britain* (New York: Random House, 1982), pp. 152–3.
27. Griffith, *Judiciary*, p. 24.
28. Remark by an official of the Lord Chancellor's office at a lecture attended by the author.
29. Griffith, *Judiciary*, p. 24.
30. C. Neal Tate, 'Paths to the Bench in Britain: A Quasi-Experimental Study of the Recruitment of a Judicial Elite', *Western Political Quarterly*, XXVIII (March, 1975), pp. 108–29.
31. Griffith, *Judiciary*, p. 31.
32. Griffith, *Judiciary*, p. 52.
33. These are both important bodies and often the prelude to significant policy changes. For a compilation of such extra-judicial activity, see David Butler and Anne Sloman, *British Political Facts, 1900–79* (London: Macmillan, 1980), pp. 274–7.
34. See Street and Brazier, *Constitutional and Administrative Law*, p. 36.
35. I have developed this more fully elsewhere. 'Change and Rumours of Change: Courts and the Rule of Law', in Donley Studlar and Jerold Waltman (eds), *Dilemmas of Change in British Politics* (London: Macmillan, 1984) pp. 211–17.
36. On natural justice, consult Paul Jackson, *Natural Justice*, 2nd edn (London: Sweet and Maxwell, 1979).
37. The first polemic was Lord Hewart, *The New Despotism* (London: Ernest Benn, 1929).
38. See Peter Robson and Paul Watchman, *Justice, Lord Denning and the Constitution* (London: Gower, 1981).
39. AC 40.
40. *Congreve* v. *the Home Office* (1976) QB 629. *Laker Airways Ltd.* v. *Department of Trade* (1976) QB 483. *Anisminic Ltd.* v. *Foreign Compensation Commission* (1969) 2 AC 147.
41. A summary can be found in the *Times* (London), 26 January 1983, p. 9 (Law Report). The refusal of appeal to the Lords is discussed in the *Times*, 12 February 1983, p. 1. *R.* v. *Boundary Commission for England* (1983).
42. Incidentally, a High Court judge serves as deputy chairman, the effective

head of the Commission.
43. *Secretary of State for Education and Science* v. *Tameside Metropolitan Borough Council* (1977) AC 1014.
44. *R*. v. *Greater London Council and Another* (1981), *Times*, 18 December 1981, p. 4 (Law Report).
45. *R*. v. *Secretary of State for the Environment, Ex parte Norwich City Council* (1981), *Times*, 19 December 1981, p. 8 (Law Report).
46. See Colin Campbell (ed.), *Do We Need A Bill of Rights?* (London: Temple Smith, 1980) and Michael Zander, *A Bill of Rights?* 2nd edn (Chichester: Barry Rose, 1979)
47. In fact, its existence was not even acknowledged until May 1983.
48. *R*. v. *Secretary of State for Foreign and Commonwealth Office and Another* (1984), *Times*, 7 August 1984, p. 15.
49. See Vernon Bogdanor, *Devolution* (Oxford: Oxford University Press, 1979).
50. This happens frequently in all federal systems. See Richard Johnston, *The Impact of Judicial Review on Federal-State Relations in Canada, Australia, and the United States* (Baton Rouge: Louisiana State University Press, 1969).
51. See, for instance, the data reported in Jorgen Rasmussen, 'Is Parliament Revolting?' in Studlar and Waltman, *Dilemmas*, 20, and David Sanders and Eric Tanenbaum, 'Direct Action and Political Culture: The Changing Consciousness of the British Public', *European Journal of Political Research*, XI (March, 1983), pp. 45–62. For a contrary view see Norton, *British Polity*, ch. 15.
52. Samuel H. Beer, *Britain Against Itself* (New York: Norton, 1982).
53. See S. E. Finer (ed.), *Adversary Politics and Electoral Reform* (London: Wigram, 1975).
54. See Philip Norton, *Dissension in the House of Commons, 1974–79* (Oxford: Oxford University Press, 1980).
55. See, for example, Patrick Devlin, *Judge* (Oxford: Oxford University Press, 1979).

7 The Courts in France
Dallis Radamaker

LEGAL CULTURE

'No author, writing on the French government, would think of devoting a chapter to the *Cour de Cassation* and to the courts.' It was this sentence that Professor André Tunc began, writing in 1959, his chapter on the Judicial Power, detailing the role of the Supreme Court, in his widely read (in France) study *The United States: How it is Governed*.[1] In thus insisting on the difference between French and United States traditional notions about the limits and extent of judicial power, Tunc did no more than repeat the observation of his country-man, de Tocqueville, made one hundred and twenty years earlier, that,

> What a foreigner has the greatest difficulty in understanding in the United States, is the status of the judiciary. There is hardly any political controversy wherein he does not hear the authority of judges invoked; and he naturally concludes that in the United States, the judge is a powerful political figure. However, when he proceeds to examine the constitution of the courts, he does not find there, at first inspection, anything other than the usual judicial power. It appears to him therefore, that judges never become involved in political questions other than by the purest chance; but this same chance seems to occur every day.[2]

In fact, the phrase 'government by judiciary' is very frequently encountered in French political discussion, where it designates a phenomenon considered by the French as typically American; to be praised or blamed, as in the United States, more often in function of the writer's political stand on the latest jurisprudential twist than on principle.

French law belongs to what the French comparatist, René David, calls the 'Romano–Germanic family' of legal systems, traditionally referred to as 'Civil Law' systems, and its practitioners as 'Civilians' by English and United States scholars in recognition of its evolution from the *Corpus Juris Civilis*, the final and authoritative compilation of the private law of the Roman Empire written under the reign of the

Emperor Justinian. The rediscovery of this work in the twelfth century[3] and its diffusion through European universities had an enormous influence in the western European countries which had formerly constituted parts of that empire, where scholars regarded the compilation as representing law still in force, a conception which was politically possible since the feudal princes holding actual power at the time rarely saw fit to legislate in the matter of the private relations between their subjects.[4] This domain was therefore, governed by customary law, alongside which or together with which the newly discovered 'written reason'[5] of the Romans was able, with more or less difficulty, to make a place for itself.

It is this history which has given to French law its peculiarly academic flavour, i.e. throughout its development it has been more closely associated with the universities which gave it birth (or rebirth) than with the law courts; and its preoccupations have been characteristically more abstract and philosophical than administrative.

We shall see, however, that the generalisation, 'American courts are more political than French courts and French courts more academic than American courts' though an essential starting point for a comparative study, covers over complexities which reward study though they confuse comparison. Our study will begin with a description of the organisation of the French courts and the personnel who administer them.

THE STRUCTURE OF THE COURTS

At the epoch of the Revolution, the republicans deprived the law courts of jurisdiction over cases calling in question acts of the government. The aim was to free the revolutionaries of the encumbering weight of the courts, which were largely loyal to the *ancien regime*. We shall see further on that this eventually had the unexpected result of bringing acts of the administration under closer control (by the special administrative courts set up to take over the jurisdiction of which the ordinary courts were deprived) than if this division had not occurred. In any case, one effect has been the permanent separation of the French judiciary into two great divisions called *jurisdictions judiciares* and *jurisdictions administratives*. Figure 7.1 gives the hierarchies within each of these structures, of which the following is a sketch of the function and activity of each element.[6]

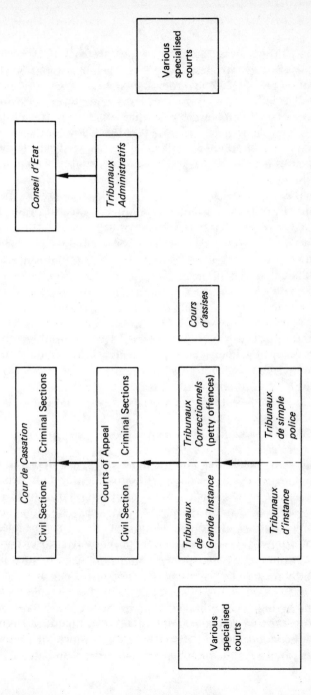

Figure 7.1 Structure of the French courts

Civil cases

There are 470 *tribunaux d'instance* which are competent to try cases
where the amount in controversy is less than approximately $1000. In
1981 there were 351,289 new complaints brought before these courts
and 328,022 judgments given. Trials are held before a single judge.

Tribunaux de grande instance of which there are 181, hear matters
involving larger amounts. Cases are decided by a panel of three judges
(ordinarily). In 1982 there were 385,502 new cases filed in these courts;
361,201 cases disposed of, and a backlog of 401,397 remaining at the
end of the year.

Cours d'appel of which there are thirty-seven, hear appeals from the
decisions of the trial courts just mentioned as well as from various
specialised courts. In 1982 there were 128,205 new cases filed; 102,615
were disposed of and a backlog of 187,661 remained.

The Cour de cassation, the French Supreme Court is headed by a
First President and six *Presidents de Chambre* corresponding to the six
chambers into which the court is divided (five to hear civil appeals and
one for criminal matters). These seven are assisted by seventy-seven
other judges and thirty-one 'counseillers réfèrendaires' who participate in the debates but may not vote. In 1981 the court received 11,738
requests for review in civil cases, of which it disposed of 11,564. The
criminal division received 16,948 requests for review, of which it
agreed to hear 5210 and finally disposed of 5505.

In addition to these there are a great many specialised jurisdictions
of which the most important are:

(1) 228 *Commercial Courts* which judge disputes between business
    enterprises (an appeal to the *Cour d'Appel* is allowed in cases
    involving more than approximately $1000). Cases are decided
    by judges elected for two to three years by an electoral college
    composed of business people. In 1981 these courts received
    221,102 new complaints and 195,000 demands for orders to pay
    debts and issued 500,000 decisions.

(2) 275 *Conseils de prud'hommes* which have exclusive competence
    in disputes between employers and employees relative to rights
    and duties under contracts of employment. Judges are elected
    for five year terms by an electoral college of employees and
    employers. Each tribunal contains an equal number of judges
    from the two camps, and the tribunals are specialised according
    to economic sector. Labour unions, more or less closely
    affiliated with the principal political parties compete furiously in

support of their candidates at elections. The number of cases has increased dramatically in recent years – 1979: 98,000; 1981: 190,000; 1982: 150,000.

Other specialised courts settle disputes involving leases of farmland, commercial rents, claims for social security benefits arising from disability to work, the supervision of minor children or incapacitated persons, family law matters and expropriation cases.

Conciliators

Outside the regular court network a system resembling private arbitrage has developed since 1970, employing in 1980 approximately 1000 *conciliateurs*, all unpaid volunteers. Most of them are retired (85.5 per cent), men (93 per cent), often jurists, civil servants or army officers. They handle cases involving disputes between neighbours, landlord/tenant problems, small debts, alimony and child visitation rights.

Criminal Cases

In 1981 the criminal courts received 13,820,000 new cases, of which 7,900,000 were heard by the police courts (*Tribunaux de Police*) which are competent in all cases where the risk of imprisonment is less than two months or the fine less than approximately $1000. The remaining cases were divided among the *Tribunaux Correctionnels*, which hear cases where the possible penalty is greater than two months imprisonment and the *Cours d'assises* which hear the most serious criminal offences (three judges and nine lay jurors). Above these are the *Cours d'Appel* and the *Cour de Cassation*. In addition, specialised courts handle cases involving minors and supervise the application of prison sentences and probation.

Administrative Law Cases

There are twenty-five administrative law courts having general jurisdiction over disputes between citizens and state agencies and employing, at the beginning of 1983, 375 administrative law judges.

These courts are subject to the appellate supervision of the *Conseil d'Etat*. The *Conseil d'Etat* was a creation of Napoleon, who gave it the task of aiding in the drafting of proposed laws and settling disputes

arising in the administration. Since that era it has been several times
reformed, even abolished and reconstituted, but has conserved and
refined both these functions.

In the period from 15 September 1977 to 15 September 1978 the
workload of these courts can be seen in Table 7.1.

Table 7.1   Administrative law cases, 1981

	Lower administrative courts	*Conseil d'Etat*
New cases brought	30200	4800
Cases decided	25500	4400
Backlog	58300	9500

The time from first bringing a complaint to obtaining a judgment
from the administrative tribunals averages about two years. About 15
per cent of all judgments are appealed. The *Conseil d'Etat* normally
takes about two years to decide an appeal.

The National 'Mediator'

Largely because of concerns over delays in the administrative court
system, a law of 1973 created the office of *'mediateur'*, which draws
inspiration from the Scandinavian institution of ombudsman popu-
larised throughout the West in the late 1960s because it seemed to offer
at least the beginning of a response to the increasing sense of
powerlessness of individuals in their dealings with monumental and
seemingly monolithic bureaucracies.[7]

Under the system, citizens not receiving satisfaction to which they
believe themselves entitled from the administration, may ask a
member of the National Assembly or of the Senate to refer the matter
to the office of the Mediator. Already, by interposing a parliamentarian between the citizen and the mediator the French system differs
from that prevailing in Scandinavia, where the ombudsman is directly
accessible. In fact, the Mediator receives several hundred requests for
action sent directly from citizens each year, and in each case he is
obliged to advise the complainant to address himself first to a
parliamentarian. The effect on someone, already sufficiently exasper-
ated by bureaucratic immobility of this stumbling block between
himself and the office responsible for straightening things out for him

can be imagined, and in practice the mediator often accepts and begins work on cases thus received without waiting to be officially contacted by a parliamentarian.[8]

The mediator has no power of compulsion over the administration. He may only make recommendations as to how a particular dispute should be resolved. Since 1976, however, he has had the power to bring a disciplinary action against an official believed to be guilty of misfeasance. He may also render his recommendation public if, after a certain delay, an adequate response has not been received from the administration concerned, which amounts to a sort of moral pressure.

The office of the Mediator is rather small, employing thirty-six people full-time (in 1979). The mediators themselves have tended to be persons without special legal training – generally parliamentarians of long standing.[9] Since 1979 the office is represented by a correspondent in each of the ninety-five geographic *departments* into which the country is divided for administrative purposes. The work of this office has increased each year since its formation, which is some evidence both of the need to which it responds and of the general satisfaction of the citizens with the service provided. In 1980 there were 6410 cases referred to the office, which represented an increase of 28.5 per cent over the workload of the previous year. The overwhelming majority of the cases referred involve money claims against the government related to social security payments, pensions, unemployment compensation and the like. The Mediator also proposes reforms of the law suggested by the cases brought before him. By the end of 1979 the office had proposed 158 such changes in the law; 68 of which had been carried out and 44 rejected leaving 46 pending before the legislature.[10]

In an interview with the press in February 1985 on the occasion of the submission of his annual report covering 1984, the Mediator complained of a certain 'stagnation' in efforts to make the bureaucracy more responsive.[11] 'Certain of the departments' he said, 'are dragging their feet, and more than just changing their methods they are going to have to change their general comportment and mentality.' He also declared himself in favour of a proposal recently put forward by the Prime Minister, that all *functionaires* who deal directly with the public be required to wear badges with their names on them in order to promote a sense of individual responsibility for the way in which citizens are treated. This suggestion, coming from the highest level of government, provoked a surprising amount of discussion both in the press and on television, which indicates how deeply the problem it addresses is felt by the public.

PERSONNEL

The administration of justice in France is assured by a corps of professional civil servants which is centralised and hierarchical. Rather than forming a constitutionally independent third branch of government, the entire corps is placed under the authority of the Minister of Justice, who nevertheless is bound to respect its liberty of decision. The contradiction inherent in a system which makes the executive power, always the most substantial and constant threat to the independence of the judiciary, the guarantor of its independence, has often been pointed out.[12]

The term 'magistrate' in France, is used to apply to the whole judicial corps, which lumps together persons whose job is to hear cases and render judgments (called 'sitting magistrates') and others whose job is to represent the government before the courts (standing magistrates). In 1975 the size of this corps was approximately 5000 persons.

Access to the profession is gained automatically upon graduation from the National School for the Magistracy, which welcomes every year some 250–275 students – the highest scorers in a competitive examination for which more than 1000 recent law graduates annually present themselves. The school provides a two-year programme, the first year being devoted to theoretical study of general problems of the administration of justice in its political, social and economic context, and the second year to a practical apprenticeship in a court or prosecutor's office. The social origins of members of the magistracy can be seen in Table 7.2.[13]

Geographically, the class admitted in 1973 came 22 per cent from the region of Paris and for the rest, was rather heavily inclined toward the

Table 7.2   Paternal background of judges

Occupation of father	1935 %	1973 %
Magistrate	17	13
Civil servant	27	26
Liberal profession	9.4	10.74
Middle management	12.9	13.7
Upper management	21.36	12.4
Farmer	7.69	1.66
Working class	2.55	12.77

south of France, with relatively few students from the north and east (the school is located in Bordeaux, on the Atlantic coast, far south of Paris). Young people leaving the school begin at the lower ranks of the judicial hierarchy and, if all goes well, advance regularly until they arrive at the *Cour de Cassation* or at the Presidency of a Court of Appeals just before retirement. Normally a new member of the corps makes an initial choice for either the sitting or standing magistracy which determines his career pattern thereafter, but it is not rare for individuals to cross over from one to the other, and a recent First President of the *Cour de Cassation* had never been a 'judge' properly speaking, before attaining that high office.

Women have been admitted as magistrates only since 1946, but have made rapid progress in the profession. In 1975 they represented 15 per cent of all magistrates in France. The last several classes received at the school of the Magistracy have been effectively half female, so that inevitably the entire corps will reflect this proportion within a few decades. In 1984 the first woman President of the *Cour de Cassation* acceded to that office, so that at the time of writing the highest judicial officer of France is a woman.

The process by which magistrates are promoted and assigned responsibility for particular cases has for many years been a subject of controversy. The present constitution provides for an organ called the *Conseil Superieur de la Magistrature* (CSM), one of the functions of which is to protect judges from external influences on the advancement of their careers. The protection it provides is, however, rather feeble.[14] The President of the Republic is its normal presiding officer, though he is replaced by the First President of the *Cour de Cassation* in cases where disciplinary action is considered against magistrates accused of malfeasance.[15] A majority of the members of the CSM are themselves magistrates, but the relative independence this provides is limited by the fact that they are appointed by the President. It has power to make recommendations to the government concerning appointments to be made to posts at the highest level of the judicial system and to approve or disapprove the annual promotion list drawn up by the Ministry of Justice. Its recommendations are not binding,[16] however, and so the executive power retains firm control over the career development of particular judges. This control is all the more firm in view of the size of the corps of professionals involved. In fact it is not really possible for the CSM to supervise realistically promotions throughout the system, and an investigation carried out by the judges' union (about which more below) reveals that members of this body have very little familiarity with the great majority of cases which they nominally review, so that approval of the promotion list proposed by the government is normally given with very little discussion.[17] Individuals may therefore very justly fear being passed over for promotion if their decisions are displeasing to the political power in place. Indeed, until very recently, judges were evaluated for purposes of consideration for promotion by government prosecutors who were their hierarchical superiors. At present these evaluations are done for judges exclusively by other judges, but it is still common for judges passed over for promotion to attribute the fact to their having given some decision or other which was not liked by the prosecutor.[18] The situation is difficult to evaluate neutrally, especially since the waters have been muddied by continuing controversy surrounding the 'judges' union', which is radically leftist in political colouration, and which brings frequent charges of executive meddling in the administration of justice, charges usually indignantly denied by the powers accused.

The *Syndicat de la Magistrature*

Founded in 1968, the magistrates' union, to which only a small minority of judges belong,[19] has attained a certain audience by means of its journal *Justice* and its public statements drawing in question the impartiality of the administration of justice and even of the possibility of real justice in a society dominated by the 'bourgeousie'.[20] At times members of the union have been threatened with disciplinary action, notably one who refused to sign orders for the payment of debts previously considered routine,[21] without a careful and time-consuming examination of the case which creditors found exasperating and which the judge clearly hoped would lead to an extra-judicial settlement of the affair granting concessions to the debtors. A judge who attempted to broaden a trial arising from an industrial accident to include criminal prosecution of the directors of the company on whose premises the accident had occurred provoked a similar reaction.[22] The union has been attacked frontally by a former President of the *Cour de Cassation* in the course of a speech where he said that what amounted to organised opposition to the existing social system was inconsistent with the duty to impartially apply the law thus criticised. The debate continues, but has calmed considerably in recent years with the dissipation of the radical impetus of 1968. In an article published in 1980,[23] one of the founders of the union concluded that it had served to attract public attention to the deficiencies of French justice, but that despite its work 'Justice is rendered in France in the name of the government and not in that of the French people'.[24]

SCOPE OF AUTHORITY

Judicial Review

Americans tend to strongly associate protection of individual liberties with the institution of judicial review of statutes for conformity with the constitution. So strong is this identification that teachers of comparative law and comparative political institutions often have difficulty convincing United States students that nations where the courts are not permitted to pass on this question seriously respect values similar to those announced in the Bill of Rights. But, as we shall see, in France similar libertarian values are enshrined in jurisprudence, particularly that of the *Conseil d'Etat*, which subjects the acts of individual office holders and bureaucrats to a much tighter and more effective control *vis-à-vis* the individual citizens with whom they deal than Americans have been accustomed to until very recently. That is, while Americans have always been alert to see that the letter of the law conformed to our contstitutional principles, they inherited from England a tradition of judicial non-interference in the administration of the law which has only recently begun to be broken down. The French, on the contrary, have been traditionally viscerally hostile to the notion of judicial review of legislation, an institution they perceive as anti-democratic, while to them it has always seemed self-evident that the individuals who administer the law should be subject to careful and strict controls to protect citizens against their possible corruption, incompetence or private rancor.

Nevertheless, the institution of judicial review, as practised in the United States has always been a lively subject of interest to the French, whose writings about it over time tend to mirror almost exactly those of United States writers, i.e. during the first decades of this century when United States courts were fighting a rear guard action against the new tide of legislation regulating the economic life of the nation, the 'Government of Judges' was the subject of innumerable French commentaries, generally denunciatory in the same terms as those employed by progressive critics of this jurisprudence in the United States, whereas ever since the 1960s when the United States courts formed the cutting edge of the civil rights movement, the institution has increased in prestige. There is at present no lack of French legal writers favourable to the introduction of United States style judicial review in France,[25] or at least, in some limited sense, favourable to the interesting and curious evolution in this direction of the jurisprudence of the *Conseil Constitutionnel*, which will now be discussed.

Conseil Constitutionnel or Constitutional Court

The *Conseil Constitutionnel* was an invention of De Gaulle, an expression of that powerful individual's determination to govern France unencumbered by the parliamentary factionalism which had resulted in the total paralysis of the government of the Fourth Republic at the moment of the Algerian crisis. The constitution of 1958, tailor-made, as it were, for De Gaulle, limited the sovereignty of Parliament, not *vis-à-vis* the citizens by subjecting legislation to review for conformity to libertarian norms, but rather in relation to the executive branch of government. In effect, the constitution sought to limit the legislative competence of the national assembly to certain designated matters – for all the rest the executive, that is, effectively the President, was given independent power to legislate by *decree*. In order to settle potential disputes between the legislature and the executive about the boundary between their respective spheres of competence, the *Conseil Constitutionnel* was created, to play the role of independent arbiter.

Composition of the Court

Until recently the Court has been made up exclusively of Gaullist politicians with no special claim to a particular competence in constitutional matters and only occasionally having had a legal education.[26]

There are nine members, who serve nine-year terms, staggered in such a way that three come up for renewal every three years. They are appointed, three by the President; three by the chief of the lower house of the National Assembly; and three by the head of the Senate. Thus, every three years each of these three appointing authorities names one judge. The President of the court is always named by the President of the Republic. In addition, former Presidents of the Republic are life members though up to now this has been a privilege little used by them.

The Court has certain consultative and administrative functions in addition to its judicial duties. Among other things it supervises national referenda, determines the eligibility of candidates for office and works closely with the President of the Republic in the rare and controversial case where the constitution grants him special powers to govern almost alone in a national emergency.[27] In such a case the Court, at the President's request, declares publicly whether in its opinion an emergency justifying the exercise of these exceptional powers exists, and privately advises him on the appropriateness of specific measures he may take to deal with the emergency once it officially exists. Indeed, aside from these special functions, with a few notable exceptions the *Conseil Constitutionnel* received no public notice during the first decades of its existence – because cases could only be referred to it by the President of the Republic or the Presidents of the National Assembly and Senate. Since the Gaullists firmly controlled all three of these positions without interruption throughout those years, they naturally felt little inclination to request an opinion on the constitutionality of decisions they had taken and with which they all essentially agreed.

In 1974, however, an important reform was made which resulted almost immediately in an increased activity of the Court – the law was changed to permit the jurisdiction of the Court to be invoked whenever sixty members of the National Assembly or Senate agreed. So for the first time it became possible for the political opposition to demand a formal, binding judicial opinion of the constitutionality of a law passed by the majority.[28] Note that even so the constitutionality of a law can only be questioned in this way immediately after its passage and that the *Conseil* must issue its opinion within sixty days of the time it is requested. Nevertheless, even before this reform the *Conseil* had seized an occasion offered to it to present itself to the public as more than a mere weapon in the hands of the executive to control the legislature.

The widespread strikes and public demonstrations which took place in the summer of 1968 all over Europe and the United States were followed in France by a period of relative repression. The French government was extremely sensitive to whatever looked like 'subversion' during this period. It was in this climate that a local police official refused to issue a needed certificate for a newly formed club of 'radicals' which called itself 'The Friends of the Cause of the People'. Without this certificate the association could not lawfully operate. Therefore the refusal was seen as a direct attack on the freedom of association. An administrative law judge ordered the certificate to be delivered, whereupon the Ministry of the Interior obtained from the

National Assembly, voting against the advice of the Senate, a new law granting local police officials power to refuse, temporarily, to grant such certificates, until they could obtain the opinion of a court on the lawful character of the association making the request. The President of the Senate, taking a stand on principle in a case which had already created controversy, invoked the jurisdiction of the *Conseil Constitutionnel*, which seized the occasion to issue a decision which has been universally qualified as audacious ever since, even by those who do not condemn it as an abuse of judicial power.[29] In effect, the *Conseil Constitutionnel* declared that the preamble to the constitution, by which the French people are said to solemnly reaffirm the great principles of the revolution of 1789, and particularly the 'Declaration of the Rights of Man and of the Citizen' form part of the fundamental law of the land. By this interpretation a kind of French 'Bill of Rights' came into existence overnight. It was widely noted that an exactly similar affirmation in the preamble to the 1946 constitution had never been thought to have any legal force, but, in spite of the judicial 'acrobatics' involved in reaching this decision, its substance, i.e. annulment of the law for inconsistancy with the freedom of association, found to be immanent in the 1789 declaration and in 'fundamental principles recognised by the laws of the Republic' was so widely approved that the *Conseil* escaped severe censure and emerged in the public mind as a champion of liberty. It is essential to note that the Declaration of the Rights of Man is a text which, though worded more vaguely than laws generally are, has the merit of having a fixed and verifiable content, something not true at all for the 'fundamental principles recognised by the laws of the Republic'. By founding its decision on such a broad notion, the *Conseil Constitutionnel* left itself a great deal of room for manoeuvre in future cases. Indeed, henceforth it appears to be bound by no particular text at all in its appreciation of the 'constitutionality' of laws, but need only show that such and such a principle which it is inclined to recognise as 'fundamental' has been consistently respected by republican legislation since the time of the revolution.

Since that decision it has become a permanent element of French political life that every important legislative battle will be carried before the Constitutional Council by the losing faction. Such has been the case in the domain of criminal law, with the long controversy over the law 'security and liberty' (about which more below); the law nationalising a large sector of the French economy following the socialist victory in 1981[30] (nationalisation itself permitted but higher compensation required to be paid to former owners); and the very recent controversy over the socialist government's plan to limit 'monopolies' in the press,[31] which has generally been perceived as directed against a prominent conservative figure who owns many newspapers hostile to the government (a decision of 10 October 1984 seems to have preserved the status quo by determining that the law could not have 'retroactive' application).

A remarkable decision of January 1984 extends the notion of review for conformity with the 'constitution' very far indeed in that it annuls legislation seeking to *repeal* an ordinary law of 1968 relative to the organisation of university faculties. The law is said to reflect a republican tradition respectful of academic freedom. Since the law proposed as a replacement did not contain what the court regarded as 'equivalent guarantees' in that regard, the existing law could not constitutionally be repealed!

The Constitutional Council thus appears to have evolved in a few years towards a position without parallel in French legal history, towards the exercise of a supervision of the legislature which is more muscled that that exercised by the United States Supreme Court with regard to the United States Congress. Certainly United States jurisprudence offers no example of an ordinary law being held to have 'constitutional value' protecting it from repeal.

The accelerating pace of the development of the jurisprudence can be seen (Table 7.3) from the change in the number of cases presented to the court in recent years and from the number of decisions annulling laws (either partially or completely).[32]

Table 7.3   Cases decided by *Conseil Constitutionnel*

	1974–81	1981–83
Total number of decisions rendered	47	27
Number of decisions annulling a law	10	12

In spite of this evolution since the victory of the socialists in the elections of 1981, it is to be noted that, though the court has been violently criticised by leading figures of the socialist party (which has, at various times, called for its abolition) the socialist president himself has been very circumspect since coming to power in his public utterances regarding it; its abolition is not at present part of the official programme of the party and indeed, appearances indicate that its basic 'legitimacy' is more and more firmly established in the public mind.

SUPERVISION OF THE ADMINISTRATION

It is difficult to know how, in a work whose object is to describe the relations between political and judicial power, to deal with an institution which practically abolishes the distinction between them. We have seen that traditional French doctrine is resolutely hostile to the very idea of the 'separation of powers' (despite the fact that the French political theorist, Montesquieu, was the inventor, if not of the idea at least of the phrase), holding to the notion that political power, as an extension of state sovereignty, is by its nature indivisible. This traditional conviction is perfectly reflected in the integration of the law courts into the executive and the *functionarisation* of their personnel. The *Conseil Constitutionnel* in its recent comportment forms the great exception to this general French tendency. But what of the administrative courts? Born of the centralising and unifying impulse that disinvested the law courts of jurisdiction in matters directly concerning the government, these tribunals form an integral part of the state bureaucracy. The administrative law judges do not benefit even from the limited guarantees of independence provided by the *Conseil Superieur de la Magistrature* for members of the judicial order.[33] The *Conseil d'Etat*, far from exercising a disinterested control over the French administration, *is* the French administration. The President of the Republic is its titutlar head; and its effective head (its vice-president) is the highest ranking civil servant in the employ of the French state. Its members, far from regarding the workings of the bureaucracy from the outside, move with great ease from one ministry to another, enjoying opportunities denied to conventional judicial officers to appreciate the day-to-day methods of operation of the various departments of the state.

Yet at the same time, these officials are judges. They hear cases brought against the administration involving the whole gamut of possible causes of dispute – from traffic accidents involving government vehicles to charges of misfeasance against state officers. The close rapports between these courts and the administration they oversee have both advantages and disadvantages. Whereas United States and British courts have traditionally been easily persuaded to defer to the judgment of administration officials acting within their fields of specialisation, the *Conseil d'Etat* has never been embarrassed by delicate separation of powers questions when considering whether an executive agency has behaved reasonably in acting or not acting in a certain way. It controls the discretion of the agents of the state in the manner of a hierarchical superior.

Several decades ago, an English comparatist[34] writing on the *Conseil d'Etat* declared that in the matter of control of agency discretion it was 'usually possible exactly to match the decisions in the opposite sense' of the English High Court and the *Conseil d'Etat*, giving as one example a case where the English court had held unreviewable a decision of the minister to withhold a taxi licence, where the statute gave discretion to grant it or not to the minister concerned. By contrast, the *Conseil d'Etat* had upheld the right to a full hearing in the case of a woman denied a licence to sell newspapers at a public kiosk, and reserved for itself the right to review the reasonableness of the decision taken in view of all the facts, as early as 1945.

Of course, both English and United States law in the matter of review of agency discretion have come a long way since the comparison above was made in 1954. A recent treatise on British administrative law quotes Lord Diplock to the effect that its development represents 'the greatest achievement of the English courts' in his judicial lifetime.[35] A similar mushrooming development of United States administrative law is evident to any practitioner. But the traditional separation of powers doctrine has represented and still represents a formidable obstacle to effective review in many cases. For example, in the United States, persons desiring to obtain review of an agency decision which they believe to be simply arbitrary, in the absence of some specific statute granting a right of review, must rely directly on the due process clause of the Fifth Amendment, which applies only when a 'liberty' or 'property' interest is implicated. If these concepts cannot be stretched far enough to cover their case, Americans can find themselves out of court – told that the agency action in question is simply not subject to judicial review. In France it is inconceivable that anyone could thus be deprived of a forum to air such a complaint.

It would be naive, of course, to pretend that the very close relations between the French administration and the administrative courts had nothing but advantages. In fact, in cases where a choice exists, French litigants have traditionally shown a marked preference for the judicial courts, not only because delays are generally longer in the administrative courts, but also because of a persuasive conviction among the French that the latter are excessively involved with and dependent upon the administration they are supposed to judge.[36] A recent manual of administrative law addressed to a lay audience gives as one of its principal *raisons d'être* a wish to persuade the French 'man in the street' that he has 'nothing to fear from the administrative law judge.[37] The problem finely illustrated here is the same for all systems which try to institutionalise effective control of the operations of complex and specialised agencies by the people they are designed to serve. An adjudicator placed entirely outside the system is likely to be perpetually defeated by the superior access to information of the persons whose acts he nominally oversees, while a judge wholly inside the system may lose his ability to see things from any point of view except that of the bureaucracy itself.

CRIME CONTROL AND RESPECT FOR CIVIL LIBERTIES

For many years now the question of how to deal with criminality has been constantly before the public, in France as much as anywhere else in the West. In France as in the United States the judicial system comes in for a great deal of criticism, both from the 'right' which complains that it is too tender with the guilty, and from the 'left', which accuses it of being nothing but an instrument of repression whereby the powerful control the powerless.

Before the election of 1981, the conservative predecessor of the present government had responded to mounting public concern over crime control (or the lack of it) by elaborating an extensive reform of the criminal law entitled euphemistically 'security and liberty' because it was supposed to reconcile these two equally noble political aims. Nearly everyone was willing to concede that the law was more preoccupied by the problem of insecurity than it was to establish new liberties. It was also plain that the law was conceived by the government in place as a key element in its re-election strategy. Unveiled shortly before the national elections with the plain intent of demonstrating in a highly visible way the government's determination to respond positively to the public apprehension with regard to violent crime,[38] it was very ostentatiously promoted by its sponsors. The Minister of Justice sent out letters defending and explaining the reform to members of the legal profession throughout France, gave numerous newspaper interviews to the same end, and undertook a veritable tour of the country making public appearances on behalf of the reform.[39] The socialists, taking up the gauntlet, denounced it as a public relations extravaganza having nothing to do with the real causes of crime but representing a serious danger to civil liberties, and promised its repeal if they won the elections.

The text at issue greatly increased the term of imprisonment for certain crimes, speeded up processing of criminal cases – notably by eliminating preliminary development of the *dossier* under the supervision of a *juge d'instruction*,[40] gave judges authority to ban from the courtroom certain defence attorneys whose 'attitude disturbed the serenity of the proceedings' and simplified the procedures for victims of crime to obtain compensation from those responsible.

The socialist opposition brought the text before the Constitutional Council, which voided several provisions, notably that concerning the exclusion of boisterous defence attorneys and another provision limiting the right of persons already convicted to benefit from a subsequent reduction of the penalty. Victorious in 1981, the socialist government, faithful to its electoral promises, promulgated a new law 'abrogating and revising' the security and liberty law. The new (present) law, restores the *status quo ante* as to most penalties, but provides in addition the possibility to condemn persons convicted of certain minor crimes to perform public service work in lieu of imprisonment, and sets out a new statute relating to police identity checks, which makes it clear for the first time that police officers cannot stop persons on the street and demand proof of their identity unless they have some objective reason to suppose the person in question is connected in some way with a crime.

Abolition of the Death Penalty

A related issue in the election of 1981 was abolition of the death penalty. In fact, there had been no executions in France since 1977. The death penalty was formally abolished five months after the socialist victory, an event of great symbolic importance to the party and particularly to the new Minister of Justice, who had been the defence attorney of one of the last men to be executed on the guillotine, and who had witnessed his client's death and written a compelling book about the experience.[41]

For some time now public opinion polls show the socialist government steadily losing popularity and 'insecurity' is one of the major themes exploited by the opposition as new national elections approach. Several of the opposition parties promise restoration of the death penalty; all promise a firmer hand against crime.

The present tone of the debate is summed up perfectly, not to say amusingly, by the incident of the quasi-riot which broke out during a nationally televised session of the National Assembly on 14 November 1984 when the Prime Minister, speaking of a recent series of murders of elderly women living alone in Paris, violently denounced the political exploitation of these crimes by the opposition and then invited the deputies thus attacked to join him in 'two minutes of silence' in memory of the victims of violence.[42]

Trial by Jury

Before leaving the domain of the criminal law it will be well to say something about the institution of trial by jury in France, since this is an institution which exists at the frontier where the judicial machinery contacts the body politic – i.e. it is a popular institution in that the jurors are non-professionals who are supposed to serve as representatives of the political community as a whole, yet it is a judicial institution in that the jurors are bound to act within a pre-established structure and in accordance with law as it is presented to them by the professionals with whom they are brought into contact at the trial.

In its original form the French jury was copied whole from the English institution as a result of the influence of that moderate class of revolutionaries who in 1789 saw the constitutional monarchy of England as a model of liberalism. As such, it quickly encountered the phenomenon of rejection so common to grafted organs, and found its power progressively curtailed by measures granting the professional judges the right to enter the jury room and participate in the debates, and restricting the right to be a juror to members of what were then called the 'propertied classes'. The latter half of the nineteenth century saw a gradual return of power to jurors, though they have never yet attained the stature foreseen for them by the founders of the institution.

The basic inability of the French to digest the notion of separation of powers has resulted in an evolution of the French jury towards a form where the lay jurors are incorporated in a single entity along with the professional judges. That is, whereas in the United States and Britain the jurors are judges of fact and the professional judges are limited to deciding questions of law (admittedly often a difficult, even nonsensical distinction) in France the lay and professional judges sit together to decide all issues relating to guilt or innocence. During the Nazi occupation the law permitted convictions to be obtained with only a minority of the votes of lay jurors, i.e. juries were composed of three magistrates and six jurors, so that a conviction (requiring only a simple majority) could be obtained if only two out of six lay jurors voted with the magistrates. This was changed promptly after the liberation but, interestingly, all that was done was to increase by one the number of lay jurors, which left it still possible to have a conviction with the votes of only three out of the seven, if those three were joined by all three magistrates. It was not until 1958 that at last reform made it theoretically impossible to have a criminal conviction unless a majority of the lay jurors consented. The present law provides for nine lay people to be impanelled along with three magistrates and retains the principle of decision by simple majority – a point in which French law now resembles that of several United States states where the former rule of unanimity for jury verdicts has been heavily eroded in recent decades.

Selection of jury persons in France is made initially by lot from the electoral lists but mayors reserve a power to eliminate names from the list[43] and it has been noted that juries tend to be older than middle-aged, predominantly male and under-representative of working-class people.

CONCLUSIONS

The French are a highly politicised people, individualistic and attached to the classic liberties, particularly that of self-expression. They have had to struggle for centuries now with institutions which appear over-centralised and hierarchical, setting up strains that have resulted in a great deal of governmental instability in alternating periods of repression and of near anarchy. The judicial institutions have conformed historically to this general pattern. Their rigidity and centralisation may be said to be expressed by the incorporation of the entire judiciary into the executive branch of government and its formal subjection to the authority of the Minister of Justice, a tendency which has sapped the independence even of the institution of the jury, subjected to the powerful influence of the professional magistrates. The individualism within this structure, by contrast, is well illustrated by the administrative courts whose broad powers of review and supervision of agency action allow a 'day in court' to anyone who claims to be a victim of arbitrary or unreasonable bureaucratic action or inaction.

The present institutions, even the radical departure represented by the recent jurisprudential adventure of the *Conseil Constitutionnel*, appear to have achieved the rare grace that their legitimacy is uncontested by any considerable part of the body politic. Whether this new stability and legitimacy can be turned to profit to deal effectively with the problems of monumentalism and mass complexity confronting all modern societies remains to be seen.

NOTES

1. André Tunc, *Les Etats Unis 'Comment ils sont gouvernes'* (Paris: Librairie Generale du Droit et de Jurisprudence, 1959), p. 56.
2. Alexis de Tocqueville, *Democracy in America* (New York: Vintage, 1945), Book I, ch. 6.
3. René David, *Grand Systems de Droit Contemporains* (Paris: Dalloz, 1964), p. 18.
4. David, *Grand Systems*, p. 47.
5. David, *Grand Systems*, p. 50.
6. Statistics on the workload of the various courts are taken from Dominque and Michele Fremy, *Quid* (Paris: Robert Laffont, 1985).
7. The mediator is compared to similar officers in numerous Western nations and in the Soviet Union in Claude-Albert Colliard, *Libertes Publiques*, 6th edn (Paris: Dalloz, 1982), pp. 148–51.
8. Colliard, *Libertes Publiques*, p. 153.
9. Colliard, *Libertes Publiques*, p. 149.
10. Colliard, *Libertes Publiques*, p. 153.
11. *Le Monde*, 20 February 1985.
12. See, for example, Charles Raymond, *La Justice en France*, 6th edn (Paris: Presses Universitaires de France, 1978), p. 17, where he notes that the independence of the 'judicial power' has never been assured under any French constitution except by a 'verbalisme honorifique'. On the same page he quotes from a speech by the Minister of Justice in 1949 speaking to an assembly of magistrates: 'La Justice n'est pas un pouvoir, car il n'y a qu'un pouvoir; elle est fonction du pouvoir, une function séparée des autres, mais partie integrante de l'Etat.' (The judiciary is not a power in itself, because power is by nature one; it is a function of power, a function separate from the others, but still forming an integral part of the state.)
    See also Pierre Lyon-Caen, 'L'Experience du Syndicat de la Magistrature: Temoignage', *Pouvoirs* (1981), no. 16, p. 59. 'How can the chief of the executive protect the judiciary against the encroachments which first tends, by the very nature of things, to make on the second?'
13. These figures are cited by Maurice Aydalot in *Magistrat* (Paris: Robert Laffònt, 1976), p. 113–14. M. Aydalot is a retired First President of the *Cour de Cassation* and the book cited is a sort of biography of his professional life.

14. 'Since 1883, the solution proposed to the problem of the advancement and discipline of magistrates has suffered an evolution with represents a veritable regression in what concerns the CSM.' Colliard, *Libertes Publiques*, p. 173.
15. Colliard, *Libertes Publiques*, p. 174.
16. Colliard, *Libertes Publiques*, p. 174.
17. From a study cited in Lyon-Cayen, 'L'Experience du Syndicat'.
18. Aydalot, *Magistrat*, pp. 245–8.
19. Since the foundation of the Syndicat de la Magistrature in 1968, other judges' unions have been formed, most of them less politically radical than the original. The number of unionised magistrates in France is given at 25 per cent of the corps by Raymond, *Justice*, 38. Administrative law judges also have a union, the Syndicat de la Juridiction Administrative which claims more than a third of such judges as members, including twenty or so members of the Conseil d'Etat. Pierre Fanachi, *La Justice Administrative* (Paris: Presses Universitaires de France, 1980). 43.
20. Lyon-Caen, 'L'Experience du Syndicat', p. 64.
21. Lyon-Caen, 'L'Experience du Syndicat', p. 64.
22. Lyon-Caen, 'L'Experience du Syndicat', p. 64.
23. See Lyon-Caen, 'L'Experience du Syndicat', *passim*. A recently submitted doctoral thesis on the judges' union by M. Lagneau-Deville has been published under the title 'Influence du pouvoir executif sur les prerogatives du juge en France sous la Ve Republique', in M. van de Kerchove, P. Gerrard, and F. Ost (eds.), *Fonction de Juger et Pouvoir Judiciare: Trans-Formations et Deplacements* (Brussels: Facultes Universitaires Saint-Louis, 1983).
24. Lyon-Caen, 'L'Experience du Syndicat', p. 68.
25. See for example, Colliard, *Libertes Publiques*, section 153 and the article of Professor Robert in *Le Monde*, 23 December 1984, written in defence of the decision of the Constitutional Council limiting the effect of the law on ownership of the press.
26. In particular, it appears that the president of the Conseil has always been a non-jurist. Louis Favoreu, 'Le Droit Constitutionnel Jurisprudentiel en 1981–82', *Revue de Droit Public et de la Science Politique en France et a l'Etranger* (1981), no. 3.
27. Colliard, *Libertes Publiques*, p. 134.
28. Colliard, *Libertes Publiques*, p. 44.
29. Colliard, *Libertes Publiques*, sections 530–31.
30. Decision of 1 February 1982.
31. *Le Monde*, 24 December 1984.
32. Favoureu, *Droit Constitutionnel*.
33. Fanachi, *La Justice Administrative*, p. 43 describes the formal guarantees of the independence of the judges as 'somewhat precarious' since they are embodied only in administrative regulations which may easily be altered by any government.
34. C. J. Hamson, *Executive Discretion and Judicial Control: An Aspect of the French Conseil d'Etat* (London: Stevens and Sons, 1954), p. 6.
35. H. R. W. Wade, *Administrative Law*, 5th edn (Oxford: Clarendon Press, 1982), preface.

36. Robert Viargues, 'Plaidayes pour les Tribunaux Administratives', *Revue de Droit Public et de la Science Politique en France et a l'Etranger* (1979), no. 4.

37. Fanachi, *La Justice Administrative*, p. 126.

38. The relationship between the intensity of the public awareness of and fear of criminality, and its objective level in the society is often difficult to discern. A year-long study of the situation in France just prior to the announcement of the 'security and liberty' law concluded that the observed level of public anxiety was unjustified since, in fact, major crime had not recently increased significantly, though there had been a sharp increase in petty delinquence. Philip Loic, 'La Decision Securite et Liberte des 19 et 20 Janvier 1981', *Revue de Droit Public et de la Science Politique en France et a l'Etranger* (1981), no. 3. Interpol statistics from the period show a crime rate in France 41 per cent lower than in the United States during the mid-1970s. Another source, however, speaks of an 85 per cent increase in violent crime in France between 1972 and 1979. George W. and Jean H. Pugh, 'Measures for Malaise: Recent French 'Law and Order' Legislation', *Louisiana Law Review* (1982), vol. 42, p. 1303.

39. Loic, *La Decision*, p. 655.

40. These 'investigating magistrates' have charge of the police investigations of crimes. They are the very lowest ranking judicial officers and thus tend to be very young. It was believed by many that the provision of the 'security and liberty' law permitting their part of the usual criminal proceeding to be leap-frogged by the prosecutor was a way of avoiding a magistrate relatively more likely than his older, higher ranking colleagues, to be a member of the judges' union or at least to have 'leftist' sympathies. Recently, these magistrates have been the subject of attacks from the left calling for more controls over their authority, notably over their authority to decide that an accused person shall be held in prison pending trial. See *Le Monde*, 19 February 1985.

41. Robert Badinter, *L'execution* (Paris: Grasset, 1973).

42. *Le Monde*, 16 November 1984.

43. This power is exercised since 1980 by a Commission made up principally of judges, but to which, nevertheless, the mayors are invited to make 'recommendations'. M. Aninat, M. F. Deschamps, and F. Devron, *Les Jurés* (Paris: Presses Universitaires de France, 1980), p. 104.

8 The Courts in Italy

Giuseppe Di Federico and
Carlo Guarnieri

Before starting our analysis we wish to point out that our work will refer mainly to the ordinary courts. Indeed, it is in this field that we have concentrated our efforts of research, so that our statements can be supported by a great amount of empirical knowledge. In fact, as regards the administrative courts and the Constitutional Court, our work will rest more on formal data. However, this qualification by no means reduces, we believe, the general value of our study. Indeed, we have to take into account that the ordinary magistrates are by far the largest corps: in 1983 they were 6682 against 842 administrative court judges.[1] Thus, at least from a quantitative point of view the decisions made by the ordinary judiciary possess obviously a greater impact. But also from a qualitative point of view the political impact of our ordinary courts is not to be underrated: ordinary magistrates completely control the criminal process, since, as we shall see, in Italy the prosecution of criminal cases is monopolised by the ordinary judiciary, besides which the highest ordinary court, the Court of Cassation, plays a major role in the overall judicial system. It is then clear that, even though we must not neglect the role of other institutions, like the Constitutional Court, our ordinary judiciary shows, especially in the day-to-day functioning of the judicial system, a higher degree of political significance.

THE LEGAL CULTURE

The role of the judge in Italy traditionally has been defined as limited to the mere interpretation of existing law, a role definition which excluded any sort of 'creativity' on the part of the judge for the solution of the concrete cases brought before him, apart from that arising from his technical ability to find in the existing law the correct legal answer. Actually, one can say that such a role definition has been the fundamental myth or value in reference to which the very legitimation of the judicial function has been based.

To be sure, the myth of the 'neutral' and purely technical role of the judge is certainly not peculiar to the Italian legal system, connected as it is to the doctrine of the separation of powers, which, in its orthodox configuration, especially influential in continental Europe, rejects judicial lawmaking. In Italy, however, a series of very complex factors, active within and without the judiciary, have converged to maintain – without dissent until the early 1960s – this role definition intact and to induce a conformistic adherence within the judiciary both to the image of the judge as *la bouche de la loi* totally aloof from the socio-political context, as well as to a work and life style formally characterised by social and political agnosticism.

As to the 'external' factors, we shall limit ourselves to recall that in Italy legal scholars, through their writings (the so-called 'doctrine') as well as through their activities *qua* technical consultants of legislators – or legislators themselves – and leaders of the practicing bar, have always had a dominating influence on the nature of the legal process, of which the judge is but one of the actors. It has been rightly pointed out that 'doctrine is not law in Italy in the way that legislation and judicial decision are law, but it pervades the legal process, strongly influencing legislators and judges, who tend to conform to the doctrinal model not only of what law is but of what their functions are.'[2] In spite of the diversified opinion and approaches that one can discern in the writings of the legal scholars, some orientations have been traditionally common to the overwhelming majority of them: in the first place, that legal science and legal reasoning should not be concerned with the concrete phenomena which might have legal consequences, nor with the social or political consequences of legal reasoning or judicial decisions, the raw material of legal science and legal reasoning being the positive legislation of the state which is to be studied in order to explain its inherent principles and relationships. (As has been remarked, 'one of the most venomous polemic devices in use among legal scientists is that of accusing a certain thesis of sociologism'.)[3]

Three basic assumptions, or dogmas, of legal reasoning bearing directly on the expected behaviour of the judge have been constantly reasserted. First, the completeness of the codified legislation, with the consequence that 'if the code is complete, then the answer to any problem can be found in the code. Where the answer fails to leap to the eye, close examination of the code will find it'.[4]

Secondly, the absolute need for the certainty of the law; which among other things implies that only the general and abstract norms made by the legislators can be certain. The entire body of Italian legal 'doctrine' is pervaded by an attitude or complex of superiority *vis-à-vis* the common law legal systems and the principle of *stare decisis*.

Thirdly, that the relation between social needs and legislative regulations, as well as any consideration regarding the 'justness' of existing norms, pertains to the exclusive responsibility of politicians or legislators and in no way should concern the scholar *qua* legal scientist or the judge in the adjudicative process.

The institutional teaching of law – a monopoly of legal scholars – being permeated by such ideas, has traditionally served (this is of course only one aspect of the influence of legal 'doctrine' on the legal process) as a powerful instrument of socialisation of university law students in general and of would be judges in particular with respect to their future role as neutral, agnostic interpreters of a supposedly systematic, inherently gapless, legislation.

The scene we have just painted began to change in the first half of the 1960s. The traditional assumptions of the Italian judicial folklore came under strong attack from a new generation of scholars, finding a good reception among an increasing number of judges. The incompleteness of the codified legislation has been revealed by pointing out the illusory nature of that assumption in a situation in which the judge is confronting an enormous amount of legal norms, often the by-product of hurried parliamentary compromises. It is then completely unreal to depict the judicial role as a purely technical activity. In fact, judges enjoy wide discretionary powers due to the intrinsic nature of legislation. Thus, judges make policy and, at the end, should make it according to the values embodied in the Constitution, as the followers of this new 'school of thought' maintained.

Even the principle of the certainty of the law began to be criticised under the charge of being a means of enforcing 'conservative' or even 'reactionary' values. Since a large part of Italian legislation has had – and, to some extent, still has – a fascist imprint even after the demise of Fascism, this charge was not unfounded. In this context, the duty of the judge is to interpret existing norms according to the democratic spirit of the republican Constitution of 1948, even by contradicting other interpretations, or, in the case the norms in question are in no way compatible with this spirit, to suspend the judgment and submit those norms to the consideration of the Constitutional Court.

To be sure, the majority of the Italian magistrates still identify themselves more or less with the traditional image of the judge as the neutral and agnostic interpreter of the existing body of positive legislation and see the present situation as a transient one, due to 'pathological' reasons, like the malfunctioning of the parliamentary and governmental systems. Moreover, a number of them still tend to react strongly against the prospect of seeing the judicial function polluted by 'politics'. On the other hand, a significant minority among the magistrates undoubtedly have deviated clearly and visibly from the traditional pattern of life and work once common to the judiciary as a whole. They variously and often vocally advocate and practice a greater involvement in the social and political context as a condition for the proper exercise of the judicial function. In many ways they maintain that the evaluation of the social and political relevance of the phenomena considered by the judge, as well as an attentive scrutiny of the social and political consequences of judicial decisions, must be an integral part of the adjudicative process.

These developments, together with other changes we will deal with later, have led to a growing self-assertion by the Italian judiciary, even *vis-à-vis* the academic doctrine, once, as we have seen, the most influential element in the legal system. Differently from the past, the magistrates have increasingly participated in the political and ideological debate, championing different interpretations of the judicial role and emancipating themselves, at least in part, from the cultural domination of traditional academic circles.

Of course, what we have said so far does not mean that the traditional conception of judicial role has been definitely superseded. In fact, not only a large part of Italian magistrates still adhere to it, but even among the 'innovators' it is easy to find vestiges of the traditional definition of the judicial role. An example is the scarce attention given to the problem of the political legitimation of policy making judges. Few observers, inside and outside the judiciary, have confronted the problem of justifying the presence of independent and policy making judges in a democracy. Very often, the problem is 'solved', even through sophisticated argumentations, by claiming that 'at the end' judges do not 'really' make policy, because they limit themselves to passively interpreting the law, or because they act only according to the prescriptions of the Constitution.[5]

THE STRUCTURE OF THE COURTS

The organisational units of the ordinary judiciary – or, as we call them, 'judicial offices' to include both the courts and the public prosecutor offices – are ordered according to the principle of the hierarchy, i.e. starting at the bottom of the organisational pyramid: 901 courts of limited jurisdiction (*preture*); 159 courts of general jurisdiction and adjunct public attorney offices (*tribunali* and *procure della Repubblica*); 24 courts of appeal and adjunct general attorney offices; the Supreme Court of Cassation and adjunct general attorney office.

At the bottom of the pyramidal organisation of the ordinary courts are the *conciliatori*, competent only in some civil cases that involve claims up to one million lire. Appeals from the *conciliatore* are taken directly to the Court of Cassation. Parties may agree to have a *conciliatori*, who serve for prestige and in fulfilment of a civic duty, are not paid and are not necessarily law school graduates.

The *preture* are courts of limited jurisdiction and serve as courts of first instance, with some exceptions, in cases involving claims up to five million lire and in certain other cases specifically provided by law. They are competent in criminal matters for which the penalty is three years imprisonment or less and for some specific crimes. The *pretori*, like the *conciliatori*, adjudicate alone. Except for a certain number of honorary appointees, they, like the judges of the higher courts, are career members of the judiciary.

The tribunals are courts of general jurisdiction and are competent in all civil cases that are not within the competence of the *pretori* or *conciliatori*, and are exclusively competent in some areas specified by law. They hear civil, but not criminal, appeals on questions of fact and law from the *pretori*. Three judges sit on the panel that adjudicates a case. Large tribunals – as well as large *preture* – are often divided in sections that in practice specialise in particular subject matters. Criminal cases that are not within the competence of the *pretori* are allocated to the tribunals and the courts of assizes. The courts of assizes are organised as special sections of the tribunals (but not all tribunals

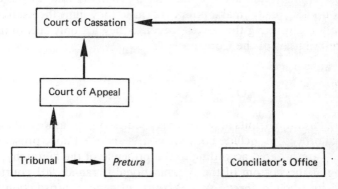

Figure 8.1   Italian civil courts

have them); nevertheless, there is a division of competence between the tribunals and the courts of assizes. Many of the most serious criminal cases are heard by the courts of assizes. Here, two ordinary judges and six laymen, acting as 'popular' judges, sit on the bench for a case. All eight vote on all questions of facts and law involved in the case. A tie vote acquits.

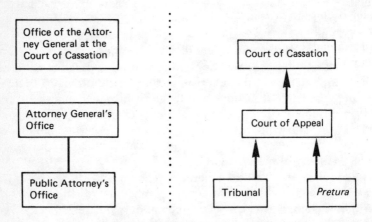

Figure 8.2   Italian criminal courts

The court of appeal, sitting in panels of three, hears appeals on questions of fact and law from the courts of first instance (*preture* and tribunals). They have also a limited competence as courts of first instance (enactment of decisions of foreign judges). Courts of appeal of assizes, in panels of two ordinary judges and six laymen, hear appeals on questions of law and fact from the courts of assizes and are organised as special sections of the courts of appeal.

Criminal cases involving defendants under eighteen years of age are decided by the juvenile courts that, together with specialised public prosecutor offices, are attached to each court of appeal and that have also jurisdiction in some civil and administrative matters concerning minors. Each case is adjudicated by a panel consisting of two ordinary judges and two social workers – one male, one female. Appeals are taken to the court of appeal. A section consisting of three judges and two social workers adjudicates the appeal.

The highest of the ordinary courts is the Court of Cassation, often called the Supreme Court, which may either uphold or quash decisions of the lower courts. Since there is a constitutional right to obtain the direct and immediate review of all provisional orders relating to personal liberties and the review of all judgments of the ordinary courts, the Court must adjudicate every case brought to its attention. The result is a heavy workload: the incoming annual load is over 8000 civil cases and over 40,000 criminal cases. The Court is staffed by more than three hundred judges and it is divided into a number of sections, criminal (six) and civil (four). A panel of five judges sits on each case. In an attempt to favour the uniformity of interpretation of the laws – which is, as we shall see, its main institutional function – united civil and criminal sections, composed of judges (nine) of each of the regular sections, hear and determine cases that involve particularly controversial issues.[6]

Judicial review of administrative acts in Italy is organised according to the European continental tradition, on a fundamentally different basis from that in the United States. Special courts have been instituted to review administrative acts, and the ordinary courts may also entertain certain actions against the state or a public body. The jurisdiction of the administrative courts and the ordinary courts are related to the dichotomy between the Italian concepts of 'rights' and 'legitimate interests'. A right is defined as an interest directly guaranteed by law to an individual, whereas a legitimate interest is defined as 'an individual interest closely connected with a public interest and protected by law through the legal protection of the latter'.[7]

In an action against the state in the ordinary courts, only declaratory judgments and judgments for a sum of money may be obtained. The administrative court may vacate the administrative act attacked and sometimes may substitute its own. In determining whether a legitimate interest has been violated, the administrative courts determine whether the administrative organ issuing the act (1) was incompetent, (2) exceeded its powers, or (3) violated the law. In some cases the courts may determine whether or not the administrative act involved a wise exercise of discretion.

The *Consiglio di Stato* (Council of State) is the highest administrative court. Cases are first heard by the *Tribunali Amministrativi Regionali* (TAR) (Regional Administrative Tribunals), one for each region. Their decisions may be appealed to the *Consiglio di Stato*. The judges of the TAR are recruited through competitive examinations among law graduates. The Councillors of State are appointed by the government (a quarter of the vacancies), recruited through a competitive examination reserved to people having some professional experience (a quarter), or promoted from the ranks of the judges of the TAR (half).

Independent of the Council of State is the *Corte dei conti* (Court of Accounts) which is primarily concerned with the handling of public money. The Court of Accounts in Rome decides the appeals from its regional branches. The recruitment of the judges of these courts is similar to that of the other administrative courts.

Judicial review of the constitutionality of laws is relatively new to. Italy.[8] Before 1948, the Constitution of Italy was the Statuto, granted in 1848 by Carlo Alberto, King of Sardinia. Since the Statuto was a 'flexible' constitution, no court could refuse to enforce, or strike down, a law as opposed to the Constitution. Such an attempt would have been regarded as a violation of the principle of separation of powers. This was the traditional Italian view until Fascism showed the dangers of legislative powers unchecked by some form of binding legal control.

The present Constitution, which can be amended only by a special procedure, is said to be 'rigid'. In creating a separate Constitutional Court, the framers of the Constitution not only were motivated by the fact that in Italy *stare decisis* is not a recognised principle and that, at least theoretically, the highest ordinary court (Court of Cassation) might find a law unconstitutional, and lower courts or the highest court itself in subsequent decisions might refuse to follow the decision, but also took into account that the ordinary judiciary had neither the prestige nor the importance of the United States judiciary, and moreover that the incumbent Italian judges had been selected, trained, and promoted under Fascism and were unlikely to interpret the Constitution in the progressive spirit intended by the framers. Consequently, a Constitutional Court with power to abrogate law *erga omnes* was felt to be necessary.

The Constitutional Court consists of fifteen judges who at present serve for a nine-year term. Five are chosen by the President of the Republic, five by Parliament, and five by the judges of the highest ordinary and administrative courts. Judges of these courts, law professors, and lawyers with twenty years of legal practice are eligible.

The Constitutional Court may not rule on the constitutionality of a law except with reference to concrete cases. Each party in a case pending in front of an ordinary or administrative court may raise an objection claiming that the law or laws applicable to the case is or are unconstitutional. The judge himself may raise the same objection *ex officio*. If the issue is considered relevant and not patently groundless, it would be considered by the Constitutional Court. This preliminary finding was designed in order to avoid the raising of constitutional issues for merely dilatory reasons.

In addition, the Constitutional Court adjudicates conflicts of competence between: regions; regions and the state; and the fundamental organs of the state, such as the President of the Republic, Parliament, the Council of Ministers, the Court of Cassation, and the Constitutional Court itself.

When compared to the activities of Parliament and of the Council of Ministers, the Constitutional Court, although having principally the negative function of abrogating laws, is seen by the majority of commentators as being the body that has done most to enact the provisions of the 1948 Constitution. In fact, the Court has decided that it has a power to abrogate laws enacted prior to the promulgation of the 1948 Constitution. Since political inertia has prevented Parliament from repealing and replacing much of the legislation of the Fascist era, it has been the Court's function, especially in the years immediately following its inception, to declare many of these laws unconstitutional.

PERSONNEL

As pointed out before, our analysis deals mainly with the ordinary judiciary. However, we can safely maintain that the general characteristics of the personnel of administrative courts are not substantially different from those of ordinary magistrates, even though this contention is not grounded on the same amount of empirical data but mostly on the formal set-up of the administrative judiciary.

In the last fifteen years the number of law graduates per year has consistently been between 5000 and 7000, and the percentage of law graduates to the total of university graduates per year has often exceeded 20 per cent. The tendency to pursue a degree in law is far greater in the economically less developed areas of the country. As a general indication of this phenomenon, suffice it to note that around fifty per cent of the degrees in law are granted in the universities of the southern party of Italy and of the islands (Sicily and Sardinia), as compared with only a little over 20 per cent in the universities of the north.[9]

The majority of the graduates in law – mainly those of southern origin – seek employment in state and local agencies of government, security of employment being, generally speaking, one of their primary motivations. As a rule they do not enter only one competition for public employment, but several. This is not due necessarily to a lack of preference for this or that particular kind of public office. It is rather, on their part, a question of expedience: by entering more than one competition immediately after graduation, they increase their chances of limiting the period of unemployment, and, in the case of success in more than one, may even be in a position to choose. On the other hand, to prepare for more than one competition does not require much additional work. In particular, one can note that most entrance examinations for the admittance to the 'directive careers' (*carrière direttive*) of most Ministries and to the judiciary have an identical basic pattern and test the knowledge of the candidates on subject-matters that are to a great extent the same. Most of them, that is, test the general scholastic preparation of the candidates in several branches of the law, and several of these branches are common to most competitions, such as civil law, administrative law, and constitutional law.[10]

In view of what we have said so far, it comes as no surprise to find that the territorial and social origins of the magistrates (judges and public prosecutors) are by and large the same as those of the members of the 'directive careers' of most Ministries: they are prevalently from the southern and central parts of Italy (over 80 per cent) where traditionally job opportunities other than public offices have been quite meagre for university graduates.[11] They come almost exclusively from middle-class families; and in about 55 per cent of the cases the father of the recruitee is, or was, himself in various capacities on the public payroll (see Table 8.1).

If, on the one hand, the social and territorial origins, as well as the general motivations, of those who enter the judiciary do not differ substantially from those of recruitees of the various branches of public administration at the administrative class level, on the other hand, neither do the structural and functional characteristics of the Italian judicial organisation differ substantially from those of the several branches of public administration of national scope. Actually, as has been remarked, 'the Italian judiciary emerges from an analysis of its structure and functioning as an organisation modelled after the great public bureaucracies that, first shaped during the period of absolutist monarchy, assumed a definite structural pattern codified by legislation in the nineteenth century.'[12]

No wonder that even a summary account of the main traditional characteristics of the Italian judiciary – such as can be outlined briefly here – is bound to appear as a step by step exemplification of Weber's

Table 8.1   Comparison between the occupation of magistrates' fathers and of the overall male working population (1951 census) (percentages)

Father	Magistrates	Overall population	Ratio
Magistrate	13.9	.04	347.5
Lawyer	10.6	.2	53.0
Law clerk	2.5	.05	50.0
Army officer	5.1	.2	25.5
Teacher	9.1	.7	13.0
NCO	3.6	.5	7.2
High civil servant	17.6	2.5	7.0
Businessman/professional	10.0	2.3	4.3
Executive (private sector)	9.4	4.7	2.0
Civil servant	3.9	3.4	1.1
Small businessman	9.9	2.5	.4
Employee (private sector)	4.4	60.5	.1
TOTAL	100.0	100.0	

Number of valid cases 1782, missing 889

Note: Table refers to magistrates recruited in the period 1967–82 (N = 2671). Source: A. Marino, 'Le origini familiari dei magistrati', in Il reclutamento della magistratura Italiana (Bologna: Centro Studi e Ricerche sull'Ordinamento Giudiziario, University of Bologna, 1984).

ideal type of bureaucracy. In undertaking such a presentation, we shall first try to illustrate the most general traits of the organisational set-up of the Italian judiciary holding until the beginning of the 1960s, and the conception of the role of the judge ensuing therefrom. We shall then proceed to describe, again in a rather synthetic and approximate fashion, the partial organisational changes that have been introduced since then, in order to provide evidence of some of the unresolved ambiguities that at present entangle the configuration of the role of the judge in Italy.

(1) As we have already pointed out, applicants for the judiciary are selected on the basis of their general institutional knowledge of several branches of the law as tested by written and oral exams, and guaranteed by a university degree in law. Professional training and experience is to be acquired within the judicial organisation, starting from the bottom of the career ladder. The recruiting system is such that candidates for the judiciary enter the competition soon after graduation and in any case before thirty years of age. In fact, if one considers only those who win

the competition, it may be seen that by far the great majority – over 70 per cent – enter the competition between the ages of twenty-three and twenty-six, and start exercising full judicial functions between the ages of twenty-six and twenty-nine after a cursory, one-year on the job, practical training period. Practical professional training acquired in other branches of the legal profession is in no way considered valuable for the judicial career. One may even suggest that actually it is penalised, if only implicitly, *vis-à-vis* other types of work experience, by pointing out that while on the one hand no viable way is provided for the insertion of practicing lawyers in the judiciary, on the other, the main exception to the general age limit of thirty for application is provided in favour of holders of other public offices (including the military and secondary school teachers) for whom no age limit is set (see Table 8.2).

Table 8.2   Social origins of deputies and magistrates (percentages)

Classes	Deputies	Magistrates
Upper class	6	36
Upper-middle class	34	30
Lower-middle class	38	28
Working class	17	5
Peasants	6	1
Total	100	100
Number of cases	1753	1782

Source: M. Cotta, *Classe politica e Parlamento in Italia* (Bologna: il Mulino, 1979) Table 5a, p. 139. Data refer to members of the Chamber of Deputies from 1946 to 1976. (Aggregated data in conformity with Cotta's categories.)

(2) The organisational units of the judiciary, as has been seen, are ordered according to the principle of hierarchy.
(3) Organisational roles are ordered according to a hierarchy of ranks to which different degrees of material and psychological gratification are attached. There is a very specific relation between hierarchy of ranks and hierarchy of judicial offices in the sense that holders of higher ranks are assigned to judicial units which are higher on the jurisdictional ladder, or are assigned to lower jurisdictional offices and functions only in a supervisory capacity.

(4) Advancement up the career ladder *traditionally* has been competitive and promotions *traditionally* have been granted, following a strict legal procedure, according to formal criteria combining seniority and merit, merit being assessed with a great latitude of discretionary judgment by hierarchical superiors on the basis of an analysis of the written judicial works of the candidates (opinions, pleadings, etc.). However, as we shall see later on, this is the facet of judicial organisation where rather drastic changes have been introduced in recent years.

(5) The approach to work performance and role assignment is of a 'generalistic' type: participants are supposed to be capable of playing indifferently all organisational roles that are formally associated with their rank. They are supposed, in other words, to adjust without strain to an extreme variety of diverse tasks – be they to adjudicate a criminal case, a bankruptcy case, a family case, a fiscal case, or to perform as public prosecutors – and at the same time compete for higher status and positions. Consequently, differentiation among members of the judiciary formally takes place only along the vertical dimension of the organisation.

(6) General and abstract norms regulate in an impersonal fashion both the relations among participants in the organisation and their official performance as judges and prosecutors.

As to the mechanisms which, active within the judiciary, have traditionally served the functions on the one hand of upholding the image of the judge as the mere interpreter of the existing legislation and the guarantor of the certainty of the law, and on the other of inducing conformity to a style of work and life detached and aloof from the social and political context, we shall limit the analysis to recall the most apparent mechanisms in a most simplified and synthetic way. Some of these are connected to various aspects of the administration of the judicial personnel, while others are embodied in the structural characteristics of the judicial process itself.

The *main* formal tools traditionally used to ensure an image of the judge detached from and uninfluenced by the social and political context in which he operates are to be found in the discretionary criteria provided by law (1) for the admission of candidates applying for entrance to the judiciary; (2) for the evaluations of the judges considered for promotion to the various ranks of the judicial career; and (3) for the evaluation of the behaviour of the judges in the disciplinary proceedings. Thus, to be admitted to the entrance

examinations the candidates must meet, among others, the requirements of an 'irreprehensible morality of conduct' and of belonging 'to a
family of undiscussed moral esteem'. Similarly, the judge's 'conduct',
his 'public esteem', his 'prestige', have always been among the several
elements to be considered in the context of the processes of evaluation
for promotion to the next rank. And finally, the basic norm regulating
the initiative of disciplinary action and stating the deviances in relation
to which disciplinary sanctions are to be taken, vaguely affirms that a
member of the judiciary 'who fails to fulfill his duties, or behaves in the
office or elsewhere in a way which makes him unworthy of the trust and
consideration he must enjoy, or that in any way undermines the
prestige of the judiciary, is subject to disciplinary sanctions'. Such
sanctions range from simple written admonition to expulsion from the
judiciary.

Such discretionary evaluations – backed by a complex system of
information-gathering on the official and private conduct of the
members of the judiciary – were traditionally concentrated, until the
beginning of the 1960s, exclusively in the hands of the higher echelons
of the judicial hierarchy and (often more formally than substantially)
in the hands of the Ministry of Justice. An analysis of the use of such
discretionary powers which we have conducted with reference to the
various types of evaluation for periods ranging from eleven to twenty-
two years clearly shows – and this is a finding that will not surprise the
student of public bureaucracies – that while traditionally there always
has been a rather benevolent attitude in the evaluation of those aspects
pertaining to the lack of diligence in the performance of official duties
(mainly if they had not given rise to 'public clamor'), there has been an
almost unfailing tendency to penalise: the private conduct of the
magistrate eliciting widespread negative gossiping in the community
where he held office; utterances couched in non-technical terms by
which members of the judiciary would publicly expose the social and
ideological implications or the 'conservative' leanings of judicial
pronouncements; involvement in political activities (especially if in
connection with parties of the moderate or extreme left).[13]

Traditionally, two of the steps in the judicial career ladder have been
more crucial than others in determining the career success of Italian
judges: promotion to *magistrato d'appelo* (appeal magistrate) and to
magistrato di cassazione (cassation magistrate). In fact, the possibility
to accede thereafter to the top echelons of the judicial hierarchy
depended almost exclusively on passing those two very harsh and
extremely selective competitions at the first or at most at the second

attempt. Until the beginning of the 1960s the task of evaluating judges for those promotions was exclusively in the hands of the judicial elite. The merit of the candidates meeting the requirements of 'irreprehensible conduct', 'prestige', and 'public esteem' has traditionally been assessed on the basis of a careful analysis of their judicial opinions. Our analysis of the written records of the promotion committees reveals quite clearly that negative evaluations were frequently made on, among others, three accounts which are of particular interest here: (1) because the judicial opinions of the candidates had disregarded or not taken into proper account the 'correct' interpretation of the law as rendered in the opinion of the Court of Cassation; (2) because the judicial opinions of the candidates dealt with extra-legal issues (i.e. because the language in which they were couched revealed too evidently that the decision had been influenced by the socio-political orientation of the judge); (3) because the judicial opinions of the candidates lacked judicial interest (i.e. because the opinion, though substantively correct, consisted prevalently or exclusively in the assessment of facts easily classifiable from a legal point of view and therefore did not permit the committee to evaluate whether the candidate was technically capable of dealing in a learned, scholarly, systematic fashion with issues of 'pure' law).

In sum, we can say that institutional mechanisms of behaviour control typical of bureaucratic structures placed in the hands of the higher echelons of the judicial hierarchy have traditionally been highly effective in inducing conformity to the image and folklore of the judge as an 'applied scientist' uninfluenced by the social and political implications of the cases he decides, intent above all on assuring the 'correct' application of positive legislation and on guaranteeing the attainment of the certainty of the law as a basic value of the legal system.

So far, we have often made reference to some recent modifications of the organisational set-up of the Italian judiciary. We shall mention the two most important ones, trying thereafter to note briefly how such modifications seem to be changing the way in which judges traditionally have defined their role.

The first modification consists in the creation, in 1959, of the Higher Council of the Judiciary (*Consiglio superiore della Magistratura*), provided for by our 1948 Constitution in order to guarantee the so-called 'external independence' of the judiciary. At present, this unit is composed of thirty-three members: three members *ex officio* (the President of the Republic, and the President and the Attorney General of the Court of Cassation); ten elected by Parliament (the electoral *quorum* is such that representation is assured also to parties of the left, i.e. socialists and communists); and twenty elected by all the magistrates (eight high-ranking, four middle-ranking and eight lower-ranking magistrates). Its main institutional function is to make all decisions concerning judicial personnel (recruitment, promotions, transfer from one judicial office to another, disciplinary sanctions, and so on).[14]

The mere summary indication alone of the functions and composition of the Higher Council indicates a breach in the traditional bureaucratic structure of the judiciary, in so far as lower- and middle-ranking magistrates for the first time participate in decisional processes regarding the distribution of organisational gratifications and sanctions, not only with respect to their peers, but also with regard to higher-level magistrates. Furthermore, an analysis of the evolution of judicial personnel management as practiced by the Council shows, among other things, two important developments. On the one hand, there has been a progressive diminution of discretionary power in the decisions concerning the organisational life of the magistrates, resulting from the adoption of detailed, publicised regulations concerning the use of such power. On the other hand, the Council has drastically curtailed the previous formal and informal systems of information gathering on the official and private behaviour of the members of the judiciary, proceeding, at the same time, to expurgate the magistrates' dossiers of information previously collected, and to regulate the use, for decisional purposes, of information still collected.

The second major modification in the organisational set-up of the Italian judiciary regards the system of promotion. In the midst of increasing public concern for the inefficiency and ever-growing slowness of the judicial process, and in the context of an often heated debate on the 'conservative' and even 'reactionary' leanings of the judiciary – viewed simplistically by many as a mere function of the dominance of the judicial elite and of the pervasive influence of the jurisprudence of the Court of Cassation – Parliament passed between 1963 and 1973 a series of laws dismantling step by step the traditional system of promotions. It was variously deemed by those who supported such laws in Parliament that the changes would, among other things, promote a greater efficiency in the judicial machinery, and meet the growing expectations in society for a 'less formalistic' and 'more substantive' rendering of justice which would be more attentive to the socio-political implications of the adjudicative function. Such hopes have been based on the simplistic assumption that the achievement of those goals could be facilitated (1) by relieving, at least to some extent, the great bulk of judges from their dependence on a judicial elite professionally acculturated during the years of Fascism; (2) by diminishing the pressures which, for career purposes, induced the judges to concentrate on the more formalistic aspects of their work and to invest a great deal of their time in making their judicial opinions appear as 'scientific' dissertations in 'pure' law; and (3) by reducing the need for the better qualified judges to avoid the exercise of those crucial aspects of the judicial function, such as criminal jurisdiction, which gave little chance in the writing of judicial opinions to demonstrate the ability to deal in a scholarly way with elegant issues of 'pure' law.

The cumulative results of the new regulations is that, at present, the evaluation of candidates having the seniority requirements to compete for promotion at the different levels of the judicial hierarchy of ranks is no longer based either on written and oral exams, or on the consideration of their written judicial works, but on a 'global' assessment of judicial performance. All candidates who qualify are to be promoted. Those promoted in excess of the existing vacancies attain all the material and normative advantages of the new rank, but remain *pro tempore* to exercise the lower judicial functions of their previous rank. An analysis of the actual working of the new system of promotion at all ranks unmistakenly shows that, beyond the smokescreen of the cumbersome rituals of the evaluation processes, the simple fulfillment of the seniority requirements provided for by the law has come to be the *only* criterion regulating the career development of the members of the judiciary. (Exceptions are indeed so rare and depend on such extraordinary circumstances that they are not worth mentioning here.) In other words, nowadays the young graduate in law, by simply passing an entrance examination where his or her general scholastic knowledge of some basic principles is tested, often in a rather benevolent, unsystematic fashion, can more or less rest assured that the mere passing of time will ensure that in twenty-eight years he or she will reach the peak of the judicial career, until recently reserved for only a little over 1 per cent of the magistrates.[15]

The main implications of the aforementioned changes are that in a rather short time interval, while the other traditional characteristics of the judicial machinery and of the judicial workflow have remained substantially unchanged, judges have in many respects been relieved of their traditional anxious dependence on the higher echelons of the judicial hierarchy, and of the need of anticipating in their behaviour and performance the expectations of the judicial elite in order to attain organisational gratifications. As for the hoped for consequences we mentioned, one can certainly say that the partial dismantling of the traditional means of organisational control over judicial performance has further accentuated the already lax work habits of the majority of the magistrates.

SCOPE OF AUTHORITY

It has often been pointed out[16] that a typical civil law nation is characterised by a set of administrative courts, entirely separate from the ordinary judicial system and exercising an independent jurisdiction. The basic reason behind this arrangement is the doctrine of separation of powers that emerged from the French Revolution and that has been so influential also in Italy. Indeed, one of the objectives of the revolutionary reforms was to deprive ordinary judges of any power to determine the legality of administrative action or to control the conduct of government officials. Thus, also in Italy the influence of this doctrine gave way to the system of administrative courts that are now illustrated.

Undoubtedly, 'the rules which govern access and establish the procedural framework of adjudicative bodies are variables of critical importance. What kinds of disputes are to be decided, who can bring these disputes, and what kinds of solutions are possible, are among the most important determinants' of the political significance of the judicial system.[17] As we have seen, traditionally, in continental Europe, administrative courts – staffed with judges more open to be influenced by the executive – have lessened considerably the political impact of ordinary courts. But, in order correctly to understand the role presently played by administrative courts in Italy we have to point out that their judges *de facto* enjoy the same degree of independence as the ordinary judges – more specifically, they cannot be removed by the government without due process – and that the authority of defining the jurisdictional controversies regarding whether an action is properly brought before an ordinary court or an administrative court is given to the Court of Cassation. Therefore, the presence of a separate system of administrative courts cannot be interpreted as leading to a low degree of political significance of the Italian judicial system.[18] In fact, the potential political impact of our courts remains strong, as we shall see, due also to the peculiar institutional setting of prosecutorial structures.

From the unification of Italy in 1861 until 1946 the public prosecutor (*pubblico ministero*) was considered to be the representative of the executive in the judiciary. The Judiciary Act of 1865 explicitly entrusted to the Ministry of Justice the direction of the activity of the public prosecutor. The prosecuting officers were members of the judiciary, followed the same career as the judges, but could be transferred into the ranks of the latter group only under exceptional circumstances. The prosecuting offices were structured according to hierarchical principles. The Attorney General attached to each court of appeal had powers of direction and supervision over all subordinate offices of its district.

After the fall of Fascism, in 1946 and in 1948 substantial changes were introduced. In 1946 the new democratic government, reacting against the abuses caused by the dependence of the public prosecutor on the executive, abolished that dependence. In 1948 the Constitution reaffirmed that the prosecutors were to be considered members of the judiciary, proclaimed their substantial equality with the judges and guaranteed them autonomy from every other branch of government. Thus, today prosecuting offices are not only recruited in the same way and together with judges but also enjoy the same guarantees (e.g. independence, irremovability and salary) assured to the judges. Transition from one role to the other has become frequent and widespread.

As shown in Figure 8.2, prosecuting officers are organised on three levels, following the structure of the courts: (1) a *procura generale* is attached to the Court of Cassation, composed of a *procuratore generale* (attorney general), who is the head of the office, and his assistants; (2) a *procura generale* at each court of appeal, directed by a *procuratore generale*, who is in turn aided by assistants; and (3) a *procura della Repubblica* attached to each *Tribunale* and headed by a *procuratore* with help from several assistants. We wish to point out that today, after the powers of the Minister of Justice in this field have been abolished, the prosecuting offices enjoy a wide autonomy. No hierarchical relationship exists between the Attorney General at the Court of Cassation and the other offices. Only the twenty-four attorneys general at the court of appeal have supervisory powers over the offices of their district.

The Italian public prosecutor is concerned with a vast array of activities even though his principal task is, of course, the prosecution of criminal cases. The peculiarity of the officials' institutional setting emerges plainly from a comparison with the prosecuting structures operating in all significant democratic regimes: only in Italy are prosecuting and judging roles entrusted to the same corps of independent magistrates.[19] In addition, in the specific case of the *pretura*, prosecuting and judicial roles coincide in the same person: the *pretore* first starts the criminal prosecution, then instructs the case, and finally decides it in court. Thus, the Italian example is not characterised by that degree of passivity which normally distinguishes the setting of the judicial system in a democratic regime.

In this context, another element to take into account is that our criminal process is formally governed by the principle of compulsory prosecution. This principle is currently interpreted in Italy as denying to the public prosecutor any discretion in deciding whether or not to start a criminal prosecution. It is maintained, at least by the great majority of Italian jurists, that in every case where a suspicion arises that a crime has been committed the public prosecutor must request a decision from the judge, even if he is convinced of the innocence of the accused. Nothwithstanding the ideological and unrealistic nature of this belief, it is important to point out that it has played a major role in legitimising the independent status granted even to the magistrates exercising prosecutorial functions.

At this point it is far from surprising that, for example, more and more *pretori* and prosecuting officers intervene in administrative and political affairs, both at the local and national levels, by starting criminal investigations and by actually 'invading' areas before reserved to traditional administrative controls. These developments have to be understood not only in view of the high degree of institutional independence enjoyed by the Italian judiciary but also with reference to the fact that judging and prosecuting functions are entrusted to the same corps, when not to the same person. It is obvious that it is precisely because of these structural and institutional arrangements that the political impact of judicial and prosecutorial behaviour in Italy is great and is increasing, leading to recurring tensions between the judicial and the political branches of government.

DECISION-MAKING

Collegiate judging is one of the most prominent features of judicial decision making in Italy. In fact, all judgments, with the sole exception of those handed down by the courts of limited jurisdiction (*preture*) are rendered by panels of judges which vary in size depending on the level of jurisdiction (from three to nine). Two aspects of the functioning of panels are, more than others, relevant in the context of our present brief analysis. The first is that all decisions taken in the panels must appear externally as unanimous – even those taken by a majority vote – not only because the institution of dissenting and concurring opinions is foreign to the Italian judicial process, but also because the participants are bound by law to observe absolute secrecy as to the internal dynamics of the judging panel. As a consequence, a reversal of any judgment at the next level of jurisdiction can more easily appear in our system simply as the *correction* of a judicial mistake brought about by higher and *therefore* more competent judges.

The second relevant aspect concerns the role of the judges who preside over the working of the panels at all levels of jurisdiction. They are always of a rank higher than that of the other members, and one of their many functions is that of re-reading, prior to their publication, the opinions by lower ranking members in order to make sure that they exactly portray the appraisal of the facts and the legal reasoning on the basis of which the panel has reached its decision. Traditionally, in performing this task, the presiding judges introduced all the modifications they deemed necessary, including those of a stylistic nature, intended both to render the opinions more rigorous under the profile of legal reasoning and to eliminate, if present, those parts that too evidently might reveal the value orientation of the judge. In fact, the modifications to the judicial career introduced in the last years have diminished the influence enjoyed *de facto* by presiding judges. However, the higher rank magistrates can affect the decision making process by influencing the assignment of cases. It is obvious that this prerogative, always politically important, becomes more relevant in the case of prosecuting and instructing offices. Indeed, the chiefs of these offices not only are entitled to distribute cases to the magistrates assigned to them but can, if they wish, also seize a case again and, possibly, reassign it to another magistrate. Even in this respect, however, the modifications of magistrates' careers have *de facto* diminished the power of the chiefs.

Another factor to take into account in analysing Italian judicial decision making is the Court of Cassation. The Court of Cassation is a *sui generis* court in the sense that it does not hear cases on their merit, but only judges with respect to the 'correct' interpretation of the law rendered in single cases by lower level judges, its main institutional objective being to ensure, on a national basis, 'the uniform jurisprudential interpretation of the law'. When this court finds what it considers a mistaken interpretation of the law, it proceeds to state the correct interpretation but does not itself reverse the decision: normally the case must be reconsidered and rejudged – according to the interpretation of the Court of Cassation – by the same lower court whose judgment has been found defective. Such interpretations of the law are formally binding for lower courts only with respect to the single cases sent back for reconsideration. Actually, however, the body of such interpretations – published in the form of 'abstracts' by the court itself and couched in highly technical legal terms with little or no reference to the facts of the cases – are widely circulated among the judges and lawyers alike and tend to constitute, so to speak, a *de facto* normative sub-system serving as the key for the interpretation of the law. A reading of any sample of judicial opinions rendered by Italian courts, as well as of the written pleadings of the lawyers, shows continuous references to the interpretations of the law as formulated in the opinions of the Court of Cassation. Naturally, as is the case in all civil law systems, judicial decisions are always formally justified with reference to the law as directly interpreted by the judge who adjudicates the case. More often than not, however, in writing their opinions Italian judges tend to qualify their interpretation of the norm relevant to the case by *adding* citations from concurring interpretations rendered by the Court of Cassation, as if to stress that they have made the 'right' interpretation.

The pervasive influence of the opinions of the Court of Cassation as the key for the 'correct' interpretation of the law has many causes. Suffice it to say here that over and over again in the course of our interviews judges have explained their tendency to adhere to the interpretation of the law rendered by the Court of Cassation, even in cases where they doubted its correctness, by pointing out that otherwise they would have taken upon themselves the grave responsibility of deceiving one of the parties concerned for many years, i.e. until their decisions were reversed by the Court of Cassation. We may add that such preoccupations on the part of many judges are borne out by two significant considerations: the first regards the staggering slowness of the Italian judicial process; the second is that recourse to the Court of Cassation, in the absence of any legal limitation on such recourse, is extremely frequent.

Moreover, we should not forget that the possibility of acceding to the higher echelons of the judicial hierarchy of ranks depended, until the beginning of the 1960s, on passing some examinations controlled by the judicial elite. As stated before, our analysis of the written records of the promotion committees[20] reveals quite clearly that negative evaluations were frequently made on, among others, the charge that the judicial opinions of the candidates had disregarded or not taken into proper account the 'correct' interpretation of the law as rendered in the opinions of the Court of Cassation.

Thus, even though we have to take into account the modifications that have released the great majority of the magistrates from the controls exercised by the judicial elite, it seems doubtful that judicial precedents are *de facto* less binding in the Italian judicial process than in countries where judges are formally bound by judicial precedents, but where the institutional mechanisms of influence on their behaviour are less cogent. In other words, it would appear that at least some of the traits by which scholars distinguish civil law from common law legal systems still need a great deal of verification at the empirical level. In fact, the Court of Cassation exercises always a great deal of influence upon the lower courts, since at least some of the mechanisms illustrated above are still at work.

Generally speaking, it is difficult to assess the effects of the aforementioned changes in the institutional and organisational setting of the Italian judiciary on the substantive aspects of the adjudicative process and on the life and work style of the judges, at least for two reasons: in the first place because those changes are relatively recent, while modifications in the work and life habits are, as we know, always rather slow to come about; and in the second place because what modifications can be discerned in this area cannot certainly be attributed *solely* to the changes that have taken place *within* the organisational set-up of the judiciary. However, there is no doubt that these changes, by minimising institutional sanctions for deviances, have played a major role in paving the way for a reconsideration, on the part of the judges, of their traditional role.

We have already observed that the conception of the judicial role is today much more diversified than fifteen or twenty years ago. The last years have seen the deepening of a tendency already manifested in the 1960s: the grouping of Italian magistrates in organised factions (*correnti*). Now, there are three such factions: *Magistratura Democratica* (leftist), *Unita per la Costituzione* (centre-left), and *Magistratura Indipendente* (centre-right), all inside the same association, the powerful *Associazione Nazionale dei Magistrati Italiani*. These *correnti* exercise a varying but certain influence on judicial behaviour, for example, by organising study meetings on the legal process, by publishing periodicals and by trying to make proselytes among the magistrates in the Higher Council of the Judiciary. Indeed, the Higher Council presently in charge is composed of three members of *Magistratura Democratica*, nine of *Unita per la Costituzione* and eight of *Magistratura Indipendente*. From this point of view it is obvious that the *correnti* heavily influence all the decisions that currently affect a magistrate and consequently play a decisive role in the process of appointment to the strategic posts of chief of the prosecuting and judicial offices. They are a definitively new factor to take into account – even if not an easy one – in the analysis of judicial decision making.[21]

It is far from surprising that the growing political significance of the Italian judiciary, in both its main roles: prosecutorial and judicial, has triggered a new attention on judicial activity from political groups. As we will see, various facts, especially in the most recent years, are signalling that the attempts by interest groups, unions and political parties at influencing the behaviour of our magistrates are actually multiplying. Of course, it is difficult to assess the degree to which they can have success. An overall assessment of the complex power interactions between the judiciary and its political environment can be made only through a detailed reconstruction of the political and institutional context in which our judges and public prosecutors operate.[22]

LINKS WITH OTHER POLITICAL INSTITUTIONS

What we have said so far confirms the high level of institutional independence enjoyed by the Italian judiciary.[23] Italian magistrates – judges and public prosecutors – are recruited through competitive examinations controlled by the judiciary, cannot be removed or disciplined by any other authority except that of the Higher Council of the Judiciary, enjoy a *de facto* automatic career which leads them to an enviable economic treatment which in turn is largely determined by the judiciary itself.[24] The legitimate influence which the other branches of government – the executive and the legislative – can exert over judicial activity is very small. Traditionally, there have always been connections and steady contacts between members of the judiciary and the political class. Such contacts have occurred, prevalently but not exclusively, in the form of a continuous, largely institutionalised, collaboration between the higher echelons of the judicial hierarchy and the Ministry of Justice. One needs only to recall here that the heads of the several divisions of the Ministry of Justice must by law be chosen from among top-level magistrates, and that the Ministry traditionally has selected among them also its head of Cabinet – a position with clear political connotation. In this way the judicial elite, while monopolising the contacts between the judiciary and political power right where these contacts are most effective, traditionally enjoyed the comfortable advantage of having the phenomenon pass by almost unnoticed, their daily contacts and collaboration with the Ministry and, through the position they hold in the Ministry, with other influential members of the political class being after all part of their official duties *qua* members of the judiciary. Today, the Ministry of Justice is still staffed, in its top positions, by magistrates, but the Minister – a politician with often scarce experience in judicial matters – has only limited authority over them since he cannot influence their career. The institutional mechanisms that once assured also in Italy, as in almost all civil law countries, the concrete subordination of the judiciary to the executive are no longer working.

Meanwhile, the resources that judges and public prosecutors can exploit in order to enlarge their power are increasing. First of all, the Italian judiciary has obviously profited from the expanded judicial creativity that is characterising nearly all judicial systems in the western area.[25] Thus, not surprisingly, its relative power, *vis-à-vis* the other branches of government, has notably increased in recent years.

However, the Italian case distinguishes itself through some specific developments that give a peculiarly strong position to its judiciary. First, the judicial review of legislation – that, as we have seen, was entrusted by the Constitution to a special Constitutional Court, even if through a preventive check by the ordinary courts – is being *de facto* more and more exercised directly by the ordinary judges themselves. Not only do many of them orient their activity of interpreting 'ordinary' legal norms prevalently in the light of what they perceive as being constitutional norms and values, but also judges often exercise *de facto* judicial review powers by not applying legal norms that they believe to be 'patently' unconstitutional, without referring the matter to the Constitutional Court. It is impossible to make a quantitative assessment of this kind of judicial behaviour, even though it has been signalled as growing[26] but we have to consider that at least one of the magistrates' *correnti* (*Magistratura democratica*) has openly advocated this practice of judicial interpretation. Generally speaking, the relationships between the legislative and the judicial branches is presently evolving toward a new equilibrium, unforeseen by the Founding

Fathers of the Constitution and leading toward an increased autonomy of the latter *vis-à-vis* the former.

However, the power presently enjoyed by the Italian judiciary has to be better understood also in connection with the general transformations that have characterised in recent years our judicial system. Here, pointing only to some of the most relevant factors, we have to recall the modifications in the judicial organisations we have illustrated before. The near abolition of the traditional hierarchical structure has not only brought to an end even the indirect powers entrusted to the executive but has enormously increased the autonomy of judges who are not obliged any longer to submit their opinions to the evaluation of higher-ranking judges in order to advance in their career. Meanwhile, also prosecutors have been relieved of most of the duties traditionally connected with their rank and, it needs to be stressed again, are at present completely free from institutional pressures by the executive.

Finally, the present system of judicial recruitment, coupled with the lack of any organisationally relevant instrument of selection inside the corps, leads to a situation in which the guarantees that homogeneous standards of professional conduct will be observed are not very high. It is probable that these standards vary strongly among the magistrates.

Thus, in Italy the relationships between the main branches of government have been characterised, in the last twenty years, by a dramatic growth of judicial power. The political significance of our judiciary is today much higher than in other democratic regimes, even in those in which, as in the United States, the political role of the judiciary has always been more or less distinctly perceived. Indeed, to the Italian judiciary has been entrusted not only the power of judging, with complete independence, issues regarding the freedom and the wealth of the citizenry, but also the power of self-recruitment, self-evaluation, and self-discipline. Moreover, the Italian judiciary enjoys exclusive control of access to the criminal justice system, i.e. the monopoly of criminal initiative. In other words, it enjoys the power of defining and implementing a large part of criminal policy without the possibility of being held responsible, directly or indirectly – as is the case, in all other significant democratic regimes – by the political community.

It is probable that this change has been encouraged, as many magistrates are prone to point out, by the spreading of terrorist activities in the late 1970s and by the powers accordingly entrusted to the judiciary in order to fight them. The relevance of this factor cannot be denied but we have shown that other elements, inside and outside the judicial system, have pushed in this direction, some common to other democratic countries, others specific to the Italian situation. Anyway, it is more convincing to conclude that, even after the near complete defeat of terrorism, the present situation is not open to being reversed swiftly.

In this context, the reactions of the political environment to the growth of judicial power is a still more interesting field to investigate. Up to now, this phenomenon has been ambiguously confronted by political groups. Some political actors, such as the opposition parties and some interest groups, have welcomed the new judicial activism because of the belief, often shown to be correct, of having something to gain: it is obvious, for example, that the criminal prosecutions initiated against elective officials of some party are normally greeted joyously by the other, competing parties. Other actors – especially, but not only, the parties in government – have resented judicial interventions but have chosen not to react too openly against them. Instead, they have tried to extract a more benevolent attitude from the judiciary by satisfying their demands – for example, magistrates' salaries are now the highest in the state sector – or by building good relationships at the individual or group level. Many judges and public prosecutors belong to a political party and participate in political activities: some even have been elected to Parliament. Moreover, the practice of conferring extra-judicial, and often well paid, tasks to members of the judiciary is widespread: at present we find magistrates in ministerial cabinets, in inquiry and study commissions, in boards of directors of public bodies, and so on. It has been argued that this phenomenon can be better understood as an attempt, even though not always successful by the political environment – and especially by political parties – of influencing indirectly the behaviour of Italian magistrates.[27]

NOTES

1. Francesca Zannotti, 'Analisi diacronica dei principali provvedimenti in tema di retribuzioni dei magistrati e degli avvocati dello Stato', in *Arel informazioni* (Gennaio, 1985), pp. 33–4.
2. Mauro Cappelletti, John Henry Merryman and Joseph M. Perillo, *The Italian Legal System: An Introduction* (Stanford, CA: Stanford University Press, 1967). pp. 166–7.
3. Massimo Severo Giannini, 'Sociologia e studi di diritto contemporaneo', *Jus*, VIII (1957), p. 223.
4. Cappelletti, Merryman and Perillo, *Italian Legal System*, p. 191.
5. Alessandro Pizzorusso, *L'organizzazione della giustizia in Italia* (Torino: Einaudi, 1981), p. 57.

6. Giuseppe Di Federico, *La Corte di cassazione* (Bari: Laterza, 1969).
7. Cappelletti, Merryman and Perillo, *Italian Legal System*, p. 81.
8. Cappelletti, Merryman and Perillo, *Italian Legal System*, p. 75ff.
9. Giuseppe Di Federico, *Il reclutamento dei magistrati* (Bari: Laterza, 1968).
10. Di Federico, *Il reclutamento*, pp. 17–50; Giuseppe Di Federico, 'Accesso nell'Ordine giudiziario e professionalita dei magistrati', in *La magistratura: indipendenza e imparzialita* (Rome: Democrazia Cristiana-Dipartimento Stato e Istituzioni, 1984).
11. Di Federico, *Il reclutamento*, p. 113.
12. Giorgio Freddi, *Legitimacy and Opposition in the Italian Judiciary: A Study of Organizational Conflict*, PhD dissertation (Ann Arbor: University Microfilm, 1970), p. 56.
13. Giuseppe Di Federico, 'La professione giudiziaria in Italia e il suo contesto burocratico', *Rivista Trimestrale de Diritto e Procedura Civile*, XXXII (1978).
14. Giuseppe Di Federico, 'Le statut, le carriere et l'independence des magistrats ordinaires en Italie', in *Justice et politique* (Strasbourg: Presses Universitaires d'Alsace), pp. 39–41.
15. Di Federico, 'Le statut', pp. 42–51; Giuseppe Di Federico, 'Limiti ed inefficacia degli strumenti di selexione negativa dei magistrati', in *La selezione dei magistrati: prospettive psicologiche* (Milano: Giuffre, 1976).
16. John Henry Merryman, *The Civil Law Tradition* (Stanford: Stanford University Press, 1969), p. 94ff.
17. Austin Sarat and Joel B. Grossman, 'Courts and Conflict Resolution: Problems in the Mobilization of Adjudication', *American Political Science Review*, LXIX (1975), p. 1207.
18. Carlo Guarnieri, *L'indipendenzia della magistratura* (Padova: Cedam, 1981), pp. 109–19.
19. Carlo Guarnieri, *Pubblico ministero e sistema politica* (Padova: Cedam, 1984).
20. Di Federico, 'Le statut'.
21. Carlo Guarnieri, 'Elites, conflitti e correnti fra magistrati italiani', *Politica del diritto*, VII (1976).
22. Giuseppe Di Federico, *Gli incarichi extragiudiziari dei magistrati: una grave minaccis per l'indipendenza ed imparzialita del giudice, una grave violazione del principio della divisione dei poteri* (Padova: Cedam, 1981); Giuseppe Di Federico, 'Costi e implicazioni istituzionali dei recenti provvedimenti in materia di retribuzioni e pensioni dei magistrati', in *Arel informazioni* (Gennaio: 1985).
23. Guarnieri, *L'indipendenza*.
24. Di Federico, 'Accesso nell'Ordine'; Di Federico, 'Costi e implicazioni'; Zannotti, 'Analisi diacronica'.
25. Mauro Cappelletti, *Giudici legislatori?* (Milano: Giuffre, 1984).
26. Giovanni Tarello, 'Chi ci salvera dal governo dei giudici', in *Mondoperaio*, n.3 (1984).
27. Di Federico, *Gli incarichi extragiudiziari*; Francesca Zannotti, *Le attivita extragiudiziarie dei magistrati ordinari* (Padova: Cedam, 1981).

9　The Courts in Sweden
Joseph B. Board

There is a long and deep tradition of respect for law which runs through Swedish history. Whether the context is a court of law, the bureaucracy, or the canons of social etiquette, there is in Sweden a pronounced attachment to the notion that life should be conducted, as far as possible, in accordance with fixed and binding rules. Merged with the typically Swedish conception of the state as a highly centralised and positive institution, this respect for law can exert a powerful educative or tutelary force on the lives of citizens, making possible a thoroughness and comprehensiveness of social reform unmatched elsewhere. At its worst, however, the law in Sweden can add to an already pervasive paternalism which, in the words of one eminent Swedish professor of law, 'pursues the citizen far beyond the letter of the text, intruding into bedrooms, hearts, and ledgers'.[1]

The Swedish legal tradition defies any simplistic urge to classify it as belonging to the Civilian or Common Law families. It is in fact an old and largely indigenous tradition, the result of long centuries when Sweden was a European backwater, isolated from the continent, from which the great historical impulses – Christianity, the Renaissance, and the Enlightenment, to name but a few – came late to it and even then assumed a distinctively Swedish flavour. With roots in old Germanic customary law, and in Provincial Codes written as early as the thirteenth century, the Swedish legal culture, while not exclusively belonging to the civilian or common law categories, reflects some characteristics of both, and – in terms of modern practice – is compatible with both. Swedish law has been subjected to considerable codification, but – it should be quickly added – these are not the comprehensive and systematic compilations of Continental jurisprudence, such as the *Code Napoleon*, or the German Civil Code (BGB). One should not convey the impression, however, that Swedish law is a kind of half-way house between the English and Continental traditions. It really is in most respects closer to the Civil Law family; in its ways of conceptualisation, terminology, and general approach, a Continental jurist would probably feel more at home. But Sweden never really participated in that great cultural transfer represented by the reception of Roman Law in Europe. In the earlier stages, Sweden was too remote, too lacking in universities or in university-trained lawyers to be a full participant in this Continental movement. When the influence did come later, in the seventeenth and eighteenth centuries, its effect was already diluted.

SWEDEN AND THE SCANDINAVIAN SETTING

Sweden must in some respects be viewed not simply as an independent nation, which it is, but as a sub-group of a larger grouping – the Nordic countries. These nations are closely related by geographic proximity in the northern latitudes, languages (Finland excepted), and rather similar social and political histories (they were all too late to urbanise, modernise, and democratise, moving rapidly in the twentieth century from rural poverty to advanced and prosperous welfare states without abandoning an attachment to the notion of private ownership in the process). Perhaps most important, they share with each other, and with the Anglo-American democracies, a strong attachment to constitutionalism, the rule of law, civil rights, and to an independent, highly prestigious judiciary.

Although the Swedish legal system rests on a foundation of values which most Englishmen and Americans would share, there are a number of respects in which Sweden differs substantially from the United States. In the first place, Sweden is in a legal sense a highly centralised (non-federal) unitary structure, with one law of the land, one system of courts, and one career judiciary for the entire country.[2]

HOW LAWS ARE MADE

The legislative process in Sweden is quite distinctive, and in many respects unique. In the usual course of events, it is slow, thorough, pragmatic, consultative almost to the point of corporatism and reflects the deference that Swedes ordinarily accord in general to expert opinion. This process, which will have touched base with all the relevant social, political, and legal opinion before a law receives final approval, creates the basic background against which the judiciary operates. Indeed, as we shall see, judicially trained personnel will be deeply involved at several crucial steps along the way, and the special nature of the legislative process will condition the work of the judges themselves when it comes time for them to interpret the meaning of the legislation.

In somewhat oversimplified terms, the process might be described in the following way. When it seems advisable that a given matter should be studied with an eye to passage of important new legislation, the appropriate cabinet minister will issue a directive for the appointment of a Royal Commission of Inquiry.[3]

Members of these Royal Commissions may include members of the parliament, judges, civil servants, and interest groups. Well-known scholars may be appointed to direct research efforts, and the staff may include persons with legal, even judicial training. The Commission, after exhaustive investigation often taking several years, produces a draft bill accompanied by an explanatory report. This report, printed and widely circulated under the designation *Statens öffentliga utredninar* (SOU),[4] typically contains a history of the subject matter in question, the existing state of the law on the matter, and an attempt to show what laws on the subject have been passed in foreign countries.[5]

This report will be delivered to the Minister in question who will then send it out with an invitation for reactions and comments to interest groups, courts, academic departments, professional associations and any other groups who can reasonably be thought to have an interest in any eventual legislation on the subject. The process of referral is referred to in Sweden as *remiss* and is a vital link in the chain of consensus which binds most Swedish laws together.

At the next stage, legislative experts in the ministry, very often junior judges, prepare a new draft bill with commentary, often reflecting the reactions elicited by the *remiss* process. The legislation will then be sent to the *Riksdag*[6] in the form of a Government bill, or it may go first to the Law Council (*Lagrådet*), a body composed of judges from the Supreme Court and the Supreme Administrative Court, for an advisory opinion as to its constitutionality or its compatibility with existing legislation. This opinion, while not binding on the Government, will generally be given considerable weight, especially if it touches on questions which are more legal than political. The relevant parliamentary committee, itself often staffed in part with judicially trained personnel, will consider the draft, and prepare its own report. When the bill finally comes up for passage, the final vote may be largely a foregone conclusion, in part because of the group discipline and cohesion of Swedish political parties, but primarily because of the long and comprehensive efforts to obtain a consensus among the interest groups and the experts. The amount of legislative materials (*travaux préparatoires*) can be quite extensive and serves to help judges elucidate the meaning of the statute when such questions subsequently arise.

THE SWEDISH CONSTITUTIONAL TRADITION

Some form of constitutionalism has been established in Sweden since at least the eighteenth century, and there is no doubt that Swedes are as firmly attached to constitutionalist values as any people, even if the Constitution has never been the central public myth that it is in the United States.[7] Throughout the nineteenth century and a very large part of the twentieth century, Sweden was governed by a constitution enacted in 1809. This constitution, which was based on a separation of powers between the king and a four-estate *Riksdag*, lasted until the 1970s as the basis of government. Of course the constitution of 1809 was so frequently amended along the way as to be unrecognisable by the time that it was finally replaced.[8]

The pressures for a complete modernisation of the constitution to bring its letter in line with practice, began to mount after the Second World War. The first change was the enactment in 1949 of a new Freedom of the Press Act.[9] This Act 'may be described as a combined Bill of Rights, code of judicial procedure and penal codes for the printed media, i.e. dailies and other periodicals, pamphlets, and books'.[10]

Reforms came quickly in the 1970s. At the beginning of the decade the bicameral *Riksdag* gave way to a single chamber legislature. In 1974, Sweden enacted a new Instrument of Government, the product of long debate and comprehensive research. The monarchy was relegated to purely ceremonial duties, and a Bill of Rights (Chapter 2) was for the first time included in the Constitution. This Bill of Rights has been subsequently expanded by amendment.

In a 1979 amendment, the institution of judicial review was given clear constitutional status for the first time, even if it had been an occasionally used practice by the courts in recent years. In Chapter 11, Article 14, it is stated that if a court or other public organ considers that a provision is in conflict with a provision of a fundamental law, or with a provision of any other superior statute, or that the procedure prescribed for the enactment has been set aside in any important respect, then such provision may not be applied.[11] Before attaching too much significance to the possibilities for judicial review in Sweden, one should duly note the fact that up until now it has rarely been employed, and there are no significant wagers on any great increase in its use. Up to now, no Swedish court has ever declared unconstitutional a statute enacted by the *Riksdag*.

THE SWEDISH LEGAL SYSTEM

We have seen that there is some adherence to judicial review, but it is not a significant part of the Swedish legal heritage. In fact, courts are less directly involved in questions of public policy than is the case in the United States. Civil Rights are guaranteed more by Parliament and by the prevailing values of the political culture than by the courts. The Swedish people are less litigious than those in the United States, so fewer cases with topical policy concerns are likely to reach the court system. The main explanation, however, is simply that judges do not think of themselves as lawmakers, and the overwhelming emphasis in Sweden is on statutory law. The legislature has the dominant position in the Swedish polity.

The basic foundation in Swedish law was laid in the Code of Sweden of 1734, the product of a commission investigation which lasted over fifty years. Although the 1734 Code is still technically in force, it has been amended and reconstructed so often and so completely that only the original general scheme of organisation remains. It consists of nine chapters (e.g. criminal, procedural, etc.) and is incorporated in a yearly volume of over 3000 pages, entitled *Sveriges rikes lag* (*The Laws of the Kingdom of Sweden*). Although it is by no means exhaustive, this compendious volume is the point of departure for Swedish lawyers and judges when they are attempting to ascertain the law on a given subject. Judges can also take into account such other sources as precedent, legislative history, jurisprudence, foreign law, and dominant social values. While precedent is not in any formal sense binding on judges, it is a practical and economical technique of judicial decision making, whose virtues have not been lost on Swedish judges. They have always deferred somewhat to precedent, and in recent years the tendency appears to be growing.[12] Actually the same growing sensitivity to precedent has been observed on the Continent as well, and informed opinion nowadays no longer exaggerates the differences between the civilians and the common lawyers in their adherence to the doctrine of *stare decisis*. Nevertheless, it does remain true to say that the main technique by which judges legitimate their decisions in

Sweden is still their reference to statutes and the rich flora of legislative materials produced by the legislative process.

JUDGES AND COURTS

Sweden in one sense will appear quite familiar to Americans or Englishmen. Like Britain and the United States, there is in Sweden a long and deeply engrained tradition of an independent judiciary, insulated from the pressures and vicissitudes of partisan party politics. Judges are appointed for life, and removable only for cause. In fact, the Swedish Constitution specifies that appointments to any court shall be made by the Government or by an authority designated by the Government. A person with a permanent judicial appointment can be removed only if, by commission of a criminal act or neglect of official duties, he has demonstrated manifest unfitness for the post. And, if a permanent judge is removed from his post by any non-judicial authority, he is entitled to call upon a court to examine the decision.[13] They occupy a position of considerable social prestige, are highly trained, and their socialisation involves a set of professional standards which emphasise seriousness of purpose, scrupulous impartiality, and a duty to the law rather than to the commands of the government of the day. They also share a widespread Swedish bias against obstructionism or dilatory tactics. They are likely to be more actively involved in the actual conduct of a trial than their United States counterparts, in this sense at least resembling more the judges in France or West Germany.

As is also the case on the Continent, a judicial career is essentially a civil service career. And, unlike United States judges, they will very rarely have been actively engaged in the practice of law (or politics) prior to their judicial appointment. In the words of one scholar:

> The judge presiding in court is likely to consider himself as a member of a particularly select corps within the public service, and the upholder of an old aristocratic tradition of objectivity, learning, common sense and public spirit; but it should be stressed that he certainly does not look upon himself as a man exalted over other officials.[14]

Swedish judges will, however, have taken the same law degree – involving four to five years of study – as the practicing lawyer. This first decree is called the *juris kandidat* and is aimed more at theoretical understanding of the law than at practice.[15] Upon receiving the law degree, a person intent on a judicial career will ordinarily serve as an apprentice in a district court (the courts of first instance) performing largely clerical tasks for approximately two and a half years. In fact, this training has been considered so valuable that until recent years, when the number of graduates has increased so rapidly, almost all law graduates, whether their professional goal was the judiciary, private practice, or government service, would have served this apprenticeship. Nowadays perhaps one-half of them undergo this training, which for would be judges will include additional service at the appellate court level before receiving their first permanent appointment.

In several respects, the Swedish judicial career pattern diverges sharply from the Continental model. Not only do legally trained persons staff much of the administrative bureaucracy, but judges, especially from the Court of Appeals level, are frequently given leave of absence to undertake law-related tasks outside the judiciary proper. These might include service in the ministries, on Royal Commissions, or on parliamentary committees. They may also be called upon to serve as arbitrators in private commercial arbitrations, and do not regard this as in any way incompatible with a judicial career. In fact, the Stockholm Chamber of Commerce, in its efforts to popularise the use of its Institute of Arbitration as a centre for the resolution of international commercial disputes has mentioned the high quality of Swedish judges as an advantage.[16]

This kind of administrative service for judges is regarded in Sweden as desirable and prestigious, and those judges who have run such a course are good prospects for future advancement in the judiciary. Today, a majority of the present members of the two highest courts in the land have held positions as under-secretaries in the ministries, lending some support to the old Swedish adage that 'the courts of appeal are the general staff of the kingdom'.[17]

THE COURT SYSTEM

There are two judicial hierarchies of courts in Sweden: ordinary and administrative. Students of the French system will be familiar with this division, which reflects in part an old distinction between private law and public law which began with the Romans. In addition, there are also a number of special courts. The ordinary courts consist of District Courts, Courts of Appeal, and the Supreme Court.

1. District Courts

There are at the local level 100 District Courts (*tingsrätter*), which vary greatly in size; the District Court in Stockholm, with over one hundred judges, is the largest of these, and may well be one of the largest courts in the world.[18] The chief judge at this level called a *lagman* (literally, a law man). In addition the District Courts are staffed with associate district judges (*rådmän*) and judicial clerks or trainees (*tings-notarier*).

In most ordinary civil cases which do not involve family law, the court is composed of three professional judges, although in preliminary findings or small claims one judge is sufficient. In criminal and family law cases, a District Court consists of one professional judge and a panel (*nämnd*) of five lay assessors (*nämdemän*). This institution of the *nämnd* is related to the European mixed-bench rather than to the Anglo-American jury. Its members rule on questions of fact and law, and are elected (politically) by the local municipal councils for six year terms; they can be, and are, re-elected. It requires the concurrence of four of the five lay assessors to out-vote the judge, but this does not often happen, and the general practice seems to be deference to the judge by the lay members on matters that are predominantly legal in nature.[19] In addition to their judicial duties, the District Courts also handle a number of purely administrative matters such as the registration of mortgages and wills, compulsory inventories of estates, etc.[20] Appeals from judgments of the District Courts lie of right to the next level, the intermediate Courts of Appeal, but in practice fewer than 10 per cent of cases are actually appealed.[21]

2. The Courts of Appeal

All decisions, both civil and criminal, can be appealed to the intermediate Courts of Appeal (*Hovrätter*) where questions of both fact and law can be heard. There are six of these, the most ancient and important of them being the *Svea hovrätt* in Stockholm, founded in 1614. The Court of Appeal is headed by a President (*Hovrätts-president*), one or more chairmen of divisions (*hovrättslagmän*), associate judges (*hovrättsråd*) as well as a number of assistant and deputy judges. Altogether there are a total of 192 professional judges on the Courts of Appeal.[22]

In hearing those cases that were originally decided by a mixed bench, the Court of Appeals will consist of three professional judges and two lay assessors, the latter elected by the county council. In cases

Ordinary Courts*		Administrative Courts		Special Courts
100	District Courts (*Tingsrätter*) Trial Courts, with criminal and civil jurisdiction.	20	Provincial Courts (*Länsrätter*) Lowest level of administrative courts, which hear complaints against administrative authorities	Examples include: Land courts Water rights courts Labour court Insurance court
6	Courts of Appeal (*Hovarätter*) Intermediate courts of appeal, which near questions of law and fact.	4	Regional Administrative courts of appeal (*Kammarrätter*) Intermediate administrative courts of appeal, which hear appeals from the provinicial courts.	
	The Supreme Court (*Högsta domstolen*) Final court of appeal in criminal and civil cases		The Supreme Administrative Court (*Regeringsrätt*) The administrative court of last resort.	

Figure 9.1 The Swedish judiciary

* Some ordinary courts are charged with special responsibilities, e.g. all Swedish patent cases are heard by the District Court of Stockholm.

originally decided exclusively by professional judges, the Court of Appeals consists of four (sometimes five) professional judges.

3. The Supreme Court

The Supreme Court (*Högsta domstolen*, usually abbreviated as HD), established in 1789, is the highest level of appeal in the ordinary court system. It consists of a chairman (*ordförande*), who is one of twenty-five justices (*justitieråd*) operating in three divisions. A case is normally heard by five justices sitting *en banc*. Cases are appealable from Courts of Appeal only at the discretion of the Supreme Court, a decision which is made by a panel of three justices. Permission for appeal is given only when important questions of uniformity, precedent, or serious procedural error are raised. Generally speaking, the Supreme Court will take up only questions of law, although there is no formal impediment to considering questions of fact if this seems advisable. The decisions of the Supreme Court have been published in *Nytt Juridiskt Arkiv* since 1874. It should be noted that if there is some prospect that the Court may wish to overrule one of its own precedents, it may require the case to be heard by the entire court sitting *en banc*.[23] Also, as we have already seen, several justices also serve, on occasion, as members of the Law Council. Four members of the Supreme Court take terms of two years for this purpose, and then four others are rotated into these duties.

THE ADMINISTRATIVE COURTS

In Sweden, the administrative system is old – dating back to Gustavus Adolphus – powerful, and far-reaching. Although the question has been debated from time to time in Sweden, the United States approach to the judicial control of administrators by the ordinary courts has never been adopted. Instead the solution, at least in recent times, has been to establish a hierarchy of administrative courts, incorporating in it some administrative courts created in earlier eras. The system of courts operates at three levels.

The lowest of these are twenty provincial courts (*länsrätter*) which hear complaints (*besvär*) against local authorities, most often (75 per cent) those in charge of taxation (an area where Swedes, ordinarily not complainers, have become increasingly contentious). In these, the bench is usually composed of a professional judge and three lay assessors elected by the local council. These courts hear over 200,000 complaints each year.

Above these provincial courts are four regional Administrative Courts of Appeal (*Kammarrätter*) the oldest of which dates back to the 1690s. Each of these courts consists of a President, several Division Chairmen (*lagmän*) and ordinary members (*Kammarrättsråd*); ordinarily three or four professional judges will decide the cases. They hear about 22,000 cases a year, of which about a half involve taxation in some form.

The Administrative Court of last resort is the Supreme Administrative Court (*Regeringsrätt*, or RR) created in 1909 in an obvious attempt to emulate the French *Conseil d'État*. Its twenty-two members are referred to as *regeringsråd*. Generally, cases (about 4000–5000 annually) are decided with five judges on the bench. Procedure in administrative courts is regulated by the Administrative Procedure Act of 1972. In some instances, the case may involve an adversarial proceeding between, e.g. a taxpayer and a public authority, but in most cases the individual complainant is the sole party. Procedure is simple, relatively inexpensive (there are no court charges), and the judges bend over backwards to make sure that cases are properly investigated and that a layman's lack of legal skills do not impair his case.[24] In addition to the cases heard by the Supreme Administrative Court, it is possible to appeal administrative complaints of a less legal and more political nature to the Government.

Outside the ordinary and administrative court systems, there exist a number of Special Courts, such as land courts, water rights courts, Labour Court, the Insurance Court, etc. Among these it is the Labour Court, (*Arbetsdomstol*) established in 1928, which has excited the most attention abroad. The members of this court are appointed by the Government to hear disputes concerning collective bargaining contracts, and almost any other aspect involving labour law. Ordinarily this court is composed of seven members: two employer and two employee representatives; a chairman and vice-chairman with experience as judges; and a person trained in the field of labour relations.[25]

In addition to the ordinary, administrative, and special courts, there are some ordinary courts charged with special responsibilities. For example, the District Court of Stockholm has jurisdiction over all patent cases arising in Sweden. When hearing such cases, the bench is composed of three professional judges and three technical experts serving as lay judges. Similarly in maritime cases, seven specially staffed District Courts have jurisdiction, and in cases involving freedom of the press, the District Courts in the County seats have jurisdiction.

PROCEDURE IN SWEDISH COURTS

More often than not, the peculiar characteristics of a people are more clearly revealed in their procedural than in their substantive law.[26] Swedish procedure was reformed thoroughly in the Code of Judicial Procedure of 1948, which represented an attempt to move closer to common law procedural practices and farther away from those on the Continent. Procedure was to be oral, immediate, concentrated, and public – the very antithesis of the closed, strung-out civilian system dependent on a written record compiled by an intermediary judge. In civil cases, there is usually a preliminary phase (largely oral) followed by a concentrated main hearing at which *all* the evidence must be introduced. In criminal cases, the main trial will be preceded by a preliminary investigation by a public prosecutor.

Perhaps even more striking is the openness, simplicity, and informality of a Swedish court proceeding, making the court quite accessible to the ordinary citizen without legal training.

There is no legal requirement in Swedish courts that a party be represented by legal counsel. However in most civil actions, the parties do retain an attorney, and in criminal cases, one will be appointed by the court to advise a defendant (who can still conduct his own defence).

However, no party to an action, civil or criminal, need be deprived of an attorney, since in recent years Sweden has constructed one of the most comprehensive public legal aid programmes in the world. For both civil and criminal cases, the costs of attorney's fees are borne by the public, discounted by the ability of the party to pay out of his or her own resources. One can either obtain reimbursement for fees paid to a private attorney ('Judicare') or go to a public legal aid office for legal advice. The basic fees for both cases are centrally established.[27]

LEGAL ELITES IN SWEDEN

In terms of influence, it is relatively easy to measure the differences within each judicial hierarchy; the two Supreme Courts are obviously more influential than the lower courts. Even within the hierarchy there are gradations. Some of these are structural, e.g. the size and prominence of the Stockholm District Court. In other cases, power and influence are largely traditional in origin, e.g. the prestige accorded to the Svea Court of Appeal in Stockholm.

It is more difficult to assess the balance of influence *between* the ordinary and administrative hierarchies. However, since the distinction between judicial and administrative functions is, as we shall see, commonly blurred in Sweden, it may be that there is no real difference in influence between the two hierarchies. The fact that ordinary and administrative judges have about the same training and that procedures are similar in both types of court would tend to support this point.

Any attempt to compare non-judicial legal notables with judges is likely to be problematical. Unlike Britain, where a Lord Chancellor sits at the legal and political crossroads, the non-judicial elites in Sweden are quite separate from their judicial brethren.

Despite all of these difficulties, which are compounded by the fact that very little systematic research has been done on Swedish legal elites, one Swedish scholar has attempted a tentative rank ordering of these elites in terms of their influence.[28] In descending order of influence, his list, which I have slightly amended, includes:

(1) The Minister of Justice and his chief advisers
(2) The Law Council
(3) The Supreme Court and the Supreme Administrative Court
(4) The chief legal officers of the ministries
(5) The Parliamentary Ombudsman (JO)
(6) The ordinary and administrative courts of appeal
(7) The Labour Court
(8) The Attorney General (JK)
(9) The Chief Public Prosecutor (RÅ)
(10) The faculties of law
(11) The leadership of the Swedish Bar Association

It may be useful at this point to comment on those which we have not yet discussed at any length.

The Ministry of Justice occupies perhaps the most central position among Swedish elites. It is responsible not only for the courts, but for the police, correctional institutions, public order and safety, as well as insuring freedom of the press. It is staffed by some of the best trained legal talent in the country, who regard service in the ministry as advantageous to a career.

The Parliamentary Ombudsman (*Justitieombudsman*, or JO) is an office created in 1809, and discovered by scholars and reformers outside Sweden a century and a half later. It has been the subject of much investigation abroad, extensive comment, and attempts at emulation, not all of them successful. For many concerned about enhancing the prospect for holding a growing public bureaucracy accountable, it has seemed to offer considerable promise. The holders of the office in Sweden are almost invariably former judges of some prominence. They are appointed by the *Riksdag* for renewable terms of four years, and they make an annual report to the *Riksdag*. Their main responsibility is to oversee the civil service (including the courts), local government authorities, and all public executives to ensure that they are acting, *vis-à-vis* the private citizen, in accordance with the law. The means available to them include powers to investigate, to institute prosecution in a court, to publicise certain abuses of power, and to recommend legislation if this seems necessary to strengthen the rule of law.

The Attorney-General (*Justitiekansler*, or JK) is appointed by the Cabinet, and is usually a judge of some distinction. The office has considerable powers of investigation and represents the interests of the state in the court system and in the administration. It also represents the state in civil actions and provides legal advice to the Cabinet.[29]

Public Prosecutors are organised in a national hierarchy. The lowest level is the local prosecution district, headed by a Chief District Prosecutor (*chefsaklagåre*) and several district prosecutors (*distriktsaklagåre*). At the next higher level are the offices of the County Prosecutors (*lansåklagare*) responsible for prosecuting more serious criminal offences and for supervising the district prosecutors in that county. At the national level, there is a Chief Public Prosecutor (*rikšaklagaren*), whose duties include supervision of the national prosecutorial system and who commences actions in the Supreme Court. Prosecutors are in general responsible for the preliminary investigation in criminal cases, and for making the decision as to whether or not the case will be prosecuted.[30]

The Swedish Bar Association (*Sverigesadvokatsamfund*), founded in 1887, is the main professional organisation of Swedish lawyers, although some lawyers are by virtue of their employment also members of a trade union.[31] Admission to membership requires a law degree, and at least five years in the practice of law, of which three must have been spent working as an advocate. He or she must pass a fitness test, and may not hold any public or private appointment except in a state law office. The membership of the Bar is quite small (some 2100 in a country of eight million) especially when compared to a country like the United States. In part, this may be due to the fact that the Bar has no legal monopoly over the representation and advising of clients, except that all public defenders must be members. However, only members may use the title of 'advocate', there is no distinction between barristers and solicitors, and all members are admitted to a national rather than a local practice. The Board of the Association is responsible for disciplinary action against members, subject to supervision by the Attorney General and possible appeal to the Supreme Court.

The organisation is, as can be seen from the foregoing description, primarily a guild of practicing private lawyers. It does in some respects perform more public functions, mainly in its capacity as a respondent in the *remiss* stage of the legislative process. For this purpose, it maintains a special body responsible for expressing the opinion of advocates concerning proposed legislation.[32]

CONCLUSIONS

From what has been said, it is clear that lawyers and judges do not play the same role in Sweden that they do in the United States. Lawyers have never dominated politics – in 1982, only twelve of the 349 members of parliament were lawyers – politicians do not become judges, judges do not retire to practice law or lobbying, and the courts do not ordinarily confront questions of public policy. This does not, however, mean that judges and lawyers are totally deprived of political influence, especially if one is prepared to look for more indirect and subtle connections.

We have already noted the very broad involvement of judges and lawyers in the *remiss* process. In 1977, for example, the Uppsala Faculty of Law gave some forty opinions on proposed legislation and an entire division of the *Svea Hövratt* did nothing but prepare opinions on legislation.[33] Furthermore the legislative opinions of some groups, e.g. the Stockholm Court of Appeals, the JO, or the Union of Judges, are likely – especially if critical – to have a pronounced effect on pending legislative proposals. Even if their opinions do not have any more legal standing than those of other interested groups, such is their prestige and such is the Swedish deference to expertise, that they will constitute what is effectively a veto group.[34]

It is not so much in their interaction with the legislative process as in their interaction with administration that Swedish judges have their most far-reaching impact. In fact, if one were to search for a distinctively Swedish judicial characteristic, it could be found in this complex judicial-administrative relationship.

Not only do persons with legal, and especially judicial, training permeate all ranks of the administration, whether in ministries or commissions or parliamentary committees. Even more to the point, the very mentality of the typical Swedish civil servant derives from a model which is more judicial in origin than anything else. The ideal bureaucrat in Sweden is supposed to act like a judge – fair, impartial, according to law.

This predisposition has deep roots in Swedish history. It finds expression in the characteristically Swedish division between small ministries which make only general policy, and large Central Administrative Agencies, which are semi-autonomous in the execution of these policies. The division is incorporated in Chapter 11, Article 6 of the Instrument of Government, which states that 'no public authority – may determine how an administrative authority shall make its decision in a particular case concerning the exercise of public authority against a private subject or against a municipality, or concerning the application of law'.

From time to time, there have been sectarian demands for a form of justice more goal-oriented, more socially conscious, more particularised to individual circumstances and less rigidly general in its operation. Others have called for a recruitment of judges from a broader social base than the middle class from which most of them derive. But, in the final analysis, these criticisms have made few inroads on institutions which, for Sweden, are remarkably bound to tradition, and resistant to the imperatives of a modernisation process which has in recent years changed the face of Sweden in so many other ways.

NOTES

1. Stig Strömholm (ed.), *An Introduction to Swedish Law* (Stockholm: Norstedt, 1981), pp. 29–30.
2. Even if one views all of Scandinavia as one cultural unit, but politically divided, much of the potential legal diversity implied by that division has been minimised by pan-Scandinavian efforts at legal harmonisation and

unification that began as early as the middle of the nineteenth century. There is today a very high degree of uniformity in such areas as family law, torts, contracts, succession, and copyright. Strömholm, *An Introduction to Swedish Law*, pp. 33–5.

3. There has been some limited tendency in recent years for these investigations to be performed within the ministries themselves, but the reliance on the Royal Commissions is as yet under no serious threat. The process of consultation outside the ministry is so ineffably Swedish that it is likely to survive for a long time to come.
4. SOU can be translated as Public State Investigations.
5. Strömholm, *An Introduction to Swedish Law*. pp. 35–7; cf. M. Donald Hancock, *Sweden: The Politics of Postindustrial Change* (Hinsdale, Illinois: Dryden Press, 1972), pp. 156–9.
6. This is the Swedish parliament, a 349-member unicameral body which has exclusive legislative power in Sweden.
7. For a general overview in English of the Swedish Constitution, see *Constitutional Documents of Sweden*, published by the Swedish *Riksdag*, 1981; for a good Swedish account, see Erik Holmberg and Nils Stjernquist, *Vår författning*, 4th edn (Stockholm: Norstedts, 1981).
8. Among the major changes was the conversion of the *Riksdag* into a bicameral legislature in 1866, and the reforms of 1909–21, which democraticised the suffrage and established the principles of parliamentary supremacy and cabinet government.
9. The constitution traditionally consisted of three documents, the Instrument of Government (*Regeringsformen*), the *Riksdag* Act (*Riksdagsordningen*) and the Freedom of the Press Act (*Tryckfriketsordningen*). These documents were distinguished from mere statutes by the more difficult procedures required for their amendment.
10. Torbjörn Vallinder, 'Who is Included in Sweden's Judicial and Legal Elite', paper presented at an International Conference on Comparative Judicial and Legal Elites at the Bellagio Conference Center, Lake Como, Italy, 24–8 June 1985, p. 4.
11. The amendment ends, however, on a note of caution: "However, if the provision has been decided by the *Riksdag* or by the Government, the provision may be set aside only if the inaccuracy is obvious and apparent." See *Constitutional Documents of Sweden* (see note 7) p. 71.
12. Vallbinder, 'Who is Included in Sweden's Judicial and Legal Elite', p. 7.
13. *Instrument of Government*, Chapter 11, Article 9; 5.
14. Folke Schmidt and Stig Strömholm, *Legal Values in Modern Sweden* (Stockholm: Norstedts, 1964), pp. 8–9.
15. Charles S. Rhyne (ed.), *Law and Judicial Systems of Nations*, 3rd rev. edn (Washington: World Peace Through Law Center, 1978), pp. 704, 706.
16. See Joseph Board, 'Arbitration in Sweden', *International Practitioner's Notebook*, April 1982, no. 18, p. 5; cf. *Arbitration in Sweden*, published by the Stockholm Chamber of Commerce, Stockholm, 1977–).
17. Vallinder, 'Who is Included in Sweden's Judicial and Legal Elite', p. 14.
18. Per Henrik Lindblom, 'Procedure', in Strömholm, *An Introduction to Swedish Law*, p. 97.
19. Note that in addition to the *nämnd*, Sweden does have a jury system used

only in cases involving freedom of speech under the Freedom of the Press Act. Vallinder, 'Who is Included in Sweden's Judicial and Legal Elite', p. 11.

20. Strömholm, *An Introduction to Swedish Law*, p. 39–40.
21. In 1982, some 165,000 cases were filed in the District Courts. See National Courts Administration, *Facts About the Swedish Judiciary, 1983–84*.
22. Rhyne, *Law and Judicial Systems of Nations*, p. 708; in 1982 17,716 cases were filed in the Courts of Appeal. *Facts About the Swedish Judiciary, 1983–84*.
23. Some 3491 cases were filed with the Supreme Court in 1982. *Facts About the Swedish Judiciary, 1983–84*.
24. Ministry of Justice, *The Administrative Courts in Sweden* (Uddevalla: Risbergs, 1982).
25. See Folke Schmidt, 'Labor Law', in Strömholm, *An Introduction to Swedish Law*, pp. 279–302.
26. An excellent account in English is the *Swedish Code of Judicial Procedure*, rev. edn, (London: Sweet and Maxwell, 1979). See also the excellent scholarly treatments by R. B. Ginsburg and A. Bruzelius, *Civil Procedure in Sweden* (The Hague, 1965). For research on legal topics in general, as well as procedural matters, the English speaking scholar has available in English, *Scandinavian Studies in Law*, brought out annually under the auspices of the University of Stockholm School of Law, published by Almqvist and Wiksell from 1957 to the present.
27. P. S. Muther, 'The Reform of Legal Aid in Sweden', *International Lawyer*, 9 (1975), p. 475.
28. Vallinder, 'Who is Included in Sweden's Judicial and Legal Elite', pp. 26–7.
29. 'Law and Justice in Sweden', Fact Sheets on Sweden, published by the Swedish Institute, February, 1984.
30. Lindblom, 'Procedure', p. 103; 'Law and Justice in Sweden', The Swedish Institute, p. 3.
31. The trade union for lawyers is the Swedish Federation of Lawyers, Social Scientists and Economists, commonly referred to by the acronym, JUSEK. It has some 25,000 members, about half of whom are lawyers. It might be noted that, in 1985, there were 16,500 persons in Sweden with law degrees.
32. Rhyne, *Law and Judicial System of Nations*, pp. 704–5; Per Henrik Lindblom, *Procedure*, pp. 102–3.
33. Strömholm, *An Introduction to Swedish Law*, p. 36.
34. Vallinder, 'Who is Included in Sweden's Judicial and Legal Elite', p. 21.

10 The Courts in Japan
Hiroshi Itoh

THE STRUCTURE AND PERSONNEL OF THE JAPANESE COURTS

Japan is a non-Western industrial democracy. It has a unitary judicial system rather than dual judicial systems between the centre and the periphery. The present judicial system was set up by the United States occupation government without delay as part of the overall constitutional reform following the Second World War. Yet in its operation, it also reflects both indigenous and European elements. The Tokugawa feudal regime (1603–1863) relied upon the indigenous conflict resolution centering around conciliation and a primitive form of judicial adjudication.[1] The Meiji constitutional government (1889–1945) that followed the Tokugawa regime modernised the judicial system by adopting first the French system and then the German system, which still constitutes the basic framework of the present judicial process.

Entire judicial power is vested in the Supreme Court and in such lesser courts as are established by law. These lesser courts are high courts, district courts, summary courts and family courts. The family court is the only specialised court established by law while the fair trade commission, the patent office and a few others are authorised to exercise the quasi-judicial power. Further, no extraordinary courts such as an administrative court and a court martial are allowed, nor is any executive organ or agency given final judicial power.

As shown in Figure 10.1, these courts are organised in the hierarchical manner. The Supreme Court, located in Tokyo, is the highest court and the court of last resort. Situated below the Supreme Court are eight high courts serving as the courts of appeal. They divide the country into eight judicial districts and each high court exercises its territorial jurisdiction over one of the eight regions. Six branch high courts are also created to facilitate the work of some high courts in metropolitan areas.

Below high courts are district courts and family courts functioning as trial courts at the same level of the judicial hierarchy. There are fifty district courts and 242 branch district courts dispersed over the country. Each district court exercises jurisdiction over a territory

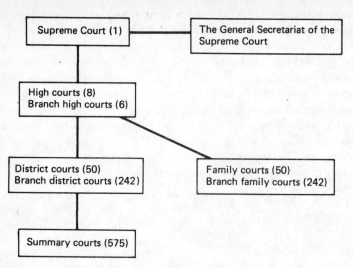

Figure 10.1   The court structure in Japan

corresponding to the subnational unit of prefecture except for the northernmost island of Hokkaido which is divided into four judicial districts. There are fifty family courts and 242 branch family courts located at the same places as the district courts and their branches. The lowest level of courts are 575 summary courts scattered in various municipalities. In addition, local offices of family courts are established at the seats of ninety-six summary courts in some remote towns and villages.

The judges of lesser courts are all nominated by the Supreme Court and appointed by the cabinet. There is no popular election of judges in Japan. A judge is a life-long occupation entered soon after rigorous training. There are altogether about 280 high court judges, about 820 district court judges, and about 220 family court judges.[2] Each high court is headed by a chief judge or president who is especially appointed by the cabinet with his appointment verified by the emperor. In addition, there are about 470 assistant judges assigned to district courts and about 150 assistant judges of family courts. Finally, the summary courts have approximately 790 judges and about 1500 probation officers.

Most law courses offered at law schools in the United States are taught at the undergraduate level in Japan. Upon passing very competitive national law examinations, all legal apprentices receive two years of legal education and training at the judicial training and research institute (JRTI), which is attached to the supreme court. Assistant judges are recruited from among those graduates of JTRI who have passed the final qualifying examinations with high marks. The judiciary is attractive to the best of the legal profession, but recruits must begin as assistant judges, each participating in proceedings as only one of a three-judge panel. Practical experience of not less than ten years as assistant judge, prosecutor, or practicing attorney is needed to become a full judge. After appointment the tenure is ten years for judges of high court, district court and family court, but these judges may be reappointed until the retirement age of sixty-five. During their tenure judges may be impeached or removed only by both houses of the Diet.

The judges of the supreme court and the summary courts are recruited differently from career judges. No special training is required of judges for family courts or summary courts. A layman of ability other than a qualified jurist may be appointed to a summary court as may a legal practitioner with three or more years of experience. A summary court judge retires at the age of seventy.

The Supreme Court consists of one chief justice and fourteen associate justices. The chief justice is designated by the cabinet and appointed by the emperor. Associate justices are appointed by the cabinet and their appointment is authenticated by the emperor. In terms of official salary and ceremonial purposes, the chief justice ranks on the same level as the prime minister, and associate justices rank on the same level as cabinet ministers. At least ten justices of the supreme court must be selected from among career judges, prosecutors, or practicing attorneys. The remaining five need not be qualified jurists so long as they are learned and have knowledge of the law. Supreme Court justices are subject to popular review by the voters at the first general election of members of the House of Representatives after such appointment. Yet, not a single justice has ever been removed as a result of popular review and this practice itself has been criticised as being ineffective.

The initial appointment of fifteen supreme court justices in 1947 resulted in rather equal distributions of five practicing attorneys, five judicial officials (i.e. four judges and one prosecutor) and five intellectuals (e.g. law professor, diplomat and bureaucrat). Political negotiations long perpetuated this practice of equal ratio, but recently it has shifted to 8:4:3 among the judicial officials, practicing attorneys, and intellectuals, indicating a trend toward domination by career judges from lower courts. Indeed an increasingly frequent path is to the secretary general of the Supreme Court, then to chief judge of a high court, especially in Tokyo, Osaka and Nagoya. This path seems to insure an appointment to a Supreme Court post.

The average age of justices at the time of appointment is the mid-sixties. It was 63.2 years old for twenty-five justices appointed in the 1970s, and has since become slightly older. Since all Supreme Court justices must retire at the age of seventy, turnover has been great. Hardly a single year has passed without witnessing the appointment of a few new justices.

With regard to the profile of Supreme Court justices, all justices appointed so far have been males. All held law degrees and a large majority of them are graduates of the University of Tokyo, probably the most prestigious school in Japan. They were all born under the Meiji constitutional government and lived through the Second World War one way or the other. Given the fact that the legal profession in the pre-war era was not so attractive to many young ambitious men, the family backgrounds of justices varied from the lower middle class to the upper middle class. However, all the justices have attained highly respectable positions, socially and economically, before they became Supreme Court judges.

Judicial administration, which was controlled by a justice minister in the pre-war days, is now in the hands of the judicial conference composed of all fifteen Supreme Court justices. This policy-making body is entrusted by the Constitution with the rule-making power to insure judicial independence and autonomy. It has established various rules of practice and procedure including matters governing attorneys, the internal disciplines of the courts and the administration of budgets and other judicial affairs. It also nominates candidates from among whom the cabinet appoints the high court chief judges and all other lower court judges while it alone appoints and removes non-judicial court staffs.

Assisting the judicial conference of the supreme court is the general secretariat of the supreme court. Its secretary general and all supervisory personnel are judges. The supreme court and these top judge-bureaucrats have been said, in essence, to have replaced the pre-war justice minister and have been criticised for influencing lower court trials. The twin processes of bureaucratisation of judicial administration and the internal policy of recruiting judge-bureaucrats from among elite judges have created a tightly-knit close working relationship between the Supreme Court justices, especially a chief justice and top levels of judge-administrators of both the general secretariat and lower courts. This triad seems to have moulded a judicial environment reflecting the preference of the Liberal Democratic Party (LDP), a very conservative party which has been ruling Japan since 1955.

For instance, the Supreme Court was criticised as having interfered with an ongoing trial in the *Suita* case (1953)[3] when it admonished Presiding Judge Sasaki of a district court for his handling of courtroom order. The Court was also criticised in 1971 when it refused to give any reason why it denied reappointment of Assistant Judge Miyamoto, the widespread presumption being he was rejected because of his membership in a leftist organisation. The Court also came under strong criticism in the 1971 Hiraga Memorandum Incident in which it imposed a much stiffer disciplinary action against a district court judge than the president of his court when the latter advised the former concerning a disposition of an ongoing trial.[4] As the court of last resort, the Supreme Court also affects lower court decisions through appeals. Although there is no formal principle of *stare decisis* in Japan, a lower court is bound by precedents of higher courts in that a disregard of judicial precedents will give rise to reversal of a lower court decision. Thus, in the eyes of court critics, the bureaucratic control of courts has from time to time allowed senior judges trained under the Meiji Constitution to influence junior judges administering the 1947 Constitution.

Finally, several training centres are attached to the Supreme Court. The judicial training research institute, mentiond above, provides legal apprentices with practical training and instruction necessary for judges, prosecutors, and practicing attorneys. It also provides judges with the advanced education and assists their research on law and practice. There are also training and research institutes for court clerks and for family court probation officers. The research training institute for court clerks trains court clerks and court stenographers, and conducts research and education necessary for the performance of these personnel. Family court probation officers are responsible for investigations necessary for the proper disposition of domestic relations and juvenile delinquency cases. The institute for family court probation officers trains them through education and research in sociology, pedagogy or psychology.

THE SCOPE OF JUDICIAL POWER AND JUDICIAL DECISION-MAKING

Currently, the range of the judicial authority is wide, ranging from civil and administrative cases to criminal cases.[5] The principle of judicial supremacy is firmly established, and the courts exercise a large degree of control and do not share authority with other institutions. Each type of trial is governed by a procedural code: the Code of Civil Procedure, the Code of Criminal Procedure, and the Code of Administrative Procedure. These rules of judicial process and procedure were initially promulgated during the Meiji constitutional era under the strong influence of the civil law tradition of Europe, particularly Germany. While the major portions of these procedural codes still remain essentially the same, the influence of Anglo-American judicial practices has been felt in some significant manner. For instance, the workload of the appellate courts was reduced by limiting grounds for appeal, thereby substantially expediting trial times. Also along with cross-examination, the adversary proceedings, with an increased responsibility placed on both litigants, were strengthened.

The Code of Criminal Procedure has adopted the following features of Anglo-American adversary practices, while retaining the European civil law practices considerably: requirement of judicial warrants for search and seizure; guarantee of state-appointed legal counsel; protection against self-incrimination by requiring evidence collaborating confession; and abolition of preliminary examination by judges. Overall, the present code has strengthened considerably the constitutional guarantees of the criminally accused persons.[6]

In the civil proceedings, the *ex officio* type of examination of evidence was abolished, and the adversary system with cross-examination was introduced. Also a method of continuous trial was adopted to expedite trials and limit the cases going up on appeal. Litigations involving commercial bills and notes were improved. Finally, dispute settlements relating to land-lease were improved in a non-litigious procedure. In addition to these general codes of procedure, the supreme court has promulgated various rules of procedure in accordance to the constitutional provisions (Article 77, Paragraph 1).[7]

A single summary court judge handles all types of cases. The summary courts have the original jurisdiction over civil cases up to 300,000 yen ($1200) and minor criminal cases with offences punishable by fine (e.g. theft or embezzlement). Summary courts generally cannot impose imprisonment. When the court finds it necessary to impose imprisonment at forced labour or a grave punishment, it must transfer the case to the district court. In civil cases, summary courts may issue an order of payment to the debtor without giving him a chance of hearing, or they may also impose a fine not exceeding

200,000 yen ($800). These summary proceedings, however, do not deprive the debtor or the accused of his right to seek an ordinary trial.

In a district court an overwhelmingly large number of cases are handled by a single judge although a three-member collegiate court sometimes is called on, depending on the type and importance of the case. For example, a three-judge court is required for exercising appellate jurisdiction. The district court exercises original jurisdiction and handles all the cases in the first instance, except for those coming under the exclusive jurisdiction of other courts. It also has appellate jurisdiction over appeals from summary courts in civil cases.

A family court has, in the first instance, jurisdiction over all domestic disputes and conflicts. Cases involving declaration of incompetence, adoption or probation of wills, for example, are handled by a means of determination while disputes over support, partitioning of estates and contested divorce are handled by a means of conciliation. A judicial divorce may be sought through an action in the district court, but proceedings for conciliation must first be attempted in the family court. The family court also handles cases involving juvenile delinquents under twenty years of age and adult defendants indicted for offences causing an injury to juveniles. All criminal cases concerning juveniles must first commence in the family court.

As a rule, a high court has jurisdiction over appeals filed from the district court or the family court. In criminal cases originating in the summary court, however, appeals come directly to a high court while appeals in the civil cases from the summary court are taken first to the district court. The high courts have original jurisdiction over cases involving either an election or an insurrection. Further, the Tokyo High Court has an exclusive original jurisdiction to review decisions of such quasi-judicial agencies as the fair trade commission and the patent office. Although a three-judge high court hears its cases ordinarily, a five-judge panel hears insurrection cases and reviews appeals from the fair trade commission.

There is no jury system in Japan, but some laymen participate in judicial proceedings as commissioners and councillors. They are all selected by the court on the basis of broad knowledge and experience. For instance, one judge of a family court, summary court or district court and two or more laymen can form a conciliation committee and attempt to secure settlement of domestic civil disputes by compromise of both parties. Also, a lay commissioner may assist a summary court judge in a civil case by bringing about a compromise or by giving his opinions to the judge. Likewise, a lay councillor may assist a family court judge by giving his opinions on competency declaration, support and the partition of the estate. In non-litigious proceedings, three or more laymen may advise judges as commissioners on disputes between landlords and tenants.

Finally, eleven laymen, picked by lot from the list of voters for the House of Representatives, form the committee of the inquest of prosecution. Their functions are to examine the propriety of the prosecutors' determination not to prosecute and, if necessary, to submit recommendations to the chief district prosecutor that the prosecutors' determination is not justified and that prosecution should be instituted. Two hundred and seven such committees throughout the country reviewed 54,913 cases between 1948 and 1977 and sent back 4320 cases for reinvestigation or prosecution.[8]

The supreme court exercises original jurisdiction only in the proceedings over impeachment of the civil service commissioners. Otherwise, it exercises appellate jurisdiction in a large number of instances. The supreme court's appellate jurisdiction is of two types: *jōkoku* appeal and *kōkoku* appeal. The *jōkoku* appeal is lodged against a judgment rendered by a high court, a judgment rendered by a district court or a family court, a judgment in criminal cases rendered by a summary court in the form of a 'jumping' appeal, appeals filed with a high court and transferred to the Supreme Court, and a special appeal made against a judgment rendered in a high court and the extraordinary appeal made by the prosecutor general. The *kōkoku* appeal is lodged on the ground of an alleged violation of the Constitution in a civil case, and is also made in a criminal case, juvenile case and a contempt of court involving maintenance of courtroom order on the ground of alleged violations of the Constitution or judicial precedents.

In civil and administrative cases, the grounds for *jōkoku* appeal are limited to a constitutional question and a question of law essential to the judgment appealed from. In criminal cases, they are limited to a constitutional issue and a conflict with the precedent of the Supreme Court or the high courts.

The Supreme Court does not decide issues of constitutionality in an abstract context. The Supreme Court and lower courts exercise judicial review only in concrete legal disputes. The supreme court has adopted a rule concerning the interest to sue, equivalent to the United States of doctrine standing to sue. A person must show a legal interest in a dispute, and the relief sought must be essential to the protection of that interest.

The Supreme Court functions either as a fifteen-member grand bench or three five-member petty benches. A case is first assigned to a justice of one of the three petty benches. The Japanese supreme court does not have any discretion for refusing to accept appeals. It automatically accepts all appeals, and then dismisses summarily a large number of them.

About thirty judge-researchers assist the fifteen justices, similar to the law clerks in the United States. They are among the most able lower court judges in the country with at least ten years of trial experiences. They are assigned to this position for four or five years. Each judge-researcher specialises in either criminal, civil, or administrative cases, and is assigned to a case, rather than to any particular justice. A judge-researcher first reads records of lower court proceedings, appeal briefs and other related documents. He clarifies disputed points and questions relating to the law, checks precedents, and reports his findings to the justices sitting on that 'petty bench' or panel.

A justice-in-charge presides over his small petty bench discussions and proposes a solution to his colleagues. Each petty bench meets twice a week, with three out of five justices necessary for a quorum. Where the appeal is to be dismissed, the Court may dispense with oral hearings; it is customary, however, to hold oral proceedings where an appeal is sustainable. The Supreme Court accepts about 300 cases in each category every year, with roughly 80 per cent of civil cases and 90 per cent of criminal cases summarily dismissed.

If the case involves a constitutional question with no precedent, it is transferred to the grand bench for adjudication. The grand bench meets on Wednesday, and the justice who is in charge of the case in question in a petty bench continues to take charge. When the chief justice presides over the case, his influence is practically insignificant. There is no established order of discussing a case nor any order of voting among the fifteen justices. Indeed, there is no practice of taking a formal vote at the end of each discussion. Nine out of fifteen justices are a quorum to dispose of an appeal. A minimum of eight justices can render unconstitutional any law or ordinance. Five out of nine justices can change the Court precedents, or decide nonconstitutional appeals. A chief justice assigns the task of writing the majority opinion. While the Japanese political culture expects unanimity as much as possible, some justices may opt to write concurring or dissenting opinions.

Law in Japan arises primarily from statutes and not from judicial decisions. The Court Organisation Law stipulates that a conclusion in a superior court decision binds a court below in respect to the case concerned but not in general (Article 4). Thus, the Anglo-American principle of *stare decisis* is not formally accepted in Japan. But the principal ground for appeal under the Code of Criminal Procedure (Article 405, Paragraphs 2 and 3) is incompatibility with established precedents of the supreme court, the pre-war Great Court of Cassation, and the present high courts. So, consistency is expected by courts at all levels and judges study and use judicial precedents, both domestic and foreign.

The grand bench decided many constitutional cases up to 1960s, establishing precedents under the 1947 Constitution, but the number of cases pending before the grand bench in recent years has decreased considerably. Also, more and more constitutional cases are being disposed of by the petty benches. In the light of the very small number of pending grand bench cases, the fifteen justices often decide administrative matters on Wednesday.

JUDICIAL REVIEW AND RELATIONSHIPS WITH POLITICAL BRANCHES

Under the Meiji Constitution (1889) there was no separation of powers nor checks and balances. The national Diet and the cabinet were reduced to state organs to assist the constitutionally sovereign monarch. The judiciary was subordinate to the executive branch and was under the supervision of the justice minister. The courts exercised judicial power on behalf of and in the name of the emperor. Judicial power and jurisdiction were therefore much circumscribed.

The Meiji Constitution did not have any provision for judicial review. The power of overseeing the constitution was formally given to the privy council, an advisory body to the emperor, but it remained virtually inactive and never passed its judgment on the constitutionality of government actions. At the same time, the authority of judicial courts headed by the Great Court of Cassation, did not extend over administrative actions. The exercise of administrative discretion was reviewed by a separate institution of the administrative court, but often remained unchecked. There were occasional jurisdictional disputes between the administrative court and the Great Court of Cassation with the result that these two courts rendered different decisions on two virtually identical cases.

Executive pressure on the judiciary was common. For instance, in the famous *Ōtsu* Trial (1891),[9] the Japanese government, for diplomatic reasons, demanded the death penalty against a policeman who tried to assassinate the visiting Russian crown prince, but the Court of Cassation did not succumb in this case to political pressure, sentencing him to life imprisonment. Yet, during the Second World War political pressures intensified to conduct what might be called political justice against critics of the military government, threatening judicial independence of some criminal trials.

On 3 November 1946 the present constitution was promulgated, taking effect on 3 May 1947. It established a constitutional monarch, with the people being ultimately sovereign. It also established the separation of powers and checks and balances. The bicameral national Diet, with the House of Representatives and the House of Councillors, is made the highest state organ with legislative power, while the cabinet headed by a prime minister is given executive power. Following the principle of parliamentary government, the prime minister is chosen from among the members of the House of Representatives and the cabinet is collectively responsible to the Diet. The House of Representatives can cause the resignation of the cabinet therefore by a no-confidence vote. The cabinet has the power to convene the Diet and to dissolve the House of Representatives.

Today, judges are not manipulated by the political branches, and judicial independence is securely established. The judges are not removable except by public impeachment and no disciplinary action may be taken by the executive against judges. On one occasion in 1948, however, the Diet invoked the constitutional power to investigate government affairs (Article 62) and intervened in an ongoing criminal trial. A district court gave a sentence of three years imprisonment and three years of stay of execution to a woman who killed her children in an abortive suicide. When the prosecutor who had sought a heavier penalty decided not to appeal, the Diet held the sentence unreasonably light and tried in vain to force a retrial. Thereupon, the Supreme Court protested the Diet's action as political interference into judicial independence, and refused to review the case.

In a vast majority of constitutional trials, the Supreme Court has upheld governmental acts and actions, largely through the doctrine of state governance. The Court has sustained the constitutionality of highly political issues by deferring to the political branches. In the famous *Sunagawa* case[10] in which the Japanese self-defence force, *inter alia*, was charged as being unconstitutional in contravention of Article 9 of the Constitution, the Supreme Court dismissed the charge by stating that this issue touches upon national survival and a vital national interest and should not be judicially reviewed unless there is obvious unconstitutionality or invalidity. Likewise, the Supreme Court has held the discretionary power of the political branches as being non-justiciable. For instance, in a taxpayer's suit, the Court upheld the actual process of decision making in the Diet as an internal matter over which the Diet has complete control.

While the courts now exercise judicial review over all administrative disputes, they have sustained administrative discretion in sub-legislation in most instances. For instance, in *Asahi* v. *Japan* (1967)[11] in which the plaintiff sought governmental welfare payments for the sick, the Supreme Court dismissed the claim by conferring a wide range of latitude upon bureaucrats. In the opinion of the Court, the authority to determine what constitutes the minimum standards of wholesome and cultured living, guaranteed in the Constitution (Article 25), is left to the discretion of the minister of health and welfare and his discretion does not necessarily bring about the question of legality. But in *Hayashi, et al.* v. *Governor, Aichi Prefecture, et al.* (1971),[12] the Court invalidated the Government Ordinance to Enforce the Agricultural Land Law as an unconstitutional delegation of the legislative power to the minister of agriculture and forestry. But, this and several other cases are exceptions and the Court has sustained administrative sub-legislations in a large number of cases.

Usually, Japanese judges have been reluctant to trust administrative experts even on highly technical matters and they have heavily relied on a trial *de novo*.[13] Only in a small number of instances have the courts, based on the substantial evidence rule, conferred finality upon administrative fact-findings without a trial *de novo*. However, following fact findings of their own, Japanese judges have sustained a great deal of latitude in administrative policy making.

Finally, the Court has exercised judicial restraint in relation to subnational governments more often than not by upholding autonomy and sub-legislative activities of prefectural and local governments. In *Ōtaki et al.* v. *Yamakita Village Assembly, et al.* (1960),[14] for instance, the Court decided not to review the local assembly's decision to temporarily suspend assemblymen on the grounds that it was an internal autonomous matter.

In view of the judicial history under the Meiji Constitution, the strong tendency of the Supreme Court toward judicial restraint is understandable. Indeed, all Supreme Court justices were born, trained, and worked under the old constitutional framework and feel strongly that the judiciary should not declare government actions unconstitutional unless it is absolutely necessary.

The conservative tendency of the Japanese courts, manifested in constitutional policy makings, reflects a legal culture in Japan in which confucianism and shintoism have formed the mainstream of the tradition of law, individual rights and authority as well as the role of courts. Confucianism has always stressed harmony in human relations. Its central concept of *gi* which focuses on duties and obligations of individuals on a status-orientated paternalistic society has permeated deeply the Japanese legal culture.[15] The status-orientated concept of traditional law in Japan was also criminal law-orientated, stressing the hierarchical human relations in a *status quo* society. The feudal law of the Tokugawa regime was butressed by shintoism, with its worship of state and emperor. In the Meiji era shintoism became the official state religion and reinforced the people's sense of obligation to the nation and to create a national identity. The stress for harmony has led to groupism in which collective interests supercede individual interests. Decisions are always group products, and a vote is seldom taken either in the cabinet or in the supreme court. The supreme court is the only tribunal in which dissents are published, but only the majority opinion is made known in lower courts.

The Japanese legal culture puts a premium on informal settlement of legal disputes based on informal controls and social sanction without legal procedure. Informal mediation or negotiation stresses compromise and proceeds on the principle that one has interests deserving protection and a right to be heard. On the one hand, the majority should not railroad wishes of minority members who, if not persuaded, should be placated by compromise. On the other, dissent is normally not allowed here.

When the traditional means of conciliation and mediation fail, the Japanese become very determined to exhaust all avenues of legal device and remedy. The way the Japanese insist on their rights becomes heavily moralistic. Since the society discourages insistence on an individual's own rights, people begin to attach excessive morality to abstract rights, to attack the immorality of the opponent, and to insist on one's rights as underdog sufferer. Law suits are no longer viewed as a conflict of relative profits.

Japanese companies seldom sue each other for the breach of contract partly because of few financial incentives. It is difficult, for instance, to win punitive damages and anti-trust suits. Contractual relations depend heavily on mutual trust and rely on informal means of dispute settlement through negotiations and mediations. At the same time, reflecting Japan's heavy industrialisation and commercial activities, domestic and international, more and more companies have thrown themselves into court battles, thereby crowding court dockets at all levels.

The non-litigious legal culture in Japan is even more explicit in relationships between individual citizens and government. Reflecting the statism of shinto and feudalistic antecedents, Japanese bureaucrats have enjoyed a special social status. Bureaucrats have tended to look down on the people while the people have looked on bureaucrats with awe. The Japanese thus seldom sue their government even though they may be strongly opposed to governmental policies.

The present Constitution was a big leap forward from the status- and criminal law-orientated laws of the Meiji and Tokugawa regimes, laws that hedged civil liberties with a great many restrictions. Yet, the legal culture in Japan is a changing mixture of traditional elements and modern Western elements. Often the two elements co-exist in the same individual citizen. For instance, formal acceptance of social equality among classes and sexes is circumvented by the traditional notions of social distinctions based on status and age.

In general, the courts have reviewed very carefully any legislative and executive actions that touch on civil liberties, and occasionally invalidated them as unconstitutional. To name a few, concerning the constitutional protection of equality under law (Article 14), the Supreme Court made the following liberal decisions: in *Kurokawa* v. *Chiba Prefecture Election Control Commission* (1976)[16] the Court declared a general election for the House of Representatives of 1972 unconstitutional on the grounds that a provision of the Public Office Election Law, Supplementary Rule, on apportionment violated the constitutional requirement of political equality (one man, one vote) in elections. Likewise, in *Aizawa* v. *Japan* (1973)[17] the Court ruled that in comparison with Article 199 of the Criminal Code, dealing with ordinary types of manslaughter, Article 200 which punishes lineal ascendant manslaughter by a penalty of capital punishment or life imprisonment is unreasonably harsh and violates equal protection under the law. Further, the Supreme Court also made liberal decisions in cases which involved the constitutional protection of freedom of occupation. In *Sumiyoshi Co.* v. *Governor, Hiroshima Prefecture* (1975)[18] the Supreme Court unanimously ruled that the provision of the Pharmaceutical Law and the Hiroshima Prefectural Ordinance enacted to implement this statute both violated the constitutional guarantee of the freedom of occupation inasmuch as there was no evidence of prevalent abuse of dispensing sub-standard drugs so as to necessitate the application of geographical regulations to the licensing of new pharmacies. The Court had also denied administrative discretion that restricted the freedom of occupation. In the opinion of the Court,[19] the Tokyo Transportation Bureau failed to give an applicant for a business licence to use his private car as a taxi-cab a chance to present his opinions and evidence concerning his eligibility and failed to produce clearly defined guidelines in granting him a licence, resulting in an unfair procedure. As a guardian of civil liberties, the Court especially has kept its eyes on law-enforcement agencies to insure constitutional rights of the criminally accused persons. None the less, over all, the Supreme Court has been very conservative on civil rights and liberties.

Judicial restraint and the judicial conservatism of the Supreme Court are rooted deeply in the nature of the post-1945 Japanese political system. Except for the first few years, the Japanese government has been dominated by the conservative Liberal Democratic Party and its predecessors. The socialist cabinet appointed the initial fifteen justices of the Supreme Court, but all others have been appointed by the conservative party's cabinets. While there is no statistically significant correlation between appointers and appointees as far as voting behaviours of individual justices is concerned,[20] a large number of constitutional decisions rendered by the Liberal Democratic Party-appointed Court have turned out to be both conservative and restrained. This finding is no surprise inasmuch as the justices feel that they are part of the Japanese government along with the Diet and cabinet and that they should fulfill their share of system maintenance functions under the present regime.

Through judicial review, the Court has performed the functions of creating legitimacy, generating support, and resolving disputes, thereby contributing to system maintenance. The Court had a formidable task in having the practice of judicial review accepted by the political branches as well as by the general public. In the absence of experience or expertise in this alien doctrine, the Court had to move very cautiously and prudently lest it should stir up political oppositions to its newly-acquired power. Self-restraint and conservatism were more or less a manifestation of self-preservation for the judiciary. The political branches have reciprocated the Supreme Court by giving it a sense of detachment and respect. Coupled with the public respect for the Court, the effects of judicial restraint and conservatism are to place stamps of legitimacy on decisions of the political branches and to generate support for the courts and for the rest of the Liberal Democratic Party (LDP) government. Yet, as can be noted from the Tokyo district court ruling convicting Former Prime Minister Kakuei Tanaka for his alleged involvement in the Lockheed Aircraft Company's bribery trial, Japanese judges are not synonymous with the LDP. According to public opinion surveys, Japanese judges enjoy the much more favourable image of being trustworthy and upright than prosecutors or private attorneys. The Supreme Court should not, therefore, be viewed as following subserviently the ruling party's lead by putting its rubber stamps on all the latter's decisions. Finally, the Court has also contributed to conflict resolution in Japanese society whenever legal disputes are brought before it. Not only has the Court reduced the backlog on its docket from 7000 cases to 2000 cases, but also has established significant judicial policies on some important social issues.

NOTES

1. Dan F. Henderson, *Conciliation and Japanese Law: Tokugawa and Modern* (Seattle, WA: University of Washington Press, 1965) pp. 47–55.
2. Supreme Court of Japan, *Justice in Japan*, 1978, pp. 13–14.
3. *Hanrei Jihō*, no. 357, p. 13.
4. Hiroshi Itoh and Lawrence W. Beer (eds), *The Constitutional Case Law of Japan: Selected Supreme Court Decisions, 1961–1970* (Seattle WA: University of Washington Press, 1978), pp. 17–18.
5. John M. Maki (trans. and ed.), *Japan's Commission on the Constituton: The Final Report* (Seattle, WA: University of Washington Press, 1980), pp. 319–23.
6. Hideo Tanaka, *The Japanese Legal System: Introductory Cases and Materials* (Tokyo: University of Tokyo Press, 1976) p. 444.
7. Takaaki Hattori and Dan F. Henderson, *Civil Procedure in Japan* (New York: Matthew Bender, 1983) ch. 3.
8. *Justice in Japan*, p. 10.
9. Great Court of Cassation; 27 May 1981; *Hōritsu Shimbun* no. 214.
10. *Japan* v. *Saketa, et al*; Supreme Court, Grand Bench; 16 December 1959; 13 *Keishū* 3225.
11. Supreme Court, Grand Bench; 24 May 1967; 21 *Minshū* 1043.
12. Supreme Court, Grand Bench; 29 January 1971; 25 *Minshū* 1.
13. Kiminobu Hashimoto, 'The rule of law: Some aspects of judicial review of administrative action', in Arthur Taylor von Mehren (ed.), *Law in Japan: The Legal Order in a Changing Society* (Cambridge, Mass.: Harvard University Press, 1963), p. 267.

14. Supreme Court, Grand Bench; 19 October 1960; 14 *Minshū* 2633.
15. Walter F. Murphy and Joseph Tanenhaus, *Comparative Constitutional Law: Cases and Commentaries* (New York: St Martin's Press, 1977) p. 38.
16. Supreme Court, Grand Bench; 14 April 1976; 30 *Minshū* 223.
17. Supreme Court, Grand Bench; 4 April 1973; 27 *Keishū* 265.
18. Supreme Court, Grand Bench; 30 April 1975; 29 *Minshū* 572.
19. *Chief, Tokyo Ground Transportation Bureau* v. *Kawakami*; Supreme Court 1st. Petty Bench; 28 October 1971, 25 *Minshū* 1037.
20. Glendon Schubert and David J. Danelski, *Comparative Judicial Behavior: Cross-cultural Studies of Political Decision-Making in the East and West* (New York: Oxford University Press, 1969), p. 150.

11 The Courts and Political Change in Post-Industrial Society

Jerold L. Waltman

Modern democracies appear to be plagued by the onset of acute political change. The stable political systems of the post-Second World War world which concentrated on managing economic growth and expanding the welfare state, all in a complacent society predominantly dedicated to democratic values, are now under stress from several directions. The economic difficulties of the last decade have undoubtedly been partly responsible. However, there has also been an erosion of the elite and mass consensus on how government should operate and what goals it should pursue.

It is inevitable that all governmental institutions will be affected by these events, including the courts. When social dislocations occur, political change follows in its wake. And during any period of institutional uncertainty it is unlikely the courts could remain aloof, no matter what the judges might desire. Law, it is true, and the courts to a degree, have a life of their own.[1] A routine exists there which has its own driving force. None the less, the legal system is not totally insulated from the society, and becomes less so during periods of stress.

The role of courts in each polity differs, as the chapters of this book demonstrate. However, all societies require the courts to perform three important functions: (1) they provide a forum for the settlement of disputes, (2) they are part of the system of administration of criminal justice, and (3) they provide, as custodians of the law, a symbolic legitimacy for government.[2] In all these areas, the changes brought about by post-industrial social and economic change and the political repercussions stemming from the seeming decline of political order stand to have a major impact on the courts.

All of the societies analysed in this book are entering a post-industrial economic phase, albeit some more rapidly than others.

Much of the change reported in these chapters is directly or indirectly attributable to this development. The exact contours of, and even the name given to, post-industrial society differ from one theorist to another.[3] However a general consensus can be organised around the following characteristics:

(1) The dominance of the service sector of the economy.
(2) The replacement of blue collar workers by white collar ones.
(3) The enlarged role of theoretical knowledge and research and development.
(4) Widespread affluence.
(5) High levels of education.
(6) A 'post-bourgeois' value structure.

If the post-industrial society takes the form outlined above, significant changes in the political role of the courts lie ahead. First, changing patterns of political participation stand to flow from increased levels of education, heralding perhaps a march to the courts. Secondly, social cleavages will take on an altered character from the emphasis on communication and information, leading to new types of conflict in society. Thirdly, executive government is likely to expand even further, stimulating an expansion of administrative law. Post-bourgeois values may shift the substance of political conflict – what is fought over – and the processes of politics – how the authoritative allocations of values are made – in ways that would make courts major actors.

On top of these changes wrought by socio economic factors are two others. Ignored by the theorists of post-industrial society but not by Western publics has been a resurgence of crime. Effective policing measures largely brought crime under control from the late nineteenth century until recently; however, these same measures have appeared ineffective in the last two decades.[4] Finally, most intangibly but perhaps most importantly, there is a growing concern about governmental legitimacy. No government can survive if its legitimacy evaporates, and it is to law and religion that the state has always looked for legitimation.[5]

My purpose in this essay is to examine the probable changes in courts created by the socioeconomic developments associated with post-industrialism, the surge in crime, and the perceived decline in legitimacy. Taken together, they could stimulate a growth in all three political roles. Judiciaries cannot, of course, assume the central role in governing modern societies any more than they could any others; yet their role may well be greater than it has been in the immediate past.

CHANGING MODES OF POLITICAL PARTICIPATION

The nineteenth and early twentieth century were consumed with the issue of participation.[6] From the United States the practice of representative government spread to Western Europe (and beyond). Moreover, participation has had an inflationary effect, spreading to ever wider circles in society. First, property requirements fell, then those barring women and, where applicable, racial minorities, and finally the age limit was pushed downward. We have now arrived at a point where there are no adults to whom the right to vote may be given.

Participation is also a deeply held political value in modern society. Indeed Daniel Bell identifies it as the motif of the post-industrial political order.[7] Under the influence of Rousseau, it has gradually become an ideal in itself, not only a technique to insure wise policy. It has therefore become a matter of the quality and impact of participation more than the right to exercise it, a right which is assumed in all Western political discourse.

Traditionally, participation has meant voting in elections. In all democracies, this has led to the rise of political parties to channel the participation and make it meaningful. For most observers, democracy is inconceivable without parties, and their health therefore constitutes a barometer of the state of democracy.[8] While there are numerous problems, conceptual and practical, with the way parties translate public preferences into public policy, they remain the cornerstone in the schemas of democratic theorists.

Paradoxically, though, in an age devoted to participation, identification with the prime instruments of participation, the majority parties, appears to be on the wane. In several countries new or outcast parties have begun to garner a large percentage of the vote. More disturbing to many observers is the decline in the number of citizens bothering to vote at all. According to a widely held view, this signals a spread of alienation and is a harbinger of mass disaffection from the political system. There is, however, an alternative view.

One result of governmental policies in the last half century has been increasing levels of education. However we measure it, there are more people with higher levels of education than ever before. Analyses of the effects of education point to two conclusions: first, the more education an individual has the more likely he or she is to participate; secondly, the more highly educated a person is the more likely he or she will join organisations.[9]

Now the first element would lead us to project higher levels of participation, which seems to contradict the reported decline in voting. However, the proposition equates participation with voting. If it is true that the educated join more organisations and that their commitment to those organisations is greater, it could follow that they channel their participatory energies there. Since they have the leisure time and the income to pursue the issues that are of concern to them through organisations, voting is less necessary. Thus, voting may not be the same measure of participation it was fifty years ago. Participation, if the organisational thesis is valid, may have actually increased. The fact that the United States is usually cited as the leader in post-industrial trends and the fact of the rise of 'single issue' politics and pressure groups in that country may be directly correlated.

The implication for the courts is that litigation is quite likely to be a strategy of these organisations. Relatively well financed and relatively sophisticated, they have the resources to fight government agencies, business corporations, or each other in court. This will mean, for one thing, that the number of important political conflicts coming to court will grow. In turn, this will itself create excess demand for court services, which can only be reduced by limiting access or enlarging the provision of the service. Both options are difficult to implement. The first, whether accomplished by queuing or financial disincentives, can lead to severe complaints among the effectively disenfranchised. Also, it can have an impact on the other users of court services as well as the administration of criminal justice. The second runs the risk inherent in altering the supply of any public good (which is essentially what governmental funding of dispute settlement is):[10] demand increases to match supply. In short, multiplying courts and judges could produce more overload, not less.

It also means that courts will feel the intensity issue to a greater degree than ever before.[11] Some of the groups will be fighting for or opposing decisions touching on quite sensitive matters, and losers cannot be expected always to end their battle in the courtroom. Pressures will, in turn, mount on executives and legislators to appoint judges with the 'proper' policy views, a move that itself will further politicise the judiciary.

Furthermore, groups with well-defined goals will pursue litigation as only one strategy. While this removes some necessity for judges to make final decisions, in that their decisions will be part of an ongoing chain of decisions, it also means litigation is not self-contained. It will become part of a stream of pressures exerted on legislators, executives, and administrators. Dragging judges into ongoing decision making will mean, in turn, that they will have to be aware of the reactions others will have to their holdings.

THE CHANGING BASE OF SOCIAL CLEAVAGES

It is also likely that the changing cleavage structure of post-industrial society will impinge on courts and their work. Industrialisation bred a bourgeoisie based on manufacturing and a mass proletariat. This fact alone precipitated new legal issues in contract and tort law as well as cases involving more overt forms of class conflict. Post-industrial economies are spawning new classes, particularly those whose social status and income are rooted in their possession of technical knowledge and skills. During periods of such transitions, as old power configurations give way to new ones, conflict can take one of three forms, as Samuel Huntington reminded us.[12] First, there is the matter of rising groups versus declining ones; secondly, rising groups can be pitted against each other; and thirdly, declining groups may struggle among themselves.

Undoubtedly, most of these conflicts will be fought out in the legislative and executive arenas, but within the first two categories the issue of property rights could pull the courts into these struggles. Those who have property, Harold Laski noted, always claim a right to govern. 'That surely is the lesson of history; for every class which possesses property will claim that it has an abstract right to power.'[13] Indeed one of the ways to read the crises of the *ancien regime* was the presentation by the bourgeoisie of claims to participate in governing by virtue of their ownership of property. At the same time, it seems an equally valid proposition of history that those who have property always insist that the authorities protect their employment and enjoyment of it.

Property in aristocratic society was measured largely by titles and land; in bourgeois society it has been measured by bank accounts and contract rights convertible to money. In post-industrial society, credentials and technical skills are the keys to income and status, becoming functionally equivalent to the older property rights of money and physical goods.

The institutions and bodies which provide access to those credentials and knowledge will find themselves beleaguered. Since they sort out winning and losing individuals, their decisions will become intensely controversial. Surely much of the litigation in the United States over the admissions policies of professional schools derives from the increased value of the skills they inculcate and the degrees they award. As alternative paths up the social ladder decline in significance it would seem that these issues will only grow in importance.

The fourteenth amendment to the United States constitution provides an automatic entryway into this arena for the courts there. But other countries' courts are not likely to remain immune from the controversies. If administrators, under colour of law, are making decisions vitally affecting people's lives, appeals to the courts will certainly come. It will be an area of administrative law that will pose knotty problems, even if the courts throw the ball back to universities and certifying bodies.

The welfare state, perhaps the crowning achievement of industrial society, has added another stream to changing property relations. Many persons are now dependent on entitlements set up through various government programmes – veterans' benefits, health care, pensions, and so forth. Charles Reich, for one, has argued that these too should be recognised as property, and treated so judicially.[14]

Whether or not that route is taken, these issues may enter the courts, especially if economic growth slows. As long as economic growth provided a larger social dividend each budget year, more and more claimants could be satisfied. If, however, the economic slowdown of the 1970s recurs, then groups dependent on the welfare state will have to fight each other. Again, legislative and executive battles will be paramount, but no country will likely be devoid of judicial battles also. To take one example applicable to any country, what if a financially pressed government tinkers with programmes financed by payroll contributions? Would not those who previously contributed assert a legal right to those benefits? When governments became trustees, the possibility of such an issue became a fact of life.

Social cleavages in post-industrial society may become so strong that they replace those of industrial society, but it is more likely they will be grafted onto the others. A residue of heavy industry and mining will remain. Moreover, many jobs in the service sector will essentially be proletarian, not technical. Thus, the legal complexity of managing the relations among social groups will be similar to that experienced during the early years of industrialisation, as businessman and worker replaced lord and serf. Who has the right to be protected against what, for example, and under what circumstances will pose knotty problems in tort law that the judiciary will have to face. Even in countries with more emphasis on legislative development of rights and obligations, there will be the ongoing task of interpretation. Given the complexity of the issues and the political conflict that will attend the passing of such laws, statutes will necessarily be vague. Courts will be called on to fill in more than details, pulling them into an important emerging area of public policy.

THE GROWTH OF EXECUTIVE GOVERNMENT

Executive institutions everywhere became dominant during the mature phase of industrialisation. Governmental responsibilities grew in tune with the growth of social complexity and interdependence. Economic regulation and management led to the creation of new executive agencies for information gathering and planning while the welfare state added its own corpus of administrative organisations. In the polity as a whole, an increasing need for expertise translated into a system of bureaucratic dominance.

If anything, post-industrial society is likely to exacerbate this tendency. Government may not grow at the rate it has in the past; indeed it could not. But the technical complexity of society cannot help but further enshrine the power of public and quasi-public institutions. In many service areas – basic education, health care, welfare – there may well be a slight contraction of the bureaucracies. In a plethora of areas, though – occupational safety, pollution control, energy, trans-portation, to name a few – the size and scope of bureaucratic institutions will not diminish. The continuing power exercised by these organisations would seem to have three important consequences for administrative law.

First, as the penetration of society by public bureaucracies has grown, the number of conflicts between agencies and citizens has grown also. 'As the number of contacts between individuals and government agencies increases', Richard Rose writes, 'the frequency of misunderstandings, friction and conflict between individuals and government is likely to increase, and to increase at least in proportion to the frequency of interaction'.[15] With this increase comes the question of the citizen's rights. And, once again, if citizens are more educated, they are more likely to challenge administrative deter-minations.

In countries with an administrative law tradition, there is likely to be a sharp increase in the number of cases. This will entail a need for expanded services or new procedures. In countries without separate administrative courts, we are likely to witness an increased debate on the regular courts' role in administrative law, a phenomenon already occurring in Britain, the United States, Canada, and Australia.[16]

Secondly, administrative law will have to adjust to the array of new organisational forms governments use. Government administration has always been complex in Western societies, with a panoply of types of public bodies existing alongside traditional executive departments. But the number and the diversity of these has grown dramatically, and the line between public and private is blurred. At the margins of the state are a whole range of service organisations which often have their own sources of revenue and make decisions virtually outside the normal system of accountability.[17] Then, too, many institutions remain ostensibly private but receive public funds.[18] Naturally, the pattern of these developments varies from country to country; however, the post-industrial state is likely everywhere to find a growth in administrative organisational complexity. Consequently, the rules of administrative law will have to take cognisance of this fact.

Thirdly, the expansion in the number of administrative agencies will strain the system of adjudication by top executives. Public bureaucracies, like all organisations, pursue organisational goals above others. Given the multiplicity of public organisations in the modern state, conflicts are bound to develop among them. Traditionally, they have passed those conflicts that could not be settled by bargaining up the line to top executives. As the number of executive agencies grows, though, that channel is increasingly clogged. Peter Self, in fact, has listed this adjudicatory function as one of the causes of overload on chief executives.[19]

When time constraints effectively close this channel, it is natural that an alternative forum will be sought, and the courts are likely to be it. This is especially true in that many conflicts between agencies involve questions of jurisdiction, where the natural ambiguity of statutory words leads to many cases of overlap.

Thus, in the bargaining process, the legal character of many disputes can easily lead to threats to go to court. As any chip used in bargaining, the threat will have to be carried out on occasion. When it is, courts will be settling a specific dispute to be sure, but at stake will also be the parameters for future inter-agency bargaining. Indeed, the bargaining of public bureaucracies will logically come to parallel closely that of private parties who know potential litigation is always an option for one or both. The calculation each makes of likely success is crucial to the substantive outcome. In essence, court decisions in cases of this sort will have important consequences for any number of administrative organisations.

Furthermore, since governmental bureaucracies are normally allied with clients or other interest groups, these rulings will have important political and policy consequences. Since who decides is rarely disconnected from what gets decided, shifting power to make decisions from one agency to another could signal important policy shifts.

CHANGING VALUE PATTERNS

Ronald Inglehart has been a strong proponent of the thesis that values are undergoing a steady and important shift in post-industrial society.[20] Substantively, the people he labels 'post-moderns' de-emphasise bourgeois values of material accumulation and in their stead place more stock on quality of life issues. Since these values tend to increase as one moves up the prosperity scale, a spread of prosperity would raise the number of post-moderns. If this phenomenon were to be coupled to the shift to organisational participation depicted above, important political consequences follow.

Quality of life issues such as the environment and consumer product safety seem especially open to litigation.[21] In the environmental area, for instance, it is necessary to settle questions such as who is affected by what pollution and to set standards for emissions from plants and vehicles. If an executive agency is established to decide such issues, it will be an agency facing powerful economic organisations. There are vastly different traditions in various countries concerning co-operation and conflict between governmental agencies and business firms, and this will no doubt frame the relations here.[22] In some nations, especially the United States, the tendency has been for continual hostility, and usually the capture of the agency by the businesses. In others, the authority of the state has been assumed and regulators have worked more hospitably with business people. What is different now is that everywhere private environmental organisations are following these conflicts with continuing interest. They possess both the resources and the inclination to go to court if agency-industry collusion appears to be detrimental to environmentalism, a development far advanced in the United States but likely to invade other societies as well.

On the issue of consumer protection, again countries vary in the protections they offer and the procedures to be followed.[23] For many years, consumers were the heroes of economic theory but poorly organised politically. It was only with the organisation of activist elites that the issues were brought onto the political agenda. However, because so much of this area involves tort law, courts will of necessity become deeply involved. The sheer economic and technological complexity of post-industrial society will insure that consumer issues will be the subject of many intense struggles. Even if administrative agencies are erected to police markets, the administrative law system will then become the vehicle for court participation.

In short, changed value patterns are to be expected during any period of social transformation. It is problematic, of course, whether or not they will shift in the direction predicted by Inglehart. Nevertheless, increased levels of education alone create a larger pool of people likely to pursue court activity to protect their interests. And when these people join together in organisations, that likelihood seems to increase markedly.

THE RESURGENCE OF CRIME

Maintaining order is a basic function of government, for without public order no form of civilised society is possible. Threats to public order are therefore threats directed at the most basic of values, generating a strong governmental response. Fundamentally, there are two types of threats: overt political violence and ordinary crime. Analytically, at least, these are separable, although they may converge in practice.

Since the quelling of the disturbances of the late 1960s and early 1970s, there has been no serious outbreak of the former on a large scale – and even those episodes, except possibly in France, pale beside the more violent upheavals of the past. None the less, individual acts of terrorism have escalated dramatically. The Irish Republican Army has expanded its terrorist activities to Britain; assassinations and assassination attempts as well as kidnappings have rocked Italy; anti-Semitism has reared its ugly head in France; tax protestors and survivalists have killed tax authorities and battled police in the United States; bombings have occurred in Germany; planes leaving Canada have carried concealed bombs. While all of these are the work of small extremist groups with no real political base (except the IRA), they focus public attention and spread fear. Most importantly for our purposes, they often bring the judiciary into the public eye, as when a conspirator or assassin is apprehended and tried. Terrorist acts have generated proposals in several countries to grant the courts and other law enforcement agencies sweeping powers. Courts are naturally viewed as a major weapon in society's fight against terrorism. This pushes courts into a sensitive political position for the proposals often run counter to the traditional canons of due process. Political pressures work both ways, to make the courts an important instrument of social control and a bulwark of liberty; there is thus no escape into a judicial role that denies the political.[24]

Of equal import has been the growth of ordinary crime. Whatever its cause – and many have been suggested – the rise of crime, and especially violent crime, is a disturbing fact of contemporary life.[25] It seems to be nearly universal, invading even tranquil Sweden. Courts should be viewed in this context as a public bureaucracy. When, as here, the area the bureaucracy is responsible for administering causes negative public reaction, the bureaucracy will feel pressure to 'do something'. If water supplies are contaminated, if disease spreads, if children cannot read, water authorities, health officials, and educators will be called upon to react. Similarly, as a portion of the administration of justice system, courts are under growing political pressure to help stem the occurrence of crime.

The issues are often complex and made more difficult for the courts by the fact that they are only part of the administration of justice system. Police, prosecutors, public defenders, probation officers, and prison officials are also involved. Thus, an issue such as sentencing, aside from raising what seem to be insoluble philosophical difficulties, touches several public bureaucracies.[26] Yet, it is often the courts that are the focus of public attention.

If crime continues to grow, or even if it subsides but public concern remains high, then political pressures are also bound to grow. Conceivably, judges will not want or seek new powers (unlike many bureaucracies). Normally, judges are more sensitive to the complexity of criminal issues than the pundits. However, wanted or not, a debate over new powers and/or a grant of expanded powers will propel courts into what may become a central issue of post-industrial society.

POLITICAL AUTHORITY AND LEGITIMACY

It is ironic that the same generation that witnessed the enshrinement of democratic governments has also witnessed a decline of governmental legitimacy. Hardly had the former fascist states been welcomed firmly back into the democratic fold than the alarms over the legitimacy of all Western governments were issuing forth. Harold Bermen connects this trend to a general decline of legitimacy:

> It is impossible not to sense the social disintegration, the breakdown of communities, that has taken place in Europe, North America, and other parts of Western civilization in the twentieth century. Bonds of race, religion, soil, family, class, neighborhood, and work community have increasingly dissolved into abstract and superficial nationalisms. This is closely connected with the decline of unity and common purpose in Western civilization as a whole.[27]

These conditions flow from two related sources; the triumphs of procedural democracy and positivist law. Procedural democracy (both its pluralist and consociational variants)[28] finds the good in correct procedures. The resolution of competing claims is the goal of government, with whatever substantive outcome results sanctified, since it was arrived at by democratic procedures. Positivist legal thought elevates human law to the highest plane.[29] In denying that an absolute standard exists, or contending that if one does exist it is unknowable, positivist law in the end makes criticism pointless.

Both of these trends are rooted in the rationalism which grew out of the eighteenth century. Without question rationalism has contributed heavily to human liberty by breaking the bonds of both secular and religious oppression. It forced a retreat of aristocratic power and freed people from the fear inculcated by an other-worldly religion. Voltaire once reportedly said that man would be free when the last king was strangled with the entrails of the last priest. At the same time, this triumph of rationalism had two other political consequences: a breakdown in the power of symbols and a denial of absolutes (a natural law).

Governing is more than managing economic aggregates and providing material benefits, no matter how expertly done. Perhaps traceable to Marx's influence, the focus of political scientists has been on the economic aspects of governing, neglecting often the issues that touch people most profoundly. Matters such as the flag dispute in Canada, an issue about which one Member of Parliament reported he received more mail than for any other,[30] stir people deeply. Effective government must flow from and reinforce a sense of community, something in which symbols and purpose interact. By concentrating on economic well being, the epitome of which is government by social indicators,[31] democratic rationalism underestimates or even denies the place of symbolic and emotive features of politics.

Natural law has been used for a number of vile purposes as well as benign ones. A well-known scholar put it this way:

> Natural law has had as its content whatever the individual in question desired to advocate. This has varied from a defence of theocracy to a defence of the complete separation of church and state, from revolutionary rights in 1776 to liberty of contract in recent judicial opinions, from the advocacy of universal adult suffrage to a defence of rigid limitations upon the voting power, from philosophical anarchy in 1849 with Thoreau to strict paternalism five years later with Fitzhugh, from the advocacy of the inalienable right of secession to the assertion of the natural law of national supremacy, from the right of majority rule to the rights of vested interests.[32]

John Hart Ely cites this passage and other cases to buttress the position that natural law cannot be used as a standard of constitutional interpretation.[33] More generally, the position is that it cannot be used in any society to measure the wisdom of the laws and their moral authority.

However, it is one thing to argue over what the natural law is, quite another to deny its existence. To posit the first is simply to assert that people disagree about values and the political good; to take the second tack loosens men from any ethical base. Detractors of natural law find a substitute in 'fair' procedures, and this does provide a referent of sorts. It does not give government unlimited power to do anything, in that it cannot obviate procedural fairness. In the realm of ordinary law, though, and it is there it should be remembered that most governing is done, it deprives us of any measuring rod, casting us into a sea of relativism. To what should human law conform, beyond passing the procedural test? Standing alone, procedural fairness leaves us adrift.

Governing a constitutional and democratic polity requires that democratic and constitutional beliefs be held by governors and governed alike. The governors have a right to a measure of discretion and an expectation that they will be obeyed; the governed have a right to expect that the governors have a basis for their actions. Carl Friedrich put the second point eloquently.

> As long as we maintain a sense of authority, that is to say as long as those who wield power recognize their responsibility for discretion-

ary acts in the sense of an obligation to retain the regard for the potentiality of reasoned elaboration, a constitutional order can be maintained. Once this regard is lost . . . the night of meaningless violence is upon us.[34]

The 'reasoned elaboration' he views as fundamental can only come if certain common elements of political discourse and some shared expectations exist between those who exercise power and the citizenry. Otherwise, the ultimate criterion becomes the very act of government that is in need of explanation. 'Unless people regain the sense that the practices of society represent some sort of natural order instead of a set of arbitrary choices, they cannot hope to escape from the dilemma of unjustified power.'[35]

Symbols have been an important aspect of society since organised human existence began, with law and religion always being central in the providing of symbols of political authority. Indeed, the two are inseparable, linked in a number of ways. Analogies abound, for instance, between judges and clergy. It is impossible, as a further example, to define crime and justify punishment without reference to religious values. The modern state, though, finds itself stripped of symbolic referent points, and its authority is thereby weakened.

If the hypotheses of political anthropologists are correct, symbols linking governmental action to absolute values are as necessary in contemporary society as they were under primitive conditions.[36] Instrumentalism works as a governing philosophy only when it sprouts from a base of absolute values. When it replaces the absolute values it dissolves the connection with absolutes. Psychologists, in fact, seem to be taking the position that the distinction between the emotional and the rational is not firm,[37] meaning that a political order based on only one or the other is in a precarious position. Rational society, in fact, as Samuel Huntington argued, may find itself having irrational politics.[38] If the symbolic aspects of life are denied in most spheres, they may end up being projected into the political arena with high intensity.

Someone once said that letters might for a while lose their place as the centrepiece of intellectual life, but that they would inevitably return for they speak to the deepest aspects of human existence. So it is with symbols and the absolute values associated with natural law theories. They may be eroded but they will return. It is not a question of whether symbols and absolute political values will be important in the politics of the future, but what symbols and what absolute political values will find wide acceptance.

Contemporary Western governments seem to sense their need for legitimacy, as their exhortations evoke diminishing levels of response. Deprived of religion as a prop, they turn increasingly to judges. In Australia, for instance, it was seen that judges were being called upon to aid in sanctifying decisions in a number of policy areas. The Italian judges, likewise, are being asked to serve in a variety of capacities, and similar trends could be recounted in other nations.[39] This strategy, of course, may be sterile in the long run. There is a danger that pulling judges into the political arena will only diminish judicial legitimacy.

The courts remain, then, the major symbolic actors in the modern state and the guardians of the only element of public policy, the law, that has a perceived link with both the past and the divine. The debilitating lack of symbolic, and hence real, authority of other institutions of government will heighten the need for courts. Unless governors choose to draw on symbols of excessive nationalism or racial superiority, which would undermine severely the democratic state and the quality of modern life, it is largely the courts that can provide the symbolic base for governing. Democracy and rationalism have been partners in the political development of the last century, and on the whole are healthy ingredients for an enhanced life for the many. But as philosophical rationalism burns itself out, it will be vital not to let democratic ideals succumb to nihilism. The need to transcend procedural democracy is evident, and the democratic future can only be built on a foundation of natural law that points to the more humane, more liberating side of human nature.

CONCLUSION

Our age, in sum, is one of transition for the modern democratic state, and courts are likely to play an important role in the reclamation of political authority. There are signs of growing recognition of law as an important mechanism of social control, indicated by the renewed social scientific analysis of its role in society.[40] Furthermore, the writings of Ronald Dworkin, generally acknowledged as the most important legal philosopher of our day, have spurred a resurgence of thinking about basic rights.[41] His absolutist position returns individual rights to the political pantheon, and has served to focus attention on questions that are far more important than how to fine tune the economy. The achievement of justice cannot be disconnected from law, and law cannot be disconnected from judicial institutions.

Courts and democracy have always represented an uneasy mixture, for at their bases lie incompatible approaches to governing. Yet, all societies must have law; and since law is built on ethics it is important to retain a belief that the ethical impulses behind democracy represent our finest political achievement. As symbolic features and absolute values are reintegrated into Western politics, the role of the courts will likely grow. How that increased role is handled by judges and non-judges will determine the future structure of authority in the West.

NOTES

1. See Alan Watson, 'Comparative Law and Legal Change', *Cambridge Law Journal*, 37 (November, 1978), pp. 313–36.
2. There are other ways to classify courts' roles, but this one draws on the governmental or political system perspective. Herbert Jacob's widely used distinction between 'norm enforcement' and 'policy making' elaborates a case perspective. Martin Shapiro takes an institutional view, seeing the courts as a form of third party dispute settlement. Herbert Jacob, *Jusice in America*, 2nd edn (Boston: Little, Brown, 1972), p. 31. Martin Shapiro, *Courts: A Comparative and Political Analysis* (Chicago: University of Chicago Press, 1981), ch. 1.
3. See Daniel Bell, *The Coming of Post-Industrial Society* (New York: Basic Books, 1973); Zbigniew Brezinski, *Between Two Ages: America's Role in the Technotronic Era* (New York: Viking Press, 1970); and John Kenneth Galbraith, *The New Industrial State*, 2nd edn (Boston: Houghton Mifflin, 1971). The list of traits is from Samuel Huntington, 'Postindustrial Politics: How Benign Will It Be?' *Comparative Politics*, 6 (January, 1974), pp. 163–4.
4. See Ted Robert Gurr, *Rogues, Rebels, and Reformers: A Political History of Urban Crime and Conflict* (Beverly Hills, Calif.: Sage, 1976).
5. Harold Berman, *Law and Revolution: The Formation of the Western Legal Tradition* (Cambridge: Harvard University Press, 1983), p. vi.
6. The best recent study of participation is G. Bingham Powell, *Contemporary Democracies: Participation, Stability, and Violence* (Cambridge: Harvard University Press, 1982).
7. Bell, *The Coming of Post-Industrial Society*, p. 12.
8. See Walter Dean Burnham, 'American Politics in the 1970s: Beyond Party', in W. N. Chambers and Walter Dean Burnham, *The American Party System: Stages of Political Development* (New York: Oxford University Press, 1975) and Everett Carl Ladd, *Where Have All the Voters Gone?* (New York: Norton, 1978). But see Max Kaase, 'The Crisis of Authority: Myth and Reality', in Richard Rose, ed., *Challenge to Governance: Studies in Overloaded Polities* (Beverly Hills, Calif.: Sage, 1984), ch. 8 for an argument that party identification has not declined.

9. Sidney Verba and Norman Nie, *Participation in America: Political Democracy and Social Equality* (New York: Harper and Row, 1972), p. 100, and more generally, Sidney Verba, Norman Nie, and Jae-On Kim, *Participation and Political Equality: A Seven Nation Comparison* (Cambridge: Cambridge University Press, 1978).

10. For an argument that courts are public goods, see Richard Neely, *Why Courts Don't Work* (New York: McGraw-Hill, 1983).

11. The issue of intensity has disturbed democratic theorists for some time. See Robert Dahl, *A Preface to Democratic Theory* (Chicago: University of Chicago Press, 1956), ch. 4 for a lucid discussion.

12. Huntington, 'Postindustrial Politics', pp. 177–82.

13. Harold J. Laski, *Authority in the Modern State* (Cambridge: Harvard University Press, 1919), p. 52.

14. Charles Reich, 'The New Property', *Yale Law Journal*, 73 (April, 1964), p. 733–87. Also see Norman Furniss, 'Property Rights and Democratic Socialism', *Political Studies*, 26 (December, 1978), pp. 450–61.

15. Richard Rose, *Understanding Big Government: The Programme Approach* (Beverly Hills, Calif.: Sage, 1984), p. 92.

16. See Harry Whitmore, 'The Administrative Law Explosion', in A. R. Blackfield, *Legal Change: Essays in Honour of Julius Stone* (Sydney: Butterworths, 1983). A longer term empirical study of the United States can be found in David Clark, 'Adjudication to Administration: A Statistical Analysis of Federal District Courts in the Twentieth Century', *Southern California Law Review*, 55 (November, 1981), pp. 65–152. Additional data for more recent times is reviewed in J. Willard Hurst, 'The Functions of Courts in the United States, 1950–80', *Law and Society Review*, 15 (Special Issue, 1980–81), pp. 401–71.

17. See Ira Sharkansky, *Wither the State?* (Chatham, N.J.: Chatham House, 1979) for an analysis of these trends.

18. See Bruce L. R. Smith and D. C. Hague (eds), *The Dilemma of Accountability in Modern Government: Independence versus Control* (London: Macmillan, 1971) for an analysis of government by contract.

19. Peter Self, 'Resource and Policy Coordination under Pressure', in Rose (ed.), *Challenge to Governance*, ch. 2.

20. Ronald Inglehart, *The Silent Revolution: Changing Values and Political Styles Among Western Publics* (Princeton: Princeton University Press, 1977). Also see his 'Post-Materialism in an Environment of Insecurity', *American Political Science Review*, 75 (December, 1981), pp. 880–900 for more recent data.

21. On the environmental issues, for example, see J. Kodwo Bentil, 'General Recourse to the Courts for Environmental Protection Purposes and the Problem of Legal Standing: A Comparative Study and Appraisal', *Anglo-American Law Review*, 11 (October/December 1982), pp. 286–326.

22. See, for instance, David Vogel, 'The Law and Politics of Environmental Controls on Industry: Contrasting British and American Traditions', paper presented at the 1982 convention of the American Political Science Association.

23. See Richard Flickinger, 'The Comparative Politics of Agenda Setting: The Emergence of Consumer Protection as a Public Policy Issue in Britain

and the United States', *Policy Studies Review*, (2 February, 1983), pp. 429–43.

24. See Otto Kirchheimer, *Political Justice* (Princeton: Princeton University Press, 1961) and Theodore Becker (ed.), *Political Trials* (Indianapolis: Bobbs-Merrill, 1971).

25. On the issue of crime, see Sir Leon Radzinowicz and Joan King, *The Growth of Crime: The International Experience* (New York: Basic Books, 1977), especially Chs 1–4. For a good summary of the reasons offered, consult David Downes and Paul Rock, *Understanding Deviance* (Oxford: Oxford University Press, 1982). For an interesting survey of converging legal responses in two countries, see Gunther Arzt, 'Responses to the Growth of Crime in the United States and West Germany: A Comparison of Changes in Criminal Law and Societal Attitudes', *Cornell International Law Journal*, 12 (Winter, 1979), pp. 43–54.

26. On sentencing, for example, see the perceptive comments in Patrick Devlin, *The Judge* (Oxford: Oxford University Press, 1979), Ch. 2.

27. Berman, *Law and Revolution*, p. vi.

28. The best general works on pluralism and consociational democracy are Robert Dahl, *Polyarchy: Participation and Opposition* (New Haven: Yale University Press, 1971) and Arend Lijphart, *Democracy in Plural Societies* (New Haven: Yale University Press, 1977) respectively.

29. The modern case for positivist law is made in Hans Kelsen, *Pure Theory of Law* (Berkeley: University of California Press, 1967; first published 1960). Summaries are available in R. W. M. Dias, *Jurisprudence* (London: Butterworths, 1976), Ch. 15 and Edgar Bodenheimer, *Jurisprudence*, rev. edn (Cambridge: Harvard University Press, 1974), Ch. 7.

30. Reported to Professor Donald Smiley and noted in a conversation with the author. On the salience of emotive issues in politics, see T. Alexander Smith, *The Comparative Policy Process* (Santa Barbara: ABC-Clio, 1975), Ch. 4.

31. For an excellent review and critique see Francis Castles and R. D. McKinlay, 'Public Welfare Provision, Scandivavia and the Sheer Futility of the Sociological Approach to Politics', *British Journal of Political Science*, 9 (April, 1979), pp. 157–71.

32. Benjamin Wright, *American Interpretations of Natural Law* (New York: Russell and Russell, 1931), pp. 39–40.

33. John Hart Ely, *Democracy and Distrust: A Theory of Judicial Review* (Cambridge: Harvard University Press, 1980), pp. 48–54.

34. Carl Friedrich, 'Authority, Reason, and Discretion', in Carl Friedrich (ed.), *Authority* (Cambridge: Harvard University Press, 1958), p. 48.

35. Robert Unger, *Law in Modern Society* (New York: Free Press, 1976), p. 240.

36. On the use of symbols, see Janet Dolgin, David Kemnitzer, and David Schneider (eds.), *Symbolic Anthropology* (New York: Columbia University Press, 1977). Also see Ernst Cassirer, *The Myth of the State* (New Haven: Yale University Press, 1946).

37. Richard Sennett, *Authority* (New York: Knopf, 1980), Ch. 1.

38. It could be viewed as a paradox that in the United States, with the most powerful judiciary, there is almost no service by judges in extrajudicial

capacities. (The rules of the American Bar Association, in fact, prohibit it.) However the explanation could be that the judges already play a legitimating role there; indeed, it is often said that that is their major function. By ensuring that the vast majority of legislative and executive acts pass constitutional muster, they provide an important stamp of approval. Moreover, justices are occasionally so used, for example, on the Warren Commission, when issues are especially sensitive.

39. Huntington, 'Postindustrial Politics', p. 166.
40. Examples would be the founding of the *Law and Society Review* (US), the *Journal of Law and Society* (UK), the Canadian Law and Society Association (with a forthcoming journal), and the increasing number of articles on law related topics in political science journals.
41. See Ronald Dworkin, *Taking Rights Seriously* (Cambridge: Harvard University Press, 1977). A useful discussion of contrasting views is Marshall Cohen (ed) *Ronald Dworkin and Contemporary Jurisprudence* (Totowa, N.J.: Rowman and Allanheld, 1983).

Index